LITURGY AMONG THE THORNS

ESSAYS ON WORSHIP IN THE
REFORMED CHURCH IN AMERICA

D0707745

THE HISTORICAL SERIES OF THE REFORMED CHURCH IN AMERICA

NO. 57

LITURGY AMONG THE THORNS

Essays on Worship in the Reformed Church in America

James Hart Brumm
Editor

WILLIAM B. EERDMANS PUBLISHING COMPANY
Grand Rapids, Michigan / Cambridge, U.K.

© 2007 Reformed Church Press
All rights reserved

Wm. B. Eerdmans Publishing Co.
2140 Oak Industrial Drive N.E., Grand Rapids, Michigan 49505
P.O. Box 163, Cambridge CB3 9PU U.K.
www.eerdmans.com

Printed in the United States of America

Library of Congress Cataloging-in-Publication Data

Liturgy among the thorns : essays on worship in the Reformed Church in
America / James Hart Brumm, editor.
    p. cm. -- (The historical series of the Reformed Church in
America ; no. 57)
 Includes bibliographical references and index.
 ISBN 978-0-8028-6099-6 (pbk. : alk. paper) 1. Reformed Church in
America--Liturgy. I. Brumm, James Hart.
 BX9523.L58 2008
 264'.05732--dc22

                    2007047535

For Sarah Livingston, Carol Hageman,
and all those who have supported and inspired
the creators of liturgical resources
in the Reformed Church in America

The Historical Series of the Reformed Church in America

The series was inaugurated in 1968 by the General Synod of the Reformed Church in America acting through the Commission on History to communicate the church's heritage and collective memory and to reflect on our identity and mission, encouraging historical scholarship which informs both church and academy.

General Editor
 Rev. Donald J. Bruggink, Ph.D., D.D.
 Western Theological Seminary
 Van Raalte Institute, Hope College
Associate General Editor
 Rev. George Brown, Jr., Ph.D.
 Western Theological Seminary

Copy Editor
 Laurie Baron

Production Editor
 Russell L. Gasero

Commission on History
 Douglas Carlson, PhD., Northwestern College, Orange City, Iowa
 Mary L. Kansfield, M.A., New Brunswick, New Jersey
 Hartmut Kramer-Mills, M.Div., Ph.D., New Brunswick, New Jersey
 Jeffery Tyler, Ph.D., Hope College, Holland, Michigan
 Lori Witt, Ph.D., Central College, Pella, Iowa
 Audrey Vermilyea, Bloomington, Minnesota

Contents

Illustrations

Contributors

Christopher Dorn is an adjunct member of the religion faculty at Marquette University, Milwaukee, Wisconsin.

Daniel J. Meeter is pastor and teacher of the Old First Reformed Church, Brooklyn, New York.

Dennis TeBeest is pastor and teacher of the Preakness Reformed Church, Wayne, New Jersey.

Donald J. Bruggink is General Synod professor emeritus of church history at Western Theological Seminary in Holland, Michigan, and general editor of the Historical Series of the Reformed Church in America.

James Hart Brumm is pastor and teacher of the Blooming Grove Reformed Church in DeFreestville, New York.

Martin Tel is an elder at the Reformed Church of Blawenburg, New Jersey, and C.F. Seabrook Director of Music and lecturer in church music at Princeton Theological Seminary, Princeton, New Jersey.

Jonathan Brownson is minister for prayer for the Reformed Church in America.

Paul Janssen is pastor and teacher of the Pascack Reformed Church, Park Ridge, New Jersey, and moderator of the Commission on Christian Worship of the Reformed Church in America.

Kathleen Hart Brumm is pastor and teacher of the First Reformed Church, Athens, New York.

Norman J. Kansfield is senior scholar in residence at Drew University, Madison, New Jersey.

PREFACE

James Hart Brumm

As the lily among thorns, so is my love among the daughters.

This verse from the Song of Solomon[1] was adopted as both a motto and a self-description by Calvinist churches in the Netherlands being persecuted by the Spanish. One of the earliest seals of the Reformed Church in the Netherlands depicts a lily surrounded by thorns and includes this verse.[2] So the title of this book, and of the conference that gave birth to this book, is a play on words.

That conference, held in March 2006, solicited six papers, four of which responded directly to issues that Howard Hageman[3] raised in 1966: the liturgy of the Lord's Day (including the Lord's Supper),

---

[1] 2:2, KJV. Unless so noted, scripture quotes are taken from the New Revised Standard Version.

[2] For a more complete discussion, see Edward Tanjore Corwin, *A Manual of the Reformed Church in America*, 4th ed., rev. (New York: Reformed Church in America, 1902), 3-6.

[3] Howard Hageman (1921-1992) was pastor of the North Reformed Church in Newark, New Jersey, from 1945 to 1973 and president of New Brunswick Theological Seminary from 1973 until his retirement in 1985. During his

baptism (admittedly, Hageman spoke of baptism only as a topic too big for his enquiry), architecture, and congregational song. The remaining presentations at the 2006 conference concerned the current state of worship in the Reformed Church in America (RCA) and creative contemporary worship in a Reformed framework. Fine, insightful work to put all of these papers into context was done by three respondents. The papers and their responses form the core of this volume.

To examine Reformed worship more completely, a chapter on prayer has been added, as have some materials regarding hymn writers, composers, and profession of faith (in Reformed theology, an outgrowth of baptism). A listing of suggestions for further reading has been included, and complete texts of historic Reformed Church liturgies can be found on a CD-ROM that is forthcoming from Reformed Church Press.

The title's play on words is evocative in this era of what some have called "worship wars." A careless reader could take it to be an elitist response by liturgical purists to the popular onslaught of the "praise and worship" movement, blended worship, and other forces of change. The more discerning, however, will quickly discover that such battles are not unique to our period in history. Such readers might easily guess—even without wider reading—that they are not limited to any one denomination.

A well-known, classic definition of the word "liturgy" is "the work of the people." In a sense, the people can be said to be the source of the thorns: people who are fully human and yet, since they have been called to be the body of Christ, struggle to be fully divine; people who have a difficult time with the Calvinist balance of head and heart, constantly tempted to give preference, as is human nature, to one or the other. If the Song of Solomon is to be taken as an allegory of the relationship of Christ to his church, then the church is not the lily, but the thorns. Any worship leader knows that liturgy which seems flawless on paper can be

---

career, he was also a long-time columnist in the *Church Herald* magazine; one of the founders of the doctoral program in liturgics at Drew University in Madison, New Jersey; and a member of the committee that created the 1968 *Liturgy* of the Reformed Church in America. It was in this last context that he presented a series of three lectures at Western Theological Seminary in 1966. These lectures have been pivotal to contemporary understandings of RCA worship. For a more complete biography of Hageman and the complete text of his 1966 lectures, see Gregg A. Mast, *In Remembrance and Hope: The Ministry and Vision of Howard G. Hageman*, Historical Series of the Reformed Church in America no. 27 (Grand Rapids: Eerdmans, 1988).

quite different in actual use.

The lily, however, still blossoms. Life among the thorns may be challenging, but it continues. The same can be said of liturgy among thorns, made all the more miraculous because God can work in and through the human community to make worship beautiful.

Readers will, no doubt, become acquainted with some opinions of the authors of the essays which follow. There is no such thing as an author without a point of view. Being good historians, however, none of these authors is advocating a particular orthodoxy. They are all doing their best to relate what happened and to point out where what the Reformed Church has said it was about or what it was doing does not seem to match the record—this is often where some opinion comes in. Even in the final, forward-looking chapter, Kathleen Hart Brumm doesn't so much advocate a particular liturgical style as give us tools for meeting our present situation creatively. In places, the opinions disagree, which is as it should be; good historical work should be a starting place for discussion.

In addition to the authors who have contributed to this volume and the members of the Reformed Church's Commission on History, thanks are due John Coakley, Susan Hastner, and the Center for Reformed Church Studies at New Brunswick Theological Seminary. As cosponsors of the conference, they were supportive of and patient with the commission in its first attempt at creating such an event. Russell Gasero, the denominination's archivist, provided professional, insightful, and creative support both in preparation for the conference and in production of this book, and Laurie Baron, copy editor for the Historical Series, made sure the work that followed continued to meet the fine standards of the series. My wife, Kathleen, was not only a contributor to this project but, along with our son, Christopher, was patient once again while I took time away from them for writing and editing.

This is the second time I have been honored with the opportunity to edit a book in the Historical Series, and I am once again awestruck by Donald Bruggink's ability to have worked so artfully and efficiently for nearly four decades as its general editor. He has again supported, challenged, and generally improved my work—and, of course, he wrote a chapter this time, as well. Any excellence you read in the following pages is the work of all these aforementioned folks. Any dross is certainly my own.

James Hart Brumm

INTRODUCTION

Why Worship? Why Now?

Blest be the tie that binds
our hearts in Christian love:
the fellowship of kindred minds
is like to that above.

There is an obvious reason why the above stanza, written by Joseph Fawcett in 1782, is important to any examination of a history of worship in the Reformed Church in America (RCA): it is the first stanza of the only hymn to appear in all of our denominational hymnals.[1] There is, however, another, more compelling, reason to include it here. As we answer the question of why, at this point in the life of the Reformed Church in America, its Commission on History might pause to examine our history as a worshiping people, we might think about what I. John Hesselink, General Synod professor emeritus and past president of Western Theological Seminary, said to the General Synod

---

[1] The term "denominational hymnals," for our purposes, refers to hymnals created at the behest of or approved by the General Synod (or the Provisional Synod, prior to 1800) for the use of the whole church during services of the Lord's Day.

1

in his report as its president in 1996. His overarching concern was how we as a church were being challenged by "greater pluralism and diversity, both ethnically and religiously....Ours is 'a strange new world' fraught with dangers as well as with exciting new possibilities."

> Our response must not be a knee-jerk reaction to the challenges of our time and what some people believe is a crisis in the church. Rather, we must go back to our Reformation roots in order to face the future with a fresh vision of what it means to be the church of Jesus Christ in the twenty-first century.
>
> I am convinced that we can do this and be truly Reformed and relevant at the same time. Or, to put it a little differently, we can be both Calvinian and contemporary. (By "Calvinian," I am indebted more to the Genevan reformer than to later strands of Calvinism.) This means, among other things, that we will reflect on the challenges of our time biblically and theologically. This has always been one of the strengths of the Reformed tradition— that we take theology seriously, convinced that right thinking will result in right living.[2]

The chief concern of Hesselink's report to the synod was how to maintain intelligently unity within the Reformed Church and also unity with the church catholic and apostolic. He would foster this unity neither by retreating into our past, nor by retreating from it, but by using it and—first and foremost—scripture to embrace and engage the future. Nor has maintaining the unity of the denomination been a concern of Hesselink alone: it was addressed repeatedly by the General Synod and its leaders throughout the twentieth century.[3] Nevertheless, that desired unity continues to be challenged, so much so that the 2006 synod authorized the creation of a special committee to answer the challenge of covenant breaches among RCA assemblies.[4]

Significant to Hesselink's premise in 1996—one of only two areas of the report to produce recommendations to the synod—was that worship is central to our unity, indeed, central to who we are as

---

[2] I. John Hesselink, "Report of the President," in *Acts and Proceedings of the General Synod of the Reformed Church in America* (hereafter, *Acts and Proceedings*), 1996, 30-31.

[3] As was pointed out elegantly by Lynn Japinga in her address, "Telling the Story of the RCA: A 376th Anniversary Conference," at New Brunswick Theological Seminary, January 29, 2004.

[4] *Acts and Proceedings, 2006*, 67-68.

believers. He argued, therefore, that we must expand the paths into that center.

> We may never be a "popular" church that appeals to all classes of society. The Reformed faith in some ways is un-American. That is, it does not emphasize the individual, free choice, and "doing your own thing."
>
> Nevertheless, we must be more intentional in reaching beyond our Anglo-Saxon, Dutch-American borders. This means more than simply intensifying our efforts to reach people of Hispanic, African-American, Native American, and Asian backgrounds. We must be flexible enough to accommodate to some of their cultural patterns and not force them to become "just like us."...
>
> By this I do not mean an overhauling of our whole inheritance when it comes to worship, but rather a greater variety of liturgical forms that would speak to the needs of seekers and those of various cultural and ethnic backgrounds. However, this means that those new church starts—and some older traditional churches which have thrown out the baby with the bath water—must be encouraged, if not required, to utilize one of those forms of worship and not simply to "do their own thing."[5]

It is an irony of history that Hesselink's report came three decades after Howard Hageman spoke at Western Theological Seminary on the history of the Reformed Church's *Liturgy*.[6] Hageman was then pastor of the North Reformed Church in Newark, New Jersey, and a member of the committee that created the 1968 *Liturgy*, and his three lectures—arguably the most extensive examination of the development of RCA worship to be presented to the church until that time—were given in preparation for the publication of *Liturgy and Psalms*, the most extensive revision of the *Liturgy* to date. The chapters ahead will cite extensively the influence of both the lectures and the 1968 *Liturgy* on our understanding of worship. In some ways, the committee that prepared the 1968 *Liturgy* followed the pattern that Hesselink would later advocate: careful examination of what had been

---

[5]   Hesselink, *Acts and Proceedings,* 1996, 32.

[6]   Howard G. Hageman, lectures on the *Liturgy* of the RCA, delivered at Western Theological Seminary, Holland, Michigan, October, 1966. Reprinted in Gregg Mast, *In Remembrance and Hope: The Ministry and Vision of Howard G. Hageman*, Historical Series of the Reformed Church in America, no. 27 (Grand Rapids: Eerdman's, 1998), 93-169.

done before, followed by thoughtful changes made to meet present and anticipated needs. And it was done, in large part, by reaching back into the past; Mercersburg theology would make its first major inroads into Reformed Church worship with that book. And it was, to a great extent, successful: there are two generations of Reformed worshipers and worship leaders who understand their faith in terms of "remembrance, communion, and hope."[7]

An additional historical irony is that Hesselink was speaking at the ninetieth General Synod since the approval of the 1906 revisions to the *Liturgy*. This had been an earlier effort to create a wider liturgical variety, as well as possibilities for brevity; again, this will be addressed in subsequent chapters. It was the most extensive revision to be approved since the English-language liturgies were approved in 1792, and yet, despite its longevity, it doesn't seem to have had the impact of the 1968 work.

Liturgical revision has proceeded at a much faster pace in the last forty years. Readers of this book will discover more, especially in Christopher Dorn and Daniel Meeter's chapters, about the growing influence of ecumenical consensus in the United States. Shifting demands and understanding of language also have driven the upheaval; much of the language of the 1968 liturgies was substantially unchanged from 1792. Just four decades later, both the use of male language for groups of people and the use of terms such as "thee" and "thou" are almost universally recognized as unacceptable, and exclusively male language for God is debated hotly. In the last quarter-century, the Reformed Church has published three sets of liturgies that have included revisions.[8]

What hasn't happened, despite Hesselink's plea in 1996, has been serious reflection shared with the whole denomination about our particular Reformed liturgical background. In 1969, the Commission on History determined that the second volume of the then-fledgling Historical Series should be a history of Reformed worship.[9] This book is being completed after more than fifty volumes of the series have been published. The near-constant, continuing liturgical reexamination and

---

[7]   A phrase that introduces the structure of the "Meaning of the Sacrament" portion of the "Liturgy for the Lord's Supper," which first appeared in *Liturgy and Psalms* (New York: Reformed Church Press, 1968), 27.

[8]   *Worship the Lord* (1987), *Liturgy and Confessions* (1992), and *Worship the Lord* (2005).

[9]   Minutes of the RCA Commission on History, October, 1969.

rewriting[10] has been ably overseen by the Commission on Christian Worship, which has held our liturgical history clearly in mind. That discussion has not taken place in the whole denomination, however.

If our worship is central to who we are as Reformed Christians, even a unifying element, and if understanding our heritage is a key to building worship tools that strengthen our unity into the future, then this study is not only relevant but overdue. The conference that gave birth to this book celebrated the fortieth anniversary of Hageman's lectures at Western, but it was also just shy of the ten-year anniversary of Hesselink's report and a century after the 1906 *Liturgy*, the beginning of what has been a century of liturgical study and change. It is hoped that this book can fulfill what both of those teachers of the church called for and can begin a conversation that will strengthen the Reformed Church in America's unity and help it understand its roots so that it might grow into the future.

This book is hoped to be the beginning of a discussion, a starting point: this is what we have done, and this is why. Those who study what follows are encouraged to think about worship in their own congregations, how it relates to the picture painted here, and how it fits into the covenant community that is the Reformed Church in America.

That is why we should study the history of worship in the Reformed Church, and this is why we should study it now. None of our congregations worships alone: our theology of the Lord's Supper reminds us that we gather around the table with everyone who ever has or ever will share the feast. If we are all worshiping together, we need to observe Paul's instruction to be considerate, to use our spiritual gifts "for building up the church."[11] And we need to remember that our unity, our dialogue that helps us build one another up in worship and in life, is something to which scripture calls us:

> Let us hold fast to the confession of our hope without wavering,
> for he who has promised is faithful. And let us consider how
> to provoke one another to love and good deeds, not neglecting
> to meet together, as is the habit of some, but encouraging one
> another, and all the more as you see the Day approaching.[12]

[10] The Commission on Christian Worship is continuing its efforts to "broaden the scope of liturgies available to congregations for the celebration of the Lord's Supper," *Acts and Proceedings*, 2005, 310. This subject is addressed more thoroughly in chapter 6 of this volume.

[11] 1 Corinthians 14:12.

[12] Hebrews 10:23-25.

Part I

Our Core Liturgies: The Lord's Day with the Lord's Supper, and Baptism

As we reflect on worship in the Reformed Church in America, we begin, necessarily, with the Lord's Day. It is in Sunday morning worship that people typically have their first RCA experience, and the earliest references to "Reformed liturgy" meant the Lord's Supper and baptism.

The chapters that cover these oldest parts of the *Liturgy* encompass more history than any other section of the book. In chapter 1, for example, Christopher Dorn traces the roots of the Lord's Day liturgy to 1531, almost a century before there was a Reformed Church in America by any accepted measure; that makes for quite a bit of data to discuss. Readers are asked to be patient and persistent; the heavier reading at the beginning sets a historical framework for everything that follows. Daniel Meeter's chapter 2 shares story and provokes discussion over the nature of the Reformed Church's baptismal liturgies, while Dennis TeBeest's response opens up avenues for further discussions over both chapters, as well as what has been called the denomination's "semiliturgical" nature. An addendum on changes in the last quarter of the twentieth century that encouraged local congregations to include children at the Lord's Table rounds out the section.

We begin with the Lord's Day, and, as readers will notice in chapter 1, the decision to discuss the Lord's Supper as part of the Lord's Day liturgy reflects a Calvinian understanding of the Lord's Day as well as the profound effect of Mercersburg theology and Howard Hageman's teachings on the modern Reformed Church in America. There are also examples of some of the thorns amidst which our *Liturgy* grows, thorns of improper use, disuse, and disagreement over what the work of the people should be about. This is the family gathered around table, font, and pulpit; thorns and all, we share God's grace.

CHAPTER 1

The Liturgy for the Lord's Day and the Lord's Supper: Critical Turning Points

Christopher Dorn

The worship tradition of the Reformed Church in America spans almost 450 years. To trace the evolution of this complex tradition from its origins in the Reformation to the present day exceeds the scope of what can be done in a brief historical survey. Here, we can focus only on three critical periods of this tradition. We begin, appropriately, at its origins in the Reformation of the Palatinate (*Pfalz*), an imperial territory in southwest Germany over which the elector Frederic III ruled from 1559 to 1576. We then consider the significance for the Reformed Church in America of the emergence of the Mercersburg movement in the German Reformed Church in the United States of America in the middle nineteenth century. Finally, we indicate the influence of the twentieth-century liturgical and ecumenical movements on the conception of liturgy and worship in the RCA. Our aim is to demonstrate by means of a brief survey of these periods that the worship tradition in the Reformed Church has undergone a real transformation.

John à Lasco

The Sixteenth Century: Reformation in the Palatinate

The sources of the liturgical tradition of the Reformed Church in America lie in a Dutch service book published by Peter Datheen, also known as Petrus Dathenus,[1] (1531-1588) in Heidelberg in 1566.[2] Having begun his vocation as a Carmelite friar, Datheen embraced the Reformed faith in 1550 and became a preacher of the new doctrine. He traveled to London during the reign of Edward VI (r. 1547-1553) and became familiar with a congregation of Dutch refugees there, one of the many "stranger churches" under the superintendence of the Polish

---

[1] Scholars of the late middle ages often Latinized their names as a sign of their learned lifestyle. Contemporary American scholarly usage often returns those names to an English form (i.e., John Calvin, Martin Luther, etc.), although some names (such as Jonas Michaelius, Zacharias Ursinus, and Caspar Olivianus) are more recognizable in the older version. "Peter Datheen" is, increasingly, the common version of this name.

[2] For a critical edition of the Dutch *Forme om dat Heylige Avendtmael te Houden*, see A.C. Honders, "Das Abendmahl nach der Ordnung des Petrus Dathenus 1566," *Coena Domini I: Die Abendmahlsliturgie der Reformationskirchen im 16./ 17. Jahrhundert*, ed. Irmgard Pahl (Freiburg, Switzerland: Universitätsverlag, 1983), 525-35. For a detailed historical account of the reception and transmission of this form for the Lord's Supper, as well as the rest of the liturgical prayers and forms used in the Reformed Church in the Netherlands and in its colonial churches in North America, see Daniel James Meeter, *'Bless the Lord, O My Soul:' The New-York Liturgy of the Dutch Reformed Church, 1767* (Lanham, Md., and London: Scarecrow Press, 1998), 1-91.

reformer, John à Lasco (1499-1560).[3] After Edward's death, his sister Mary acceded to the throne and launched a violent campaign to restore the Roman Catholic faith to England. Consequently, many Protestants were forced to flee to the continent to escape persecution. Datheen fled to Germany and became pastor of a Flemish congregation in Frankfurt from 1555 to 1562. When increasing opposition from the Lutherans there finally forced him out, Datheen and sixty families under his care moved to Frankenthal, a city in the southwest German territory of the Rhine Palatinate. Here the elector Frederic III (1515-1576) offered to the refugees the use of a former monastery for their worship services. Out of a diplomatic respect for the elector's desire for political and religious stability in his territory, Datheen translated into Dutch many of the liturgical forms and prayers contained in the Church Order of the Palatinate, which the elector had published in 1563 to consolidate the ecclesial reforms he had been promoting in his territory since his accession to the prinicipate.[4]

The Heidelberg Catechism

Included among the forms and prayers in the new church order was a new catechism. The Heidelberg Catechism was intended by the compilers of the order not only to be a compendium of private instruction, but also the standard for the doctrine, discipline, and worship for the churches in the territory. Consequently, liturgical

[3]   Ibid., 8-9. For the origin of the Reformed refugee communities in London, see Andrew Pettegree, *Foreign Protestant Communities in Sixteenth-Century London* (New York: Oxford Univ. Press, 1986), 23-76. For the career of John à Lasco, see Dirk W. Rodgers, *John à Lasco in England* (New York: Peter Lang, 1994).

[4]   *Kirchenordnung, wie es mit der christlichen lehre, heiligen sacramenten und ceremonien in des durchleuchtigsten, hochgebornen fürsten und herren, herrn Friderichs, pfaltzgraven bey Rhein, des heiligen römischen reichs ertzdruchsessen und churfürsten, hertzogen in Bayrn etc. churfürstenthumb bey Rhein gehalten wirdt* [vom 15. November 1563] in Emil Sehling, *Die evangelischen Kirchenordnungen des XVI. Jahrhunderts, Vierzehnter Band, Kurpfalz,* (Tübingen: J.C.B. Mohr (Paul Siebeck), 1969), 333-408. See also Wilhelm Niesel, ed., *Bekenntnisschriften und Kirchenordnungnen der nach Gottes Wort reformierten Kirche* 3rd ed. (Zurich: Evangelischer Verlag, 1938), 136-218. From the Niesel edition, Bard Thompson has translated into English three sections ("of Common Prayer;" "of the Preparation for the Holy Supper; and "of the Lord's Holy Supper") in "The Palatinate Liturgy Heidelberg 1563" *Theology and Life* 6/1 (Spring 1963): 49-67. For a critical edition of the German *Form, das Heilige Abendmal zu halten,* see also Frieder Schulz, *"Das Abendmahl nach der Kurpfälzischen Ordnung"* in *Coena Domini I,* 495-523.

Heidelberg in 1620

practices in these churches cannot be understood apart from an appreciation of the role envisaged for the Heidelberg Catechism in the regulation of ecclesial life in the Palatinate.

As do most catechisms, the Heidelberg provides instruction in the Christian faith by explaining the Apostles' Creed, the Decalogue, the Lord's Prayer, and the sacraments. The distinguishing feature of the Heidelberg Catechism, however, is its arrangement of this material according to a threefold *ordo salutis* scheme: "misery," "deliverance," and "gratitude." Accordingly, the subject matter of the first section is human sin, which is revealed by the Decalogue (questions 3-11); that of the second is the redemption and freedom of men and women through Jesus Christ, as taught by the Apostles' Creed and the sacraments (questions 12-85); and that of the concluding section is thankfulness and obedience, about which the Lord's Supper and again the Decalogue teach (questions 86-129). Since, according to the church order, the Word of God itself tends to arrange doctrine according to this threefold scheme, ministers are to observe the scheme attentively when treating their texts. To ensure that their program of preaching was organized on the basis of the dogmatic outline supplied by the catechism, the church order stipulates the following for its use in public worship: first, it directs the ministers to read out several questions prior to the sermon on Sunday morning, according to a set schedule that enabled them to cover the entire catechism in nine weeks; second, it mandates that every Sunday afternoon throughout the year a preaching service be held for the purpose of catechetical instruction. To aid the ministers in this task, the 129 questions and answers are further divided into 52

Lord's Days. Finally, to adapt their preaching to the understanding of the common people, ministers are instructed to cite the questions in the catechism that relate to the themes of their sermons.

Liturgy of the Lord's Day in the Palatinate

But the Heidelberg Catechism did not only serve as the blueprint for the program of preaching in the Palatinate. Many of the liturgical forms and prayers contained in the church order bear the imprint of the catechism with respect to structure, content, and even wording. In the prayers provided for the ordinary Lord's Day worship service, for example, one can see how the threefold scheme of the catechism serves as the pattern according to which worship is to unfold.

The service opens with words from 1 Timothy 1:2[5] to convey that God approaches the worshipers as their only comfort. This is to be impressed on the congregation in the word of judgment and grace in the sermon. But to be prepared for the reception of this word, the congregation must be led in a prayer of confession, which reminds the faithful of their sin and misery and need for grace. Then follows the sermon, which will expound the judgment and grace indicated in this simple prayer more extensively. After the sermon comes another prayer of confession, to which the "comfortable" words (i.e. scriptural promise of redemption) and the absolution are appropriately added. At that point, the faithful can offer the intercessions in confidence, because they have been delivered from their sins. For this reason, the service can conclude with gratitude and praise.[6]

The Liturgy of the Lord's Supper in the Palatinate

Once a month in the cities, once every two months in the villages, and in both on Easter, Pentecost, and Christmas, the Holy Supper continues this service. But the faithful can participate in the Supper only on the condition that they assemble for the service of preparation on the prior Saturday afternoon. In this service worshipers reaffirm their commitment to Christ by examining themselves and assenting to a series of doctrinal propositions as they respond to a form the minister reads from the pulpit.[7] Then, on the day of the celebration, the minister

---

[5]   In the NRSV this reads, "Grace, mercy, and peace from God the Father and Christ Jesus our Lord."

[6]   For a translation of the texts of prayers and rubrical directions for the ordinary Sunday service, see Thompson, "The Palatinate Liturgy" 49-56.

[7]   *Von der vorbereitung zum H. Abendmahl* in Niesel, *Bekenntnisschriften und Kirchenordnungen*, 187-89. ET in Thompson, "The Palatinate Liturgy," 57-58.

delivers a brief sermon on the death of the Lord and the purpose for which the Supper was instituted. A rubric directs the minister, after the sermon and the Sunday prayer, to move to the table to read the form for the Holy Supper to the congregation. This form can be outlined in the following way:

> Institution Narrative from 1 Corinthians 11:23-29
> Self-Examination in Three Parts:
>   Sinfulness and God's wrath
>   Faith in God's promise
>   Thankfulness and the Life of Love
> Excommunication
> Comfortable Words
> Exposition in Three Parts:
>   Homily on the Atonement
>   Interpretation of the Institution Narrative
>   Exhortation to Unity in the Holy Spirit
> Prayer for Worthy Reception and Lord's Prayer
> Apostles' Creed
> Reformed *Sursum Corda*
> Distribution with a Song or Scripture Readings
> Post-communion Psalm or Prayer of Thanksgiving (two forms)

In the order in which it unfolds, the form betrays a close dependence on the liturgical scheme that John Calvin (1509-1564) had drawn up in his *La Forme des Prieres*, published in Geneva in 1542.[8] In Calvin's Geneva, the celebration of the Lord's Supper begins with the Apostles' Creed and a prayer for worthy reception. Then the minister recites the institution narrative from 1 Corinthians 11:23-29. The following penitential sections, consisting in the excommunication, the self-examination, and the comfortable words, comprise the response to the Pauline admonition to everyone "to examine himself" lest he "eat and drink condemnation to himself" (1 Cor. 11:27-29). These sections then lead into a protracted exposition of the promises that relate to

---

[8]   *La Forme des Prieres et Chants ecclesiastiques, avec la maniere d'adminstrer les Sacramens, et consacrer le Mariage: selon la coustume de l'Eglise ancienne* in P. Barth et al. (eds.), *Joannis Calvini Opera selecta* volume II, 11-58. For a critical edition of the French *La maniere de celebrer la cene*, see Bürki, *Coena Domini I*, 347-67. ET in Thompson, *Liturgies of the Western Church*, 197-210 and RCD. Jasper and G.J. Cuming, *Prayers of the Eucharist: Early and Reformed* (Collegeville: Liturgical Press, 1992), 213-18.

Christ's institution of the Supper, culminating in the "Reformed *Sursum corda*," which warns the people not to look for Christ in the bread and the wine, but rather to "lift up their hearts" to contemplate him in his glory at the right hand of the Father. Calvin's form concludes with the words of distribution, Communion, and a post-communion thanksgiving.

Calvin's prolix form reflects the Reformers' strict insistence that the Supper cannot be celebrated properly unless the members of the congregation are prepared to approach it intelligently. For this reason, it is not inappropriate to interpret the Reformed rite as an extension of the proclaimed Word. Just as the biblical text precedes the sermon, so that there is no doubt that the minister proclaims the Word under the authority of the Lord, so too the institution narrative precedes the entire celebration, so that there is no question that this same Lord authorizes the words and actions associated with it. To extend the parallel between the sermon and the Supper even further, we can regard the admonitions, exhortations, and exposition of doctrine that follow the institution narrative as an extensive exegesis of the Pauline passage.

The structural and thematic affinities between the Palatinate and the Genevan forms are obvious. But this is not to suggest that the former is merely a slavish copy of the latter. A comparative analysis of the two reveals that the excommunication in Calvin's order precedes the self-examination; in the Palatinate form this sequence is reversed. Furthermore, the prayer for worthy reception, with which Calvin's order opens, occurs much later in the Palatinate form, before the *Sursum corda*.

But what constitutes above all the distinguishing feature of the Palatinate form is its close dependence on the Heidelberg Catechism. This is immediately apparent in the section on self-examination. Adopting the familiar threefold scheme of the catechism, the material in this section also corresponds closely to the examination questions addressed to the congregation at the service of preparation on the previous afternoon. The homily on the Atonement, which carries out the command "to proclaim the Lord's death until he comes" (1 Cor. 11:26), consists in a restatement of the teaching of the Heidelberg Catechism on the satisfaction made by Christ through his perfect obedience to the divine law and substitutionary death on the cross. Verbal parallels between this section of the form and the catechism can be found in questions 19, 35, 37, 38, 39, and 44. Similarly, the interpretation of the institution narrative teaches in the language of

John Calvin

the catechism how the faithful are reminded and assured of Christ's love and faithfulness to them. The content of the answers to questions 75-79 has been incorporated into this section of the form.

Since the compilers of the church order intended the Heidelberg Catechism to serve as the standard for the doctrine, discipline, and worship of the churches, it is hardly surprising to find the forms prescribed for worship deeply imbued with it. Therefore, it is legitimate to see worship on the Lord's Day, especially on those days when the Supper is celebrated, as a ritual enactment of what it means to live and die in the comfort of the Christian faith—precisely as the Heidelberg Catechism expounds it. The familiar first question of the catechism reads:

> Q: What is your only comfort in life and in death?
> A: That I am not my own, but belong—body and soul, in life and in death—to my faithful Savior Jesus Christ. Christ has fully paid for my sins with his precious blood, and has set me free from all the power of the devil. He also watches over me in such a way that not a hair can fall from my head without the will of my Father in heaven; in fact, all things must work together for my salvation. Because I belong to him, Christ, by his Holy Spirit, assures me of eternal life and makes me wholeheartedly willing and ready from now on to live for him.

The second question explains what the faithful must know to rest secure in this comfort:

> Q: What must you know to live and die in the joy of this comfort?
>
> A: Three things: fist, how great my sin and misery are; second, how I am set free from all my sin and misery; third, how I am to thank God for such redemption.[9]

We have already seen how the threefold content of the answer to this second question constitutes the pattern according to which the order for the ordinary Lord's Day worship service in the Palatinate proceeds. On the Sundays when the Supper continues the service, the faithful pledge in more concentrated expression to adhere to this same threefold pattern, just as they had learned in the catechism and heard in the preceding prayers and sermon.

Datheen adopted most of the prayers and forms from the Church Order of the Palatinate *en bloc*. However, in his Dutch rendering Datheen failed to preserve the symmetry between the Lord's Day and Holy Supper celebrations. For reasons not entirely clear, he introduced substitutes for the ordinary Sunday morning prayers provided in the church order. While his own opening prayer of confession conforms structurally with the Palatinate original it replaces, the prayer after the sermon is not so clearly marked by an acknowledgment of the deliverance from sin proclaimed in the sermon. Datheen did, in fact, draw this second prayer from the Palatinate order, but he had no regard for its designation as a prayer to be used only on special fast days. Confession and supplication for pardon predominate throughout the prayer, unrelieved by the comfortable words and the absolution. The intercessions are not preceded by a thanksgiving for God's gifts of preservation and forgiveness of sins, as in the prayer after the sermon ordinarily used for the Lord's Day. The faithful, then, can hardly approach God in supplication in any attitude other than that of dejection, thanks to their own unworthiness. The cumulative result of such a service could only have been an increased awareness of sin, obscuring from view the themes of deliverance and gratitude so critical to the Palatinate Reformers' understanding of the gospel.

---

[9] Standard English edition for the RCA is that approved in 1989 and contained in *Liturgy and Confessions* (Grand Rapids: Reformed Church Press, 1990), Part VI: "Confessions."

The Seventeenth and Eighteenth Centuries:
Historical Transmission of Datheen's Orders of Worship

Recently, Daniel Meeter has shown that the Reformed church in the Netherlands introduced very few changes to the liturgical material it had inherited from Datheen. Already at the provincial synod of Holland and Zeeland, convened at Dordrecht (Dort) in 1574, church leaders passed resolutions to adopt the prayers and forms for the sacraments that Datheen compiled for his own congregation in Frankenthal in 1566.[10] The synod, however, did require that the votum ("Our help is in the name of the Lord...") open the Lord's Day service, and the Aaronic benediction ("The Lord bless you and keep you...") conclude it.[11] The only modification to the form for the Supper was the required use of the words of distribution based on Martin Micron's London rite (1554):

> Neemt, eet, ghedenckt ende ghelooft dat het lichaem Iesu Christi ghebroocken is tot een volcomen versoeninghe aller onser sonden.
>
> Neemt, drinkt alle daer wt, ghedenckt ende gheloouet dat her dierbaer bloet Iesu Christi vergoten is tot versoeninghe al onser sonden.
>
> [Take, eat, remember, and believe, that the body of Jesus Christ has been broken for the full forgiveness of all our sins.
>
> Take, drink all of it, remember and believe that the precious blood of Jesus Christ has been poured out for the forgiveness of all our sins.] [12]

At the national synod convened at The Hague in 1586, the Reformed Church in the Netherlands mandated that its congregations

---

[10] Resolutions of the synod concerning the use of Datheen's order of worship are found in *De Kercken-Ordeninghen der Ghereformeerder Nederlandtscher kercken in de vier Nationale Synoden ghemaeckt ende ghearresteert. Mitsgaders Eenige anderen in den Provincialen Synoden van Hollandt ende Zeelandt gheconcipieert ende besloten waerby noch anderen in bysondere vergaderinghen goet-ghevonden, by ghevoeght zyn*, ed. I. Andriesz, Delft, 1622, 13ff. Cited in Bryan D. Spinks, *From the Lord and 'The Best Reformed Churches': A Study of the Eucharistic Liturgy in the English Puritan and Separatist Traditions 1550-1563* (Rome: C.L.V. Edizioni Liturgiche, 1984), 138. See also Meeter, *'Bless the Lord, O My Soul,'* 10-11.

[11] Ibid., 10.

[12] Frederik Lodewijk Rutgers, *Acta van de Nederlandsche Synoden der zestiende eeuw* (s'-Gravenhage, 1889), 147. (The translation of this formula, known as the *London aanhangsel* [London appendix], is my own.)

Synod of Dort, 1618-1619

adhere strictly to Datheen's form for the Supper, which the minister was to read at the table on those Sundays when the sacrament was celebrated.[13] In 1618-1619 the national synod of Dort officially ratified the forms for the sacraments provided by Datheen and directed that they be added to the public documents of the church. By this synodical resolution, these liturgical texts were now officially constituted as the *Netherlands Liturgy* and accorded the same authority as that of the doctrinal standards of the church, which now consisted in the Heidelberg Catechism (1563), the Belgic Confession (1561), and the canons promulgated at the Synod of Dort.[14] It is curious, however, that the new Church Order of Dort did not contain the forms for the prayers before and after the sermon, nor did it instruct them to be read. Their continued use evidently depended on the customs of the churches and the free enterprise of Dutch printers.[15]

[13]   Meeter, *'Bless the Lord, O My Soul,'* 14.
[14]   According to Meeter, among all the Protestant churches only the Dutch Reformed have consistently used the term "liturgy" to designate the forms of worship in their service books, anticipating the modern use of the term by several centuries. See Daniel James Meeter, "Is the Reformed Church in America a Liturgical Church?" in Heather Murray Elkins, ed. *Pulpit, Table, and Song: Essays in Celebration of Howard G. Hageman* (Lanham, Md.: Scarecrow Press, 1996), 199.
[15]   Meeter, *'Bless the Lord, O My Soul,'* 17.

The *Netherlands Liturgy* and the doctrinal standards accompanied the colonists who settled on Manhattan Island (New Amsterdam) shortly after the Synod of Dort concluded its sessions. Naturally, the churches the immigrants planted in the soil of the new world were subject to the authority of the governing body of the Reformed Church of Amsterdam in the Netherlands, the Classis of Amsterdam. Because of their subordinate relationship to the Classis of Amsterdam, the fledgling congregations in the new world became as Dutch Reformed in doctrine and in worship as those in the Netherlands itself.[16] The distinctive liturgical character of these colonial churches survived the annexation of New Amsterdam by the English in 1664; the new English government prescribed laws that guaranteed to the Dutch the rights to freedom of conscience and to worship publicly in accord with their own customs and church discipline.

Public worship on the Lord's Day in the Dutch American colonies usually consisted of a morning and an afternoon service, which generally followed the same order. The *voorlezer* (lay reader) opened the service by reading a scripture lesson. He then led in the singing of a psalm, after which he read out the Ten Commandments in the morning or the Apostles' Creed in the evening. There followed another psalm during which the pastor entered the congregation, offered a silent prayer, and ascended to the pulpit. From the pulpit the pastor intoned the votum and the salutation. He then introduced the *exordium remotum* (outline of his sermon) and read the prayer before the sermon. After his sermon, he read the prayer after the sermon, into which he incorporated specific intercessions, concluding them with the Lord's Prayer as a collect. The offering followed, a psalm was sung, and the pastor pronounced the Aaronic benediction. In the afternoon the congregation would hear a sermon on the Heidelberg Catechism.[17]

Throughout the colonial period most congregations could expect a measure of uniformity in their worship from Sunday to Sunday. On those infrequent Sundays when the Lord's Supper was celebrated, they would have heard the form for the Supper as it had come down to the Dutch churches from the Palatinate, since throughout the period the Classis of Amsterdam mandated that pastors read without change the forms for the sacraments. This is not to say, however, that these congregations were without exceptions. Dutch pietist preachers, including the renowned Theodorus Jacobus Frelinghuysen (1691-

---

[16]   Gerald F. De Jong, *The Dutch Reformed Church in the American Colonies* (Grand Rapids: Eerdmans, 1978), 7.

[17]   Ibid., 128-35.

1747), opposed set forms of prayer in worship, convinced that these impeded the freedom and fervor in the expression of public devotion. The pastors who favored experientialism in worship, however, did not prevail on the young colonial church to abandon its commitment to the *Netherlands Liturgy*, which remained the norm for worship throughout the period.

Eventually, the use of the Dutch language among the growing urban populations of the renamed English colonies of New York and New Jersey eroded. To adapt to the forces of social change in America during the mid eighteenth century, the consistory of the Dutch Reformed church of the city of New York issued in 1763 a formal request to the Classis of Amsterdam for a pastor able to preach and to catechize in English.[18] The classis responded by recommending the Reverend Archibald Laidlie, a Scotsman who had been serving an English church in Vlissingen (Flushing), a seaport town in the southern region of the Netherlands. The consistory extended the call. In spite of opposition from the pro-Dutch party, Laidlie introduced English preaching successfully in the Dutch congregation of New York in April 1764.

Once it had a minister who conducted worship in the English language, the church in New York had to provide an English translation of the *Netherlands Liturgy*, as well as the doctrinal standards. Three years after Laidlie began his preaching ministry, the consistory presented to the church what became known as the *New-York Liturgy*, which included not only a complete metrical psalter for congregational singing, but also translations of the Heidelberg Catechism, the Belgic Confession, and the public prayers and forms from the *Netherlands Liturgy*.[19] The appearance at this time of a service book in English was emblematic for the changes soon to come, because, in 1772, the Classis of Amsterdam approved a plan by which the Dutch Reformed church in the American colonies was to establish independence from the mother church in the

---

18   Arie C. Brouwer, *Reformed Church Roots: Thirty-Five Formative Events* (New York: RCA Press, 1977), 18. The stages in the history of the Anglicization of the Dutch American Reformed churches in New York and New Jersey, which necessitated the English version of the Netherlands Liturgy, are recounted by De Jong, *The Dutch Reformed Church in the American Colonies*, 211-27, and by Meeter in *'Bless the Lord, O My Soul,'* 37-75.

19   For the annotated critical edition of *The Liturgy of the Reformed Church in Netherland. Or The Forms used therein in Publick Worship* (1767), see Meeter, *'Bless the Lord, O My Soul,'* 98-180. Curiously, the *London aanhangsel* is not attested in the form for the administration of the Lord's Supper.

Archibald Laidlie

Netherlands. In 1788, the synod of the Reformed Protestant Dutch Church in North America appointed a committee to translate and revise the entire Church Order of Dort, as well as the doctrinal standards and liturgy.[20] In 1793, these documents were published together as the new church's official *Constitution*, consisting from this time to the present in the threefold "Doctrine, Liturgy, and Government." While it made modifications and additions to the documents to adapt to the changed political circumstances in a now independent United States of America, the committee altered neither the public prayer forms for the Lord's Day nor the form for the Lord's Supper. In fact, until the proposals for liturgical reform in the twentieth century were implemented, the traditional Supper form continued its official life in the transplanted

---

[20]   "Until 1772, the Dutch Reformed Churches in America were subject, at least theoretically, to the Classis of Amsterdam. After achieving their independence in 1772, the new denomination became known as the "Dutch Reformed Church in North America" and as the "Reformed Dutch Church in the United States of America." In 1819, it was incorporated as the "Reformed Protestant Dutch Church in North America." An attempt was made about 1840 to drop the term "Dutch" from the official title, but the proposal failed. It was not until 1867 that the present name of "Reformed Church in America" came into use." Dejong, *The Dutch Reformed Church in the American Colonies*, 236. In many published materials from the 1780s to the 1860s, the denomination referred to itself as "The Reformed Protestant Dutch Church in North America," the term being used in this book.

Dutch Reformed churches in America as an English translation of Datheen's Dutch translation of the Palatinate prototype.

The Nineteenth Century: Worship and Liturgy in the Dutch and German Reformed Churches

In the nineteenth century, the Reformed Protestant Dutch Church in North America confronted the challenge of defining its own place in an American Protestant landscape that was becoming increasingly pluralized. That the church did not entirely succeed in maintaining continuity with the sources of its worship tradition in the liturgies of Datheen and the Palatinate is reflected in some critical remarks from an address delivered in 1835 by a respected Dutch Reformed minister, George Washington Bethune.

> The Reformed Dutch Church has a liturgy adapted to all the offices and occasions of worship. It is perhaps to be regretted that its disuse has become so common among us, perhaps from a weak desire to conform to the habits of other denominations. Certainly there are occasions when the forms of prayer are at least as edifying as many extemporaneous effusions we hear from the desk [sc. pulpit], and it is evident that the wise fathers of the church did not intend that they should remain a dead letter in our [sc. liturgical] books.[21]

A layman in the denomination corroborated these observations. He reported to the *Christian Intelligencer*, the official newspaper of the denomination at the time, that he had participated in many Dutch Reformed services in New York and New Jersey during the second quarter of the nineteenth century. But the absence from them of the order of worship prescribed in the *Netherlands Liturgy* led him to conclude ironically that the Dutch had no liturgical forms of prayer of their own. He expressed regret that he had not heard the form for the Lord's Supper read in its entirety for many years.[22]

The disintegration of the order of worship prompted the synod of 1848 to appoint a committee to find ways of promoting a greater consistency of use of the traditional liturgical forms, but the committee disbanded the following year. In 1853, the issue re-emerged, and this

[21]   Gregg Mast, *In Remembrance and Hope: The Ministry and Vision of Howard G. Hageman*, Historical Series of the Reformed Church in America, no. 27 (Grand Rapids: Eerdman's, 1998), 122.

[22]   *Christian Intelligencer*, XXIII (April 28, 1853), 1.

George Washington Bethune

time the church made the liturgy the object of study and revision for
the next five years. The changes that the committee proposed were
substantial and later were incorporated in a new provisional liturgy
approved by the synod and published in 1857.[23] The synod, in a special
session in October of that year, however, determined its earlier action to
be unconstitutional and resolved that the classes vote on the new liturgy
in 1858. But the majority of the classes failed to take action, and the
synod aborted the whole project. Apart from a relatively insignificant
grammatical correction in the form for the Lord's Supper, nothing had
been changed officially.

Despite this reversal of fortune, the labors of the committee
during the previous five years had not gone to waste. The synod
did not recall the published copies, and they circulated within the

---

[23]   *The Liturgy of the Reformed Protestant Dutch Church in North America*. New York:
Board of Publication of the Reformed Protestant Dutch Church, 1857.

denomination, influencing the liturgical life of many Dutch Reformed congregations. The provisional liturgy consisted of a volume of ninety-six pages, containing forms for a wide range of services and dedications, including the traditional forms, the Nicene and Athanasian creeds, as well as a table of scripture lessons for morning and evening services each Lord's Day.

Perhaps the most significant feature of this liturgy was a complete order for public worship, appearing for the first time in the history of this tradition. The service opened with an invocation and a salutation, then proceeded to the reading of the Law. This was followed by the reading of the scripture lessons (Old Testament and New Testament), which provided the theme for the sermon. But between the lessons and the sermon was interpolated the prayer of intercessions. After the sermon came the second prayer, and the service concluded with a benediction. Rubrical directions for hymns did not appear; presumably the drafters of the liturgy decided to let local customs dictate their place in the order.

Students of classic Reformed patterns of worship will observe at least a few anomalous elements in this order. Perhaps most conspicuously, in the Palatinate order the prayer before the sermon consists of a confession of sins and a petition for a saving apprehension of the Word. Only after the sermon is the longer prayer of intercessions offered. Second, the invocation for God's presence at the beginning of worship is incongruent with the firm confidence in the already present God expressed in the votum. Finally, in the Reformed churches two scripture lessons were occasionally used, but almost always from the epistles and the gospels. Howard Hageman has pointed out that the practice of selecting one from each of the two testaments was borrowed from the Anglican services of morning and evening prayer.[24] Evidence of the Anglican influence on the Dutch Reformed would reappear later in the century when the church responded once more to the need for liturgical revision.

The Dutch were not the only Reformed Christians in America concerned about the integrity of their worship practices in this period. Palatinate immigrants who had arrived in the new world beginning in the early eighteenth century under the sponsorship of the Reformed Church in the Netherlands soon became numerous enough to establish their own church. By 1792 they organized themselves into an independent denomination, and the German Reformed Church was

---

[24] Mast, *In Remembrance and Hope*, 132-33.

born. Uncertain about its own place and mission, the German church was open to cooperation with various Protestant communions in the nineteenth century. Because of their shared heritage, it was especially close to the Dutch Reformed. These two bodies traced their origins from the Reformation in the Palatinate, and were defined confessionally by their formal adherence to the doctrine, discipline, and worship enshrined in the Heidelberg Catechism and the Palatinate liturgical forms. Because of their strong affinities, the two denominations entertained a merger and, in 1842, appointed delegates to a convention to engage in open dialogue about the issues still facing the two churches before this could happen.[25]

The plans for merger ultimately came to grief, however, due to a controversial development in the German church. In the mid 1840s, a program of theological and liturgical renewal known as the Mercersburg theology emerged in this denomination. During the next several years, the two progenitors of this theology, John Williamson Nevin (1803-1886) and Philip Schaff (1819-1893), produced a voluminous body of literature in which they argued for an inclusive, ecumenical vision of an "evangelical and catholic" church. The Mercersburg theology generated one of the most protracted and intense ecclesiastical conflicts in American church history, and opponents in both the German and Dutch Reformed churches denounced it for its "Romanizing" tendencies. Yet this theology had important consequences for the conception of liturgy and worship in both churches, consequences which would be felt especially in the twentieth century by the Reformed Church in America.

The immediate focus for the publishing activity of the Mercersburg theologians centered on foundational issues in the worship life of the Reformed churches on the American frontier. In his polemical tract, *The Anxious Bench* (1842), Nevin decried the revivalistic techniques made popular by evangelist Charles G. Finney (1792-1875).[26] The "new measures," as these techniques were called, consisted of invitational hymns, sermon, pleas addressed to sinners by name, and the use of an "anxious bench" to which the preacher summoned the convicted for improvised admonitions and prayers.

According to Nevin, the new measures not only eroded the Reformed order of worship in the congregations that adopted them,

---

[25]   Herman Harmelink, III, *Ecumenism and the Reformed Church* (Grand Rapids: Eerdmans, 1968), 33.

[26]   John W. Nevin, *The Anxious Bench* (Chambersburg, Penn.: Office of the "Weekly Messenger," 1843).

John W. Nevin

but, more seriously, they propagated a defective ecclesiology. In a revised and enlarged edition of his tract, Nevin argued that the church does not grow by means of techniques contrived to induce dramatic conversion experiences in those to whom they are applied. The church is the body of Christ and grows in unity and love by means of its own internal dynamism—the very life of Christ within it. If the churches remained faithful in sound preaching, pastoral visitation, frequent celebration of the Lord's Supper, and patient catechetical instruction, growth would happen spontaneously.[27]

Nevin and his supporters soon found a platform on which to promote their conception of church and worship. In 1847, their denomination appointed Nevin as chairman of a committee instructed to prepare a new liturgy. Ten years later, the project was completed. The provisional liturgy was published under the title, *A Liturgy, or Order of Worship*, which the synod authorized for use on a trial basis in German Reformed congregations. The contrast between the orders of worship in the provisional liturgy and the relatively simple services of prayers and sermon contained in the Church Order of the Palatinate is dramatic. An outline of the orders for worship on the Lord's Day

---

[27] Nevin, *The Anxious Bench* 2nd ed. (Chambersburg, Penn.: Publication Office of the German Reformed Church, 1844) in *Catholic and Reformed: Selected Theological Writings of John Williamson Nevin*, ed. Charles Yrigoyen, Jr. and George H. Bricker (Pittsburgh: Pickwick Press, 1978), 111-15.

Marshall College, Mercersburg, 1843

and for Holy Communion reveals a structure of worship modeled on the classic liturgies of the patristic era rather than on the forms from the Reformation. This is most conspicuous in the order for Holy Communion. Instead of a communion exhortation addressed to the people in the name of God, there is instead a eucharistic prayer addressed to God in the name of the people.[28]

The realization among the conservative members in the German church that the provisional liturgy introduced a decisive break with the traditional patterns of worship reflected in the Palatinate forms led to conflict and controversy in that denomination.[29] The critical issue in the debates was the precise place of the traditional Reformed cultus itself. For Nevin the Reformation liturgies were deficient as models for the new liturgy. By adopting this position, Nevin of course was exposing an open flank to the attacks of his opponents. But Nevin and his supporters insisted that they had no intention of undermining the substance of the Reformed faith; they only refused to defend and consolidate the liturgical traditions that originated in the Reformation. Instead they sought to establish a liturgical order of worship on the foundation of patristic sources, in order to promote their goal of an evangelical catholicity, which made the Reformation relative. They argued that they were not thereby repudiating their confessional

---

[28] *A Liturgy: or, Order of Christian Worship* (Philadelphia: Lindsay and Blakiston, 1857). The table of contents, including the lectionary of scripture lessons for the church year, is reproduced in Jack M. Maxwell, *Worship and Reformed Theology: The Liturgical Lessons of Mercersburg* (Pittsburgh: Pickwick Press, 1976), 425-33, 467-68.

[29] Ibid., 262-82.

Elbert S. Porter

heritage, but preserving and elevating its true essence. Indeed, Nevin was convinced that his own rehabilitation of John Calvin's doctrine of the mystical union, according to which union of the faithful with the risen and glorified Christ is mediated by the symbols of the bread and wine in the power of the Holy Spirit, necessitated the liturgical reforms they were advocating. The omission of the sacrament of the Lord's Supper from ordinary Lord's Day worship distorted the reception of the distinctive features of the tradition that originated in Calvin.

The liturgical ideals of Nevin and his Mercersburg circle exercised a profound influence on the Reformed Church in America through Howard Hageman in the middle twentieth century. But already in the late nineteenth century, the stimulus that Mercersburg gave to liturgical study and revision in other Reformed churches also reached indirectly into the Dutch Reformed church (by now renamed the Reformed Church in America). In 1868, the church appointed a liturgical committee, to which it called Elbert S. Porter, the former editor of the *Christian Intelligencer* and opponent of Mercersburg, to serve as chair. Two years later, however, Porter asked to be relieved of his responsibilities. The synod nominated in his place Mancius Smedes Hutton, minister of the Washington Square church in New York.

Mancius Smedes Hutton

Hutton wished to restore to the Reformed Church its character as a liturgical church. In the report of his committee to the synod of 1871 can be found three principles that Hutton proposed to guide the study and revision of the liturgy. The first provided for greater corporate participation in public worship. The second simply reminded the denomination that it should distinguish itself from other Presbyterian churches by acknowledging its tradition as a liturgical church. The third suggested that the Reformed Church possessed in Calvin's Strasbourg liturgy an exemplary model on which to base its own revisions.[30]

After two years, the committee was prepared to submit to the synod a revised liturgy, which was subsequently published in 1873.[31] Unfortunately, what transpired in the brief period between then and the first report is lost to posterity, because the minutes of the synod of 1873 do not contain any report. According to secondary sources, an elaborate liturgical order based on that of the Episcopal Church was discussed by the committee but, in the end, discarded. The committee seemed also to have deliberated on the question of whether to recommend the

---

[30] For a summary of the report, see Howard G. Hageman, "Liturgical Development in the Reformed Church in America: 1868-1947," *Journal of Presbyterian History* 47, 262-63.

[31] *The Liturgy of the Reformed Church in America as Reported to the General Synod of 1873 by the Committee on Revision* (New York: Reformed Church in America, 1873).

Anglican *Book of Common Prayer* as the liturgy of the denomination. That these proposals were even entertained by the committee illustrates the ongoing influence of Anglican liturgical life in the denomination, as we have already noted. Finally, the committee is supposed to have discussed the history of the form for the Lord's Supper. Its report was apparently accompanied by a modified form for this sacrament, but, in the end, the committee discarded this also.[32]

The content of the lost working papers and reports would have proved invaluable for achieving deeper insight into the mind of the church concerning its liturgy and its celebration of the Lord's Supper at this stage in its history. But the orders in the revised service book themselves afford clues about the direction in which the committee wished its church to proceed liturgically. The order for ordinary Lord's Day worship opens with an invocation and the Lord's Prayer. The invocation is the familiar collect for purity from the Anglican prayer book, "Almighty God, unto whom all hearts are open, all desires known...." At the head of the order appears a rubric instructing the people to recite corporately the Lord's Prayer and the "amen" after every prayer. Such a rubric reflects the desire of the committee to promote greater corporate participation in worship. To this end, a response is suggested after the reading of the Decalogue, which follows the Lord's Prayer, and a "suitable chant" is indicated between the Old and New Testament lessons. The prayer before the sermon could be free, but Martin Bucer's litany, first proposed in 1857, is suggested as an alternate, with responses from the congregation indicated. After the sermon occurs the offering. Four collects drawn from the Anglican prayer book are suggested as options for the closing prayer, after which comes the benediction. The order for evening worship varies only in its omission of the Decalogue and inclusion of the creed after the New Testament lesson.

Even if the members of the committee decided finally against recommending the *Book of Common Prayer* to the Reformed Church in America for adoption as the official liturgy of the denomination, it is clear that they were determined to draw on as much of it as they could. With Datheen's form for the Lord's Supper, however, they were more conservative. The committee proposed to divide the two most extensive sections of the form, the self-examination and the exposition, into two parts. The first was to be incorporated into a service of preparation. The

---

[32] *A Digest of Constitutional and Synodical Legislation of the Reformed Church in America*, ed. Edwin Corwin (New York: Board of Publication of the Reformed Church in America, 1906), 373.

second modification that the committee introduced was the insertion of a rubric before the Apostles' Creed, directing that both the minister and the congregation recite the creed corporately. In addition, the post-communion thanksgiving (Psalm 103) was set to be read responsively, with the Romans texts omitted. Again, the provision for corporate responses here instantiates the principle that the whole people of God—minister and congregation—comprises the royal priesthood before God, and offers together the sacrifice of praise. But, admittedly, the compression of the form seems determined more by pragmatic considerations than anything else. In the judgment of the committee, the traditional form for the Supper was simply too long and needed to be adapted to the limited capacities of the worshipers.

The Eucharistic Prayer of 1873

The committee's considerations of the order of the Lord's Supper, however, were not limited to these modifications to the traditional form. The most outstanding contribution to the revised liturgy of 1873 is a prayer designated as a "Eucharistic Prayer," which appeared in an appendix named "Prayers for Special Occasions."[33] It was not, however, the liturgical compositions of the German Reformed Church, but rather those of the Church of Scotland, that influenced the committee to introduce a eucharistic prayer to the RCA. With few exceptions, the committee adopted for its own liturgy the eucharistic prayer contained in the *Euchologion*, a liturgical book published in 1867 by the Church Service Society of the Church of Scotland.[34] This prayer has the following structure:

> Preface
> Sanctus
> Epiclesis
> Self-Oblation
> Thanksgiving for the Church Triumphant
> Statement of Eschatological Hope[35]

The puzzle here for the historian is not so much *that* the committee introduced a liturgical prayer that until then had no

---

[33] *The Liturgy of the Reformed Church in America as Reported to the General Synod of 1873*, 109-111.

[34] *Euchologion or Book of Prayers* (Edinburgh and London: William Blackwood and Sons, 1867).

[35] *The Liturgy of the Reformed Church in America as Reported to the General Synod of 1873*, 109-111.

precedent in the denomination, but for what purpose. The traditional form for the Supper already contained a prayer for worthy reception. It seems unlikely that the committee intended the eucharistic prayer as a substitute for this traditional prayer, to be chosen at the discretion of the minister. A possible clue is suggested beneath the title. There a rubric reads:

> The constitution of the Church directs that in the administration of the Lord's Supper, "after the Sermon and usual prayers are ended, the Form for the administration of the Lord's Supper shall be read, and a prayer suited to the occasion shall be offered, before the members participate of the ordinance.[36]

It is possible that this directive reflects a custom in the celebrations of the Supper in which both the traditional form and the prayer were used. The absence of permanent tables or altars in the church buildings of this period required the minister to read the entire form from the pulpit. When he finished reading the form, the minister descended from the pulpit to stand at the long tables that were set up for the communicants. This transition may have felt awkward, and so to maintain an uninterrupted flow in the rite, the minister offered another prayer as he presided at the table. The custom thus emerged that two "communion prayers" were offered at the celebration: the prayer for worthy reception read from the pulpit and another prayer offered at the table.[37] Could it be that the committee seized the opportunity afforded by this custom to propose the eucharistic prayer? There is no documentary evidence to suggest how many churches used the prayer in this manner. But the prayer was evidently popular enough to be retained unaltered when the revised liturgy of 1873 was adopted and issued in 1882 as the authorized liturgy of the denomination.[38]

In 1902, another committee was appointed to respond to the demands of the congregations for abbreviated forms, especially those for the sacraments. Mancius Holmes Hutton, son of the chair of the committee responsible for the 1882 revision, was appointed chair. Interestingly, the report and the revised forms that the committee presented to the synod of 1903 reveal a curious attempt to conflate the traditional form for the Supper with the eucharistic prayer. The committee substituted the *epiclesis* in that prayer for the Pauline version

---

[36] Ibid., 109.

[37] Mast, *In Remembrance and Hope*, 147.

[38] *The Liturgy of the Reformed Church in America Together with the Book of Psalms, for use in Public Worship* (New York: Board of Publication, RCA, 1882).

of the institution narrative with which the traditional form begins. The committee maintained that it did this in response to requests from the churches to introduce the form with a prayer instead of the scripture reading. It further claimed that reading the institution narrative at the beginning of the form was redundant, since much of the text recurred in the exposition. Following this line of reasoning, the committee also eliminated the Lord's Prayer at the end of the prayer for worthy reception, since it is offered again after the post-communion thanksgiving. Finally, it also decided to move the self-oblation from the eucharistic prayer to a place before the prayer for worthy reception, with a rubric indicating the traditional prayer as an alternate.

The traditional form now contained two parts of the eucharistic prayer, separated from that prayer and relocated in what can only be seen as arbitrary places in that form. Holmes Hutton refers to the eucharistic prayer in his report: the prayer the committee had proposed "consisted of the richer parts of a communion prayer [eucharistic prayer] already in the earlier part of the liturgy [1882 revision] among the special prayers." The opinion that Holmes Hutton had neither the liturgical scholarship nor even the basic knowledge of the forms necessary for a liturgically acceptable eucharistic celebration hardly needs defense. To remove the *epiclesis* and the self-oblation from the eucharistic prayer, refer to them as the "richer parts," and then arbitrarily relocate them in the traditional form, is to reduce the celebration to incoherence.[39]

The recommendations in the 1903 report failed to win the approval of the majority of the classes, and the Reformed Church resumed the project of revision the following year. The synod of 1904 appointed a new committee and instructed it to continue the work of its immediate predecessor. This committee endorsed the decision to introduce the celebration of the Lord's Supper with a prayer. But the committee was determined to use even more of the eucharistic prayer within the traditional form. The proposed form was now to begin with the preface and *epiclesis*. The self-oblation, however, remained in the place immediately preceding the prayer for worthy reception. The formulae omitted from the eucharistic prayer include the *sanctus*, thanksgiving for the Church triumphant, and the statement on the eschatological hope. The one other significant change was the restoration of the institution narrative to its original place at the beginning of the traditional form. The simple elimination of the section of the exposition that interprets the institution narrative effectively solved the problem of the

---

[39]   Hageman, "Liturgical Development in the Reformed Church of America," 280.

redundancy of the narrative: it now occurs only once, but appears after the preface and *epiclesis* from the transposed eucharistic prayer.

The result is the familiar "abridged" form for the Lord's Supper. It is an amalgam of formulae drawn from the eucharistic prayer that appeared in 1873 and the Palatinate/Datheen Supper form. The complicated structure can be outlined in the following way:

Preface
Anamnesis
Epiclesis
Institution Narrative from 1 Corinthians 11:23-26
Self-Examination (abridged—Excommunication omitted)
Comfortable Words
Exposition in Two Parts
The Homily on the Atonement
(interpretation of the Institution Narrative omitted)
the Exhortation to Unity in the Holy Spirit
Prayer of Self-Oblation or,
Prayer for Worthy Reception (Lord's Prayer omitted)
Apostles' Creed
Reformed *Sursum corda*
Distribution
Post-communion Psalm and Prayer of Thanksgiving (concluded with Lord's Prayer)

This form was successfully introduced into the 1906 *Liturgy and Psalms*, but only after the synod reached a compromise with the dissenting classes of the Midwest: in order to avert the conflict that it had witnessed in the German Reformed Church, the synod agreed to publish the traditional (Palatinate/Datheen) form for the Supper next to the revised one in the 1906 service book.[40] Designated as the "unabridged" and "abridged" forms respectively, these were reprinted in the 1968 *Liturgy and Psalms* as alternatives to the Order for the Sacrament of the Lord's Supper.

The Twentieth Century: Worship and Liturgy in an Age of Liturgical and Ecumenical Renewal

The liturgical and ecumenical movements of the twentieth century, and the enormous amount of biblical, liturgical, historical, and

---

[40] Hageman, "Liturgical Development in the Reformed Church of America," 283.

theological scholarship they generated, created a climate for liturgical study and reform as never before seen in the history of the Christian churches. Consequently, the members of the committee appointed in 1950 to revise the liturgy were able to carry out their assignments informed by a knowledge of both the history and principles of liturgy and the theologies of Christian worship that simply were not available to their predecessors. The eighteen-year period during which the committee labored on what was to become the new *Liturgy and Psalms* (1968) is a watershed in the liturgical history of the Reformed Church and opens up a field of research that a brief historical survey cannot adequately cover.[41] Here we can only indicate a few of the factors that account for the new appreciation of the place of the sacrament of the Lord's Supper in the denomination's conception of its liturgy.

Faith and Order and Liturgical Change in the Reformed Churches

Since the principal concern of the liturgical movement was to recover the meaning of the Eucharist as the worship event *par excellence* through which Christians renew their unity with Christ and with one another, the liturgical and ecumenical movements were intimately bound up with each other. Indeed, insofar as it maintained that the ultimate goal of all sound liturgy is to unite Christians with the church in all times and in all places, the liturgical movement was ecumenical in its very essence. One member of the Reformed Church's liturgical committee later perceived this as he reflected on the impact that the liturgical movement had on his own denomination. "Some," he observed, "see in the liturgy not only a bridge over which men may join the ranks in the Body of Christ with Christians of every century, but also the means by which a divided Christendom may be healed of its many divisions."[42]

The intent of the ecumenical movement in the twentieth century was to provide a worldwide forum in which a divided Christendom could engage in interconfessional dialogue about the doctrines and practices that to this day continue to obstruct their path toward visible unity. Between 1910 and 1948, the World Conference on Faith

---

[41] *The Liturgy of the Reformed Church in America together with the Psalter Selected and Arranged for Responsive Reading*, ed. Gerrit T. Vander Lugt (New York: The Board of Education of the Reformed Church in America, 1968). This is known popularly as *Liturgy and Psalms*.

[42] Garrett C. Roorda, "Worship and Liturgy in the Reformed Church in America," in *A Companion to the Liturgy* (New York: Half Moon Press, 1971), 1.

and Order played an instrumental role in creating possibilities for the churches to examine their differences. Since it is in the meaning and practice of the sacraments that the most intractable divisions among the churches have emerged, it is no accident that Faith and Order was intensely concerned with the problem of the sacrament of the Lord's Supper from the outset.

This sacrament received attention at the first Faith and Order conference in Lausanne (Switzerland) in 1927, as well as at the second in Edinburgh in 1937. But at both the subject was treated only in the context of a general discussion about the sacraments.[43] An avenue for more concentrated study opened up in 1939, when the continuation committee of the Edinburgh conference decided to appoint two international theological commissions to be devoted to liturgical issues. The first was instructed to study the "ways of worship" characteristic of the various Christian churches, the second to address the problem of "intercommunion."

The volume produced by the commission on ways of worship contains significant papers by theologians and liturgical historians representing the Reformed tradition. An analysis of their papers in *Ways of Worship* reveals radical changes in orientation to the historic Reformed conception of the Lord's Supper, which these contributors subjected to criticism on the basis of new insights appropriated from the liturgical movement.[44] We consider briefly here two of the contributors who were, directly or indirectly, among the most influential on the members of the liturgy committee.

Perhaps the most outstanding was the versatile scholar appointed by the continuation committee of Faith and Order as chairman of the commission on ways of worship, Gerardus van der Leeuw (1890-

---

[43] The participants at both conferences restricted their theological considerations to the sacraments of baptism and the Lord's Supper, since it was on these two sacraments that all the churches represented could agree. The statements on the sacraments are contained in the final report ("Sacraments") of the sixth section at Lausanne; those at Edinburgh are found in the final report ("The Church of Christ: Ministry and Sacraments") of the fifth section. See resp. *Faith and Order: Proceedings of the World Conference Lausanne, August 3-21, 1927*, ed. H.N. Bate (London: Student Christian Movement, 1927), 390-91; *The Second World Conference on Faith and Order Held at Edinburgh, August 3-18, 1937*, ed. Leonard Hodgson (New York: The Macmillan Company, 1938), 239-49.

[44] *Ways of Worship: The Report of a Theological Commission on Faith and Order*, eds. Pehr Edwall, Eric Hayman, and William D. Maxwell (London: SCM Press, 1951). The Reformed contributors include W.D. Maxwell, J. Schweizer, A. Graf, R. Paquier, G. van der Leeuw, and M. Thurian.

1950). Internationally known for his research in the phenomenology of religion, van der Leeuw was professor of the history of religions at the University of Groningen, and later Minister of Education and Cultural Affairs of the Netherlands. Amid all his responsibilities, he still found time to serve as mentor of the *Liturgische Kring*, a group of pastors and laypersons in the Netherlands Reformed Church (*Nederlandse Hervormde Kerk*) dedicated to the renewal of the liturgical life of that communion. This group added to the Palatinate/Datheen form for the Supper a number of eucharistic liturgies for use in Dutch Reformed congregations, and the *Dienstboek in Ontwerp* (Worship Book in Preparation) published in 1955 by the Netherlands Reformed Church bears the stamp of their labors.[45] Van der Leeuw's own *Liturgiek* enjoyed a relatively wide circulation, and members of the RCA liturgical committee studied it assiduously throughout its own work on revision.[46]

Van der Leeuw drafted the report that introduced the volume, *Ways of Worship*, and contributed one paper, which his death prevented him from revising and expanding. In this brief paper, he identified the challenge that the renewal in sacramental life posed to the Reformed churches in the twentieth century. That challenge was to unite Word and sacrament in Reformed worship. The Reformers affirmed the unity of Word and sacrament as the norm for worship on every Lord's Day, but sacramental practice in Reformed churches very soon departed from the original intention of Calvin, who denounced lay participation in Communion only a few times a year as a Roman Catholic abuse to be corrected. Against Calvin's wishes, however, infrequency of Communion remained the rule in the congregations of Reformed churches into the twentieth century. Celebrated only on special occasions in a spirit of solemn reverence, the Lord's Supper was seen as the "spiritual peak" in the life of the congregation.[47] For his part, however, van der Leeuw insisted that "Holy Communion can never be the acme of worship, since it is itself worship, and every gathering of the members of Christ's body is essentially a gathering at the Table where He laid down the law of the New Covenant in his blood."[48]

---

[45] *Dienstboek voor de Nederlandse Hervormde Kerk: in Ontwerp* ('s-Gravenhage: Boekencentrum N.V., 1955). For an overview of its contents, see Howard Hageman, "Three Reformed Liturgies," *Theology Today* XV, no. 4 (January 1959): 508-10.

[46] *Liturgiek* (Nijkerk: G.F. Callenbach, 1946).

[47] *Ways of Worship*, 225.

[48] Ibid., 226.

But the Dutch scholar subjected not only the practice but also the form for the Reformed Supper to criticism. In the Reformed churches there had been an "almost exclusive relation between the Eucharist and the death of the Lord, with a total neglect of his resurrection." For this reason, the Lord's Supper resembled more a "funerary ceremony" than a "joyful feast."[49] Indeed, the drafters of the Palatinate form conceived the Lord's Supper as a celebration of a death, as the rubric at the head of the form implied: "On those days when Holy Communion is to be celebrated a sermon shall be delivered on the Lord's death and on His Supper."[50] But van der Leeuw urged that the "resurrection is included in the sacrifice of the Lord," which helps explain why the church of the apostolic era broke bread "with exultation," as is apparent in Acts 2: 46.[51]

The Swiss Reformed liturgical scholar Richard Paquier (1905-1985) continued van der Leeuw's criticisms of the conception of the classic Reformed Lord's Supper. Paquier was the founder of *Eglise et Liturgie*, a group of Swiss Reformed pastors and laypersons who championed an "ecumenically-oriented renewal of the concept of the church and the reform of worship in line with an evangelical catholicity."[52] Paquier was drawn to the liturgical life of the Anglican world and also profoundly versed in the liturgical traditions of the churches in both the East and the West. Just as the Mercersburg theologians before them, Paquier and his group adopted an approach to liturgical reform shaped by their studies of the liturgies of the early church. Paquier claimed that authentic liturgy developed from the apostolic times and found expression in the classic liturgies of the third and fourth centuries. The goal of the *Eglise et Liturgie* was to rehabilitate these liturgical sources, from which the Reformers departed in their protests against perceived abuses in the eucharistic theology and practice of the late Middle Ages. In regard to new forms for the Lord's Supper, Paquier and his group succeeded already in 1931 in composing and distributing a "complete, ecumenically recognizable eucharistic prayer."[53] This prayer came out in several versions, and a final formulation was published in 1952.[54] *Eglise*

---

[49] Ibid., 229.
[50] Thompson, "The Palatinate Liturgy," 59.
[51] *Ways of Worship*, 229.
[52] Bruno Bürki, "Reformed Worship in Continental Europe since the Seventeenth Century," in *Christian Worship in Reformed Churches Past and Present*, ed. Lukas Vischer (Grand Rapids: Eerdmans, 2003), 49.
[53] Bürki, "Reformed Worship," 49.
[54] For complete texts of the 1931 and 1952 eucharistic liturgies, see Bruno Bürki, *Cène du Seigneur—eucharistie de l'Eglise: Le cheminement des Eglises*

et Liturgie played an instrumental role in assisting the Reformed church of France (ERF) and the French Reformed churches of Switzerland in recovering the traditional structure of the eucharistic prayer, and the eucharistic liturgies that these churches created after the Second World War are profoundly indebted to its pioneering labors. Through the mediation of the ERF, the RCA also owed a debt to *Eglise et Liturgie* for its own new order for the sacrament of the Lord's Supper. The Reformed Church's Communion Prayer is largely a translation of a eucharistic prayer that appeared in a liturgy that the ERF published in 1950 and again in 1968.[55]

Paquier's criticism of the Reformed Lord's Supper tradition is found in the paper that he contributed to the volume. He believed that the sacramental life of the Reformed churches was vitiated by a flawed conception of the relation between Word and sacrament. The Word of God in these churches is the "sole path from God to man." The sacraments do not have a value *sui generis*; rather they are accorded the status of a seal and a pledge of the grace that the Word alone is sufficient to confer.[56] This conception, according to Paquier, led those in the Reformed tradition to interpret the sacraments only in terms of the Word, as a *verbum visibile*, which God, in graciously condescending to frail human beings, instituted as a pedagogical aid, so that they might understand the promises addressed to them in Christ more adequately. By reducing the sacraments to another form of the Word, however, the Reformers were unable to prevent their churches from collapsing the one into the other. For the Reformers, in Paquier's judgment, "there [was] no difference between the Word and the sacraments, neither quantitative nor qualitative."[57]

Paquier warned that only in drawing a proper theological distinction between Word and sacrament could the Reformed churches ensure for the sacraments their proper place and meaning in Lord's Day worship. Without this distinction, the sacraments and any new liturgies accompanying them would always appear as "invaders, or as needless postscripts, in the minds of Churches which wish to be fundamentally Churches of the Word."[58]

---

réformées romandes et françqises depuis le XVIIIe siécle, d'après leurs textes liturgiques: Volume A : Textes, (Fribourg Suisse: Editions Universitaires, 1985), 127-45.

55   Ibid., 156-59.
56   *Ways of Worship*, 242.
57   Ibid.
58   Ibid., 245.

The Reformed Church and Liturgical Renewal

The Reformed Church in America was certainly sensitive to these currents circulating within the Reformed churches abroad. In 1950, a young Howard Hageman published an article in *Theology Today* on the worldwide renewal of interest in liturgy and worship. The article is an enthusiastic report of a personal encounter with the literature that emerged from the liturgical and ecumenical movements, and it reveals clearly Hageman's own commitment to liturgical and sacramental renewal.[59] Later in that same year the synod appointed him as one of four members to constitute the new Committee on the Revision of the Liturgy. Guided by his liturgical scholarship and theological acumen, this committee, after almost two decades of exacting study and experimentation, succeeded not only in integrating Word and sacrament in Lord's Day worship, but also in composing an order for the sacrament that adheres to the structure of the classic eucharistic prayers of the early church. We turn first to consider the order of worship for the ordinary Lord's Day service as it appears in the new *Liturgy and Psalms*.

The order reveals above all that the drafters were intent on restoring to the liturgy elements that are characteristically Reformed. The prayer of confession precedes the sermon; three prayers printed in boldface appear as options for the purpose, indicating that both minister and people are to recite together the one chosen at the discretion of the former. The minister then proclaims the words of assurance, after which the reading of the Law continues the service. The theological rationale for the liturgical use of the Decalogue is intimated in a rubric that prefaces the text.

As in the Heidelberg Catechism, the Law follows the forgiveness of sin. The Law and/or Summary may be read here or before the Prayer of Confession.[60]

The preference of the drafters for the Law's position after the words of assurance accords with the characteristic Reformed emphasis on the Law's function as a guide for Christian living; obedience to the commandments is an expression of gratitude to God for the remission of sins through Christ. The option of reading the Law before the prayer of confession, however, is not inconsistent with the teaching of the catechism. It is through the Law that Christians are made aware of

---

[59] Howard Hageman, "The Liturgical Revival," *Theology Today* VI, no. 4 (January 1950), 490-505.

[60] *Liturgy and Psalms*, 10.

Howard G. Hageman

sin (questions 3-11); the Law furnishes a standard for holiness and personal morality that Christians can always only fail to attain. But the Law has a salutary effect, because it continually points up the need for grace, which the gospel of the forgiveness of sins announces.

A brief prayer for a right understanding of the Word through the power of the Holy Spirit, the lessons, the confession of faith, and the sermon follow. After the sermon and prayer for blessing on the Word, there appears the following rubric:

> The movement of the service now goes from the pulpit to the table, where the minister will receive the offerings from the people, after the singing of the [doxology].[61]

The ushers return to their places, the congregation is seated, and then,

> While at the table, the minister shall lead in prayers of thanksgiving and intercession, concluding with the Lord's Prayer.[62]

The transition from pulpit to table reveals the nature of the offering. In the early church the worshipers brought their gifts to the table in thankful response to the message of their redemption through Christ, which they heard in the scripture lessons and the sermon. The

---

[61] Ibid., 14.
[62] Ibid.

gifts not only consisted in alms for the poor, but also bread and wine for Communion.[63] The presentation of the gifts thus constitutes a symbolic gesture of thanksgiving, which the presider then verbalizes in the eucharistic prayer proclaimed at the table. With this sequence, the link between offering and Communion is established, impressing on the people that the ordinary Lord's Day service is normally to be completed by the Lord's Supper. Even when the service does not move to the celebration of the sacrament, the minister nevertheless faces the congregation from the *table* to offer the prayers of thanksgiving and intercession. The members of the committee observed that if the day were ever to come when the Reformed Church decides to celebrate the Supper each Lord's Day, the people will have already been habituated by this transition from pulpit to table to expect the completion of the service with Communion.[64]

In the meanwhile, on those Sundays when the Lord's Supper is celebrated, the minister, after the doxology, reads out a statement on the meaning of the sacrament. After a hymn is sung, the minister proclaims the familiar Communion Prayer.[65]

A consideration of this prayer reveals the aim of the Reformed Church to compose a liturgy for the Supper on the basis of the classic eucharistic prayers of the early church. In accomplishing this aim, the church at the same time responded to the call of Reformed scholars for a new form for the Supper that would be devotional rather than didactic, joyful rather than somber, and oriented to Jesus' resurrection as well as to his death. Above all, the Lord's Supper is a joyful celebration of praise and thanks. Moreover, in contrast to what the Palatinate/Datheen form for the Supper envisaged, the celebration guided by the Communion Prayer is a corporate action, not a sermonizing discourse given by the minister. That is why it opens with the invitation to the worshipers to lift up their hearts. After a preface in which the minister gives thanks to God on their behalf for the gifts of creation and for the redemption accomplished by Jesus Christ, they respond with the *sanctus* and the *benedictus*—liturgical formulae that serve to express awe, wonder, and joy, thereby maintaining them in a jubilant mood. The motivation for this joyful celebration is the Christ event. But this event is not restricted to a memorial of the "perfect sacrifice that Christ offered once and for all on the cross for the sin of the whole world." "The joy of his resurrection and the expectation of his coming again" impress on the

---

[63] *A Companion to the Liturgy*, 6.
[64] Ibid., 8.
[65] For the text, see *Liturgy and Psalms*, 66-70.

worshipers that the Supper is not a funerary ceremony, but a Supper of intimate communion with the resurrected Christ who was crucified. Finally, this Supper anticipates the fulfillment of this communion on the day of redemption, depicted in the New Testament image of the eschatological Supper of the Lamb. This is why the worshipers are to await expectantly Jesus' *parousia*, when his church will be gathered from the ends of the earth into the kingdom. The doxological note on the joy of the resurrected and triumphant Christ is sustained from beginning to end in the Communion Prayer.

Conclusion

The history of worship in the Reformed Church does not end with the publication of the 1968 *Liturgy and Psalms*, but few will doubt how hard it is to trace the scarlet thread from the developments that culminated in the monumental liturgical achievement of 1968 through what has followed since then. To be sure, the publications, in 1985, of the Reformed church hymnal, *Rejoice in the Lord*, and, in 1987, of *Worship the Lord*, consolidated the gains of their predecessor, but this has not guaranteed fidelity on the level of the local congregation to the liturgical principles embodied in *Liturgy and Psalms*. Under the pressure of the cultural upheavals in the last few decades, many Reformed Church congregations have sought to reinvent themselves in an attempt to secure a place for themselves in an ever changing American Protestant landscape. This has entailed the introduction of a bewildering variety of new worship programs and the suspension of traditional liturgical practices in an attempt to attune the church to contemporary cultural sensibilities. Many congregations were impressed by the large numbers that independent "community churches" were drawing and were eager to translate into their own contexts the strategies for renewal and growth that seemed to account for the vitality of these newer churches.

Among these strategies have included the adoption of the familiar "contemporary" or "seeker-sensitive" services to replace "traditional" orders of worship. Usually this has meant that services consisting in praise medleys, dramas, personal testimonies, and emotionally uplifting messages inspired by a biblical theme have largely replaced those determined by prescribed texts and prayer formulae, traditional hymnody, and lectionary preaching. The rationale for this change is that the words, symbols, and ritual actions deriving from the classic liturgical forms of the Reformers and of the broader catholic traditions are no longer relevant or accessible to contemporary churchgoers. In order to engage people living in an increasingly secularized or pluralized world, these congregations have defended the move to adopt forms of communication that appeal more broadly to an unchurched culture.

The concern to contextualize the message of the gospel to stimulate interest in what the church is and does is valid. To be sure, the church must always remain open to accomodating those cultural sensibilities and values that may find legitimate expression in the praise and worship of God. Conversely, the church must be willing to test liturgical formulae inherited from a past age to discern their potential to speak meaningfully of God's covenant of grace through Jesus Christ in this age.

On the other hand, critics have objected that the constant creation of services *de novo* to appeal to the contemporary seeker have often resulted in a disorientation among both older and younger members of Reformed congregations. Older members were initially willing to embrace the new styles of worship in the interest of rejuvenating their congregations. But whenever the experimentation did not achieve the desired effect, the pastors and worship leaders were ready to discard the services in favor of the new and the next. The result was a perceived discontinuity in worship practice and consequent demoralization among the members. This, in turn, introduced a vicious cycle: the more the demoralized members left the congregations, the more determined the pastors and worship leaders were to experiment with ever newer programs to maintain flagging numbers.

Perhaps in response, more congregations in the Reformed Church will begin once again to focus on the hallmarks of the best of the tradition of Reformed worship—sound preaching, patient instruction, principled worship, and a more frequent celebration of the Lord's Supper. Perhaps then, as John Nevin and Howard Hageman believed, growth and renewal will happen as a matter of course.

CHAPTER 2

The Baptismal Liturgy:
Searching for Significance

Daniel James Meeter

The principal forms for the liturgy of baptism in the Reformed
Church in America are these four: 1906, 1968, 1987, and 1994.[1] These
are the dates not of their first appearance but of their widespread
publication. These are the dates of four editions of the liturgy: 1906
was the pocket-size *Liturgy*; 1968 was the idealistic *Liturgy and Psalter*,
designed for the pew-rack; 1987 was the paperback *Worship the Lord*;
1994 is included in the wonderful new 2005 edition of *Worship the
Lord*, for which the Worship Commission deserves high praise. Four
successive books, and each contains a new form for baptism. In just
under nine decades the change is total, though step-by-step you can
follow the evolution. The end result is that, in the course of ninety
years, we have switched the form and content of our baptismal liturgy
from the consensus of the Reformation to the consensus of the
liturgical movement. We have done the same with Holy Communion,

---

[1] The 1994 form first appeared in hardcover in the 2005 edition of *Worship
the Lord*, but it will be dated by the year of its adoption—1994—for the
purposes of this study.

but the results, in my judgment, have been better for the table than for the font.

In 1906 there were actually two forms—the unabridged and the abridged. The abridged form was new in 1906 and was offered as a "doctrinally identical" condensation of the original form. The original form is the classic one going back to Heidelberg.[2] It came out with the catechism in 1563. It was adopted by the Dutch in 1566, revised in 1574, endorsed at Dort in 1619, translated into English by us in 1763, and maintained in exclusive and obligatory use among us until 1906. In what follows, "1906" means the original form. Taking the original form and its abridgment together, we can say that the Heidelberg form of baptismal liturgy was in force among us for four hundred years. It has very many virtues, and I love it. But, judging by what we published in 1968 and 1987, it either was not speaking any longer or we were not listening.

These four liturgies I will compare in the second half of this chapter. The first half is more general and offers my conclusions. I do this because I expect my conclusions to be of wider interest than my analysis.

Allow me to begin with a personal story. My son-in-law is a recent immigrant from Morocco. He arrived in the United States last spring. In July, he married my daughter, and then he applied for status as a permanent resident. While waiting he could not work or go to school. He had no social security number, he couldn't get a driver's license, and he couldn't cross the border or his visa would expire, so he sat home and did nothing. How long would this take? And how would the U.S. government regard this young male Muslim? His life was in their hands. We saw him become discouraged and depressed. In December a letter came from U.S. Immigration. We gathered in our dining room to watch him open it. It was his green card. Hooray, hooray! We celebrated round the table. We took turns looking at the card, turning it over, reading every line. Just a little piece of plastic, but such power was in it. He could work now; he could travel now. A week later, he said he felt like a free man; he could even travel to Morocco now to see his mom. The government had recognized and accepted him. He had come under its sovereignty, and his status was secure.

You will understand the analogy. The green card was the "sign and seal" of his status and of everything that status comprehended.

---

[2]   For this, see my critical edition with history and commentary, in *'Bless the Lord, O My Soul.'*

His status changed not from something inside himself, but from a decision by some authority behind some desk somewhere, and his internal changes followed that. We received the change and accepted the decision and the reality belonged to us, as certainly as we held that card. We had not planned our little celebration. It hadn't even occurred to us that we would celebrate. But I'm sure that the same celebration happens in Brooklyn apartments all the time, that the ritual is generally the same, and that it is simple and direct, because everyone present at the opening of the letter has reason to know the significance of that sign and seal.

I offer this story as a window into the experience of baptism among ordinary people in the apostolic church. In Acts 16, for example, the story is told of the founding of the church in Philippi. It was a Roman military base, and two baptisms are reported. The first is the baptism of Lydia and her household, at the river bank outside of town, on a Saturday afternoon. The second is of the jailer and his family, in his own home, just after midnight. We may guess that Lydia was immersed, but in the jailer's case immersion will have been impossible, so it's clear that the mode of baptism was immaterial. Both of these baptisms were of households, thanks to the faith of the head of the house. This offers a clue to the baptisms' significance. There's another clue in how quickly St. Paul baptized, and how little preparatory catechesis there was. I submit it was because the meaning was evident. The meaning of "Lord and Savior" was very clear, but not first theological. These titles were claimed by Caesar, as was the title "son of god." To apply these now to Jesus, the Messiah of the Jews, had obvious implications, as easy to figure as getting a green card.

Baptism is first and foremost a sign of entering the sovereignty of Jesus and his effective government. Right now. In other words, it is a sign of entering the kingdom of God. Of course, baptism has more significance than that, and it has a complexity of meaning that the apostolic writers took decades to develop, but where you have to start is with entering the kingdom of God. That was its significance for John the Baptist, as well as for the disciples of Jesus in his Galilean ministry, and that was its significance for our Lord himself when he instituted it in the Great Commission of Matthew 28: "All authority in heaven and earth has been given unto me, go therefore and make disciples of all nations, baptizing them in the name of the Father, and of the Son, and of the Holy Spirit." This is kingdom terminology. Our Lord is taking his place as the exalted Son of Man from Daniel 7:13-14, the very thing the Sanhedrin had just condemned him for. Daniel 7 lies behind Luke's account of the Ascension in Acts 1, also with its kingdom talk. It lies behind the language of "all authority" and the "nations" in Matthew 28. Our Lord was instituting baptism as the sign and seal of whole nations being transferred into the realm and sovereignty that God had given him.

That was baptism's significance in Acts 16. The households of both Lydia and the jailer had been transferred from the lordship of Caesar to the lordship of the Messiah. The kingdom of Jesus was invading the empire of Rome, but under the radar, and by instruments of peace, not weaponry. The city of Philippi was oriented toward the gods and goddesses of war, and as the events in the chapter make clear, the spirits of exploitation, violence, and terror held sway there. The jailer was so terrified that he thought to take his own life. But Jesus saved him from all this. And, under our Lord's government, the jailer's home became a place of hospitality, of healing and washing and eating together, a circle of light within the darkness. Such is life where Jesus, not Caesar, is Lord. Baptism is the sign and seal of this.

The other house is Lydia's. The church in Lydia's house. The first church in what we now call Europe. From observing this little alternative community we may propose a definition of the church: the church is that community which is the first fruit of and witness to the kingdom of God. Now I am not suggesting that we replace the beautiful definition of the church in the Heidelberg Catechism. What I'm offering is a way of relating the church to the kingdom.[3] The church is that community which is the first fruit of the final population of the kingdom of God, and also the community that is the witness to the kingdom of God. This definition of the church has a vision and a mission statement built right in, a vision and mission that looks beyond the church.

The Book of Acts is not about the expansion of the church but the extension of the kingdom of God, from Jerusalem to Rome, of which the church is the first fruit and the witness. The church is not in business for itself, but for the kingdom. The harvest of the *missio dei* is not the church, but the kingdom. This way of relating the church to the kingdom effectively renders the church relative, and not everyone agrees with it. Roman Catholics and Anglicans tend to identify the kingdom

---

[3]   I am taking my definition from the magnificent sermon by Hendrikus Berkhof at Marble Collegiate Church to the General Synod during the 350th anniversary of the Reformed Church, a sermon that the synod needs to hear again, I think.

and the church. Some Reformed theologians have done so too. Think of the hymn by Jonathan Edward's grandson, Timothy Dwight:

> I love thy kingdom, Lord,
> the house of thine abode,
> the church our dear Redeemer saved
> with his own precious blood.

I am sorry to say that the relationship of the church to the kingdom is practically lost to the Reformed Church. Indeed, the doctrine of the kingdom of God, as such, is evaporating from our denominational consciousness. The RCA's Statement of Mission and Vision never mentions the kingdom of God, nor any nongendered substitute like the reign of God or even the sovereignty of God. Instead, we get a drastic innovation in Reformed ecclesiology. The Reformed Church in America is "to be the very presence of Jesus Christ in the world." A denomination as the very presence of Jesus Christ in the world, and ours, no less! This is breathtaking in its audacity or else its insouciance. It's Catholic ecclesiology in caricature.

More to the point, the kingdom of God is absent from our newest Order for the Sacrament of Baptism. By contrast, the forms in use until 1968 led with it. Our original form started like this:

> The principal parts of the doctrine of Holy Baptism are these three: *First.* That we, with our children, are conceived and born in sin, and therefore are children of wrath, insomuch that we cannot enter the Kingdom of God, except that we are born again. This the dipping in or sprinkling with water teaches us, whereby the impurity of our souls is signified....

These words edified our congregations for centuries. But our 1994 form mentions the kingdom only once, and doxologically, at the end of the final prayer, as something for the future.

Here is my first main point. In ninety-nine years of liturgical change, from 1906 to 1994, the doctrine of the kingdom of God has moved from the first place in our liturgy for baptism to almost no place at all. This reflects the general absence of the doctrine of the kingdom of God from the mind of our denomination. The absence has consequences for our denomination in general and our congregations in particular, for our vision and mission and, no less, for how our baptized members see the purpose of their membership and church participation. The implications I leave for you to work out. But I do mean to alarm you, because one central and distinctive theme of Reformed theology is the sovereignty of God, the realm of God, the kingdom of God.

My second point is a hypothesis, in fact a double hypothesis. The first part of my hypothesis is that during the eighty-eight years from 1906 to 1994, the Reformed Church has been uncertain of baptism's significance, to which its liturgical forms give evidence. The four forms show a divergence of a degree remarkable for such a small denomination with such a strong confessional constitution. For example, 1994 is practically a repudiation of 1987. We've sort of bounced around. You can compare this to the relatively organic evolution of the communion liturgy.

To be fair, there's more to go on when it comes to communion liturgies. Even though such scholars as Paul Bradshaw have shown us that the evolution of the eucharistic prayer is not as straightforward as we once pretended, our Patristic sources still give us good models for communion liturgies, and we can adequately surmise their Jewish roots.[4] But there is no such model for baptismal liturgy, and so it's up for grabs. All denominations have this problem.

The solution of the Episcopalians, for the 1979 *Book of Common Prayer*, in short, was to pattern baptism after Hippolytus. They also recast their baptismal prayer along the lines of a eucharistic prayer. The idea is that the Eucharist is the defining sacrament from which the other sacraments derive. As in the usual course of things, the Episcopalians were followed by the Presbyterians and the Presbyterians were followed by us. In our 1994 form we, too, now have renunciation, a baptismal covenant, and signation (making the sign of the cross). We too now have a baptismal prayer which is a eucharistic prayer. Well, why not? Because eleven times in the New Testament our Lord took the bread and blessed it and gave thanks for it, but never once did he do so with water. Further, it confuses the place and function of eucharistic energy in the worship service as a whole. This point I will return to at the very end of this paper.

The second part of my hypothesis is that there is a correlation between our uncertainty of baptism's significance and our complication of its ritual. Compare the structures of the four forms, and the evolution of elaboration is evident:

---

[4]   Paul F. Bradshaw, *The Search for the Origins of Christian Worship: Sources and Methods for the Study of Early Liturgy*, (New York and Oxford: Oxford Univ. Press, 1992).

1906	1968	1987
Exposition	Institution	Meaning
Baptismal Prayer	Scripture	Scripture
Exhortation	Meaning	Institution
Administration	Baptismal Prayer	Vows
Prayer	Creed	Creed
	Vows	Baptismal Prayer
	Administration	**Administration**
	Declaration	Declaration
	Prayer	Prayer

1987	1994
Meaning	Institution
Scripture	Scripture
Institution	Meaning / pouring
Vows	Presentation
Creed	Renunciation
Baptismal Prayer	Vows
Administration	Creed
Declaration	Baptismal Prayer
Prayer	Baptismal Covenant
	Naming
	Address
	Administration
	Signation
	Declaration
	Prayer
	Welcome
	Blessing

1906 has five discernible parts and no rubrics. Both 1968 and 1987 have nine discernible parts and, at first glance, the same parts, but in different sequence and with different content. The 1968 form has a few rubrics, but 1987 has rubrics gone wild and crazy. The liturgy approved in 1994 has seventeen discernible parts, some kept in their 1987 placement and others returned to their 1968 placement; 1994 has as many rubrics as 1987, but they are more sensible. The seventeen parts of 1994 are all much shorter than the five parts of 1906, except for the administration itself. We ought not compare apples to oranges, but the trend is clear. More things are said and done, but not so deeply, and the thoughts are not so well developed. I would say that the 1994 form aims lower than 1906.

What we have here is hardly unique to the Reformed Church. You see it in other denominations as well. I quote from my own article on baptism in the *New Westminster Dictionary of Liturgy and Worship*, which addresses matters beyond the Reformed Church:

> Under the influence of rationalism and pietism, the [Reformed] tradition's values have tended toward the devolution of the sacrament into a mere pastoral ordinance. Some churches do little more than the required minimum of the water act and the Trinitarian formula. The last decades have seen attempts to revitalize the ritual with new forms. The baptismal prayer is being recast in a eucharistic pattern. While the practices of renunciation, exorcism, signation, and chrismation were regarded as distractions from the divinely instituted covenantal sign, some of these are being reintroduced. How far the Reformed churches will go with these remains to be seen. At issue are whether ceremonial elaboration serves the sacrament better than doctrinal exposition, the significance of the water, the meaning of the covenant, and the form and content of the baptismal prayer. The Reformers would not have thought to give thanks for the water, quite apart from lacking any scriptural warrant, since they saw the water as the sign of judgment and purification. The questions asked of the candidates have been reformulated as vows, but this both risks Pelagianism and alters their original purpose, which was simply disciplinary and catechetical. Some American churches have borrowed the Episcopalian "baptismal covenant," but this is a different use of the word "covenant" than the historic Reformed one.[5]

The Reformed Church is not alone. All the Reformed denominations are facing similar issues, including the issue of whether ceremonial elaboration serves the sacrament better than doctrinal exposition.

My hypothesis about the correlation between the elaboration of the ritual and our uncertainty of its significance is behind my story about the green card. And it is why the connection moves from

---

[5]   Daniel Meeter, "Baptism: Reformed," in Paul Bradshaw, ed., *New Westminster Dictionary of Liturgy and Worship* (Philadelphia: Westminster Press, 2002).

there to Acts 16. When the significance of an action or event is clear and compelling, the ritual can be simple and direct. Chances are, the ritual will be sufficiently obvious and organic that its pattern may be fairly constant. But when we compare our context to that of Acts 16, we have to ask what difference does it really make in daily life if a person is baptized? In terms of safety and violence, as with the jailer? In terms of what happens in your house and who starts living there, as with Lydia? In terms of the risk to her business that she has to manage now, selling purple cloth to Roman army officers whose lord and savior she has become disloyal to? Lydia was no slouch—she will have worked in several languages and across the social classes, she will have traveled regularly between her suppliers and her market, paying workers, dealing with officials, gathering capital—she was a woman of enterprise and property, and you can expect that already at the riverside she must have sensed that baptism was both a passage to life and a clear and present danger, and that the water with the name of God will have said it well enough.

I am not proposing a return to 1987, 1968, or 1906, although I do believe that for all the good we've added to our baptismal liturgies, such as the recovery of the Creed, the action of pouring water, the question to the congregation, and the introduction of the blessing, we've taken a net loss from 1906. But God is good, all the time, and maybe we can see things now that none of us could see until now.

We now examine the four forms one by one. The 1906 form is an example of the historic consensus pattern of baptism in most of the Reformed churches. The pattern is simple and direct, and it gives a clue to the sacrament's significance. Allow me to open another window into the baptismal experience of ordinary Christians, this time not from the apostolic church, but from the Dutch Reformed Church in the seventeenth and eighteenth centuries. Once again it is an analogy from immigration.

In 1991, my wife and I and our two kids were living in Canada as landed immigrants, and we had applied for citizenship. We got a date to appear before a judge, who would examine us, and so for the weeks leading up to it we boned up on our knowledge of Canada. When the day came, we got dressed up and went to the Federal Building. We sat in a large hall and waited our turn among a couple dozen other candidates, all of us anxiously running through our Ottawa catechisms (in liturgics we call this a "scrutiny"). It was our turn, and we went into the judge's chambers where she examined and approved us. We came back out to the other candidates, excited and relieved. Ultimately, the judge came out in her robes, plus a Mountie in his hat, and we all rose, raised our hands, and repeated our oath of loyalty to Canada and to Elizabeth, our Queen. They declared us citizens, the Mountie shook our hands and gave us Bibles (or Korans or Gitas or whatever), and he stood with us for photos.

That's analogous to both the pattern and the primary significance of baptism in earlier centuries. It was about sovereignty and loyalty, whom you belong to, who has power and authority in your life and in your family's life, whose laws do you live by and under whose protection, and who gives you your rights. This is still the case today for baptism in missionary situations. Members of the church I served in Hoboken came from India, and they had stories of how costly baptism was for their families. Baptism was sometimes like a reverse green card, even in their native land.

The relationship of church and kingdom that held at Heidelberg and Dort is one we cannot go back to now. When the pastor baptized you and wrote your name in the baptismal register, that was tantamount to citizenship as well. In the Netherlands, for example, until Napoleon, the baptismal register *was* the civil register. And since, in those days, every ruler ruled more or less in the name of God, your baptism really did signify the kingdom of God. This is not to say that they did not also comprehend the eschatological sense of the kingdom. But I want to stress that baptism was not just analogous to the experience of citizenship or a green card, it actually did include those factors. Don't judge that experience and practice of baptism as if it did not make some kind of sense, at least as much sense as our baptisms make today. Of course, things changed in America with the separation of church and state. But America was still considered a Christian nation and very much an expression of the kingdom of God.[6]

Now, of course, you are protesting that baptism was always much more than that, and you're right. When you read the exposition of 1906, you see that the sacrament is the sign and seal of a real and powerful work of God in us. You have to rethink any prejudice you might have about a low view of the sacraments in the Reformed tradition. In fact, the exposition was criticized for teaching baptismal regeneration, so real and so miraculous is the baptismal work of God in us.[7] It certainly does

---

[6]   Dennis Voskuil, "Piety and Patriotism: Reformed Theology and Civil Religion," in James W. Van Hoeven, ed., *Word and World: Reformed Theology in America,* The Historical Series of the Reformed Church in America, no. 18 (Grand Rapids: Eerdman's, 1986), 120.

[7]   At the General Synod of 1855 the Classis of Schenectady asked "whether

teach a real presence and a mystical union, that we are incorporated into Christ, that we share in his death and resurrection, and that even children are baptized with the Holy Ghost.

The exposition of 1906 does not mention the institution of baptism as such. It doesn't quote scripture passages, it blends scriptural images. Its outline is simple: it explains what we will see and hear and do. What we see: the water. What we hear: the name of the Father, Son, and Holy Ghost. What we do: we enter the covenant by submitting to the water and accepting the Name. Water signifies death and washing, and it seals rebirth and washing. The Father and the Son both witness and seal their particular graces to us, while the Holy Ghost dwells in us to apply to us and assure us of what we have in the Father and the Son. Our covenantal response is to accept it, and the new kind of obedience in this covenant is an obedience of faith, of clinging and cleaving and loving.

The whole passage deserves your study and your admiration. Its tone is forceful, direct, and pastoral, just like the catechism it appeared with. It is worth notice that its explanation of the sacrament is quite different from the catechism's, which is all about the atonement and which teaches, in very Lutheran terms, that baptism points us to and joins us to the one sacrifice of Christ upon the cross. The catechism and the exposition are different because they both are context-sensitive. Finally, the exposition, like the catechism, ends with an apology for infant baptism, in a paragraph which gets added when a child is baptized. Here we get quotations of scripture like proof texts, and the tone gets a bit apologetic.

In my third parish I memorized the exposition, and on the day of a baptism I preached it as a sermon. One of our older members told me how much he appreciated it and asked where I got it, because he hadn't heard it that way before. But actually he had heard it many times before. He had grown up Christian Reformed and had heard it read in full at every baptism. But it didn't speak, and I suspect this was typical. Maybe it had been read too fast, or read from the mind instead of the heart, or read as a duty and not a delight, or maybe it was just that it was read. Whatever, the liturgical text and the liturgical experience became disconnected.

---

the Form of Infant Baptism does not teach Baptismal Regeneration," and the Classis of Westchester requested a "change in said Form, to remove the appearance of such teaching." Corwin, *Digest*, 80.

After the exposition comes the great baptismal prayer—the former great baptismal prayer. It was originally the so-called "flood prayer," written by Luther, revised by Zwingli, adapted at Heidelberg, and then a precious part of our heritage. The prayer is also forceful and direct, and it speaks of baptism as a matter of life and death:

> O Almighty and eternal God, who in thy severe judgment didst punish the unbelieving and impenitent world with the Flood, and didst of thy great mercy save and preserve eight souls to faithful Noah, who didst drown the hard-hearted Pharaoh with all his host in the Red Sea, and didst lead thy people Israel through the same with dry feet, by which baptism was signified, we beseech thee, that thou wilt be pleased of thine infinite mercy graciously to look upon these children, and incorporate them by thy Holy Spirit into thy Son Jesus Christ, that they may be buried with him into his death, and be raised with him in newness of life; that they may daily follow him, joyfully bearing their cross, and cleave unto him in true faith, firm hope, and ardent love; that they may with a comfortable sense of thy favor, leave this life, which is nothing but a continual death, and at the last day, may appear without terror before the judgment seat of Christ thy Son, through Jesus Christ our Lord, who with thee and the Holy Ghost, one only God, lives and reigns forever, Amen.[8]

What contributes to its power is the vigorous narrative that opens it. Such narratives give power to eucharistic prayers. You also find them in the Psalms: "O God, this is what you once did, now please do that again." But this prayer is not a eucharistic prayer because it does not give thanks for water. Indeed, the water of baptism is not the water of life but the water of death. It's not for drinking but for drowning. It's a sign of judgment and purification, and it's a seal of the Spirit, not something for the Spirit to dwell in.

The Old Testament typology in this prayer engages a God who is active in the world at large, a God who is sovereign in judgment and election, a God who is active in gathering, protecting, and preserving a community. Implicit in this typology is that baptism is essentially a corporate sign, though individually sealed. Tragically, the narrative section of the prayer got deleted from our standard text of the liturgy between 1789 and 1815. This was not as the result of any official synodical decision. John Henry Livingston, who was the denomination's

---

[8] Meeter, *'Bless the Lord, O My Soul,'* 119.

editor and publisher, simply deleted it, with the apparent connivance of the whole denomination.

This fact can only mean that our apprehension of baptism was evolving away from the high Calvinist doctrine of our confessions and liturgy. The connection was beginning to disconnect. The denomination was evolving. Between 1800 and 1850 the Reformed Church "made the transition from classical Reformed orthodoxy to American style evangelicalism,"[9] with an emphasis on individual conversion, experience, and the works of faith. The kingdom of God began to mean the positive sanctification of America as a writing large of the individual sanctification of the soul, although it was also a synonym for eternal life (the Heidelberg Catechism is not uncongenial to these meanings). The Calvinism that survived this evolution was the old Princeton Calvinism of the decrees as opposed to the more churchly, sacramental, and even Lutheran Calvinism of the Heidelberg heritage.

The results are predictable. Baptism can still be first about entering the kingdom of God and about the sovereignty and loyalty that come with that, but now, since entering the kingdom of God is the result of one's own conversion, then what's being signed and sealed is the individual's loyalty to God's sovereignty. Baptism is less a work of God toward us and more a work of us toward God. Baptism gets emptied of the miraculous. Yes, miracles happen, but not in church.

We return to the form. After the prayer came the exhortation, which is a set of three questions addressed to the parents. The first question asks if the parents believe the doctrines just laid out, and whether they believe that their children "as members of [Christ's] church, ought to be baptized." Notice, it's not that baptism makes them members of the church, but that as members already of the church, they ought to be baptized. The second question asks if they agree to the Apostles Creed as an expression of biblical faith, and the third question asks about their intention to instruct the child in the faith.

It is worth noting that, since 1968, our publications of this form have styled the exhortation as "vows." But they were not vows. That kind of semi-Pelagianism would have been intolerable to the church that wrote the Canons of Dort. The intention was disciplinary, to guard against baptism from out of "custom or superstition." The context was that all citizens were expected to be baptized (our rule that one of the parents must be an active member is relatively recent). These questions

---

9   James Van Hoeven, "Dort and Albany: Reformed Theology Engages a New Culture," in *Word and World*, 19.

are the interplay of two marks of the church—the right administration of the sacraments and the practice of church discipline for preventing abuses.

The administration is simple: water and the Trinity. The pastor pronounces the full name of the child and the full name of God. The prayer which follows is a prayer of thanksgiving and blessing, but it is not a eucharistic prayer. It is similar to the closing prayer in the original liturgy for the Supper. It moves quickly to petition and intercession and closes with the Lord's Prayer.

We move to the form of 1968. The form opens with the institution from Matthew 28, which was lacking from 1906. Then come these words of introduction:

> In fulfillment of our Lord's institution and command, the Church, acknowledging God's gracious covenant with his people, recognizes the Sacrament of Baptism as a sign and seal of membership in the body of Christ both to believing adults and to children of the faithful.

Notice the shift in significance. Baptism is now first about membership in the body of Christ, that is, the church. The Reformed Church has switched to the modern consensus that baptism is basically Christian initiation. This does not contradict the Belgic Confession, but it's a change in priorities from both the original liturgy and the catechism.

After this comes a string of five scripture quotations to select from. It might be unfair to call these proof texts, but we can say that this string of quotations, quick upon the institution and introduction, betray a felt need to shore up baptism in the denomination. By locating baptism in the doctrine of the covenant it resorts to a trusted bastion against the worst of American evangelicalism. At issue is how to keep baptism properly sacramental, that is, more about God's miraculous activity than about our intention. But how is this done without seeming to be Catholic or even Lutheran?

The solution is the Dutch Reformed tradition of the church as the covenant people, the new Israel. This has several virtues. It integrates the Old Testament into familiar doctrine. It underscores the communal aspect of baptism. It offers an attractive defense for infant baptism. And the confessions certainly regard the sacraments as covenantal signs. But which covenant? For the confessions, it's the covenant of the cross. But the Dutch Reformed tradition tended too often to jump over the cross and understand it in terms of the covenant with Abraham, or the covenant with Israel. There are subtle distinctions here, but the danger of the Dutch Reformed tradition may be seen in the custom among us that adopted children should not be baptized until they were older, or, worse, the apartheid theology of South Africa. Not that the 1968 form is guilty of this, only that this is the significance of baptism that the Reformed Church turned to in order to hold on to it.

The exposition is replaced by something called the "meaning of the sacrament." It maintains much language from 1906, but the passage comes across as a doctrinal review, instead of more dramatically pointing to what will be seen and heard. Both God's kingdom and the Trinity are mentioned in passing, but the language is softer and smoother and lacks the drive of 1906.

The main baptismal prayer is not based on the flood prayer. It thanks God for Christ and blesses God for the covenant of grace, which baptism signs and seals. It then asks God to

> sanctify with thy Word and Spirit this Sacrament to the use for which thou hast ordained it; and grant that this child now to be baptized may through the power of thy Holy Spirit be made a true member of Christ's body, the Church; and being kept in thy love, finally obtain his inheritance in thine eternal Kingdom.

This is a prayer of consecration, though it is not yet eucharistic. Notice two things. First, Christ's body is equated with the church, and we enter it by baptism. This contradicts the first question of 1906. Second, the kingdom is equated with eternal life.

Next comes the Apostles' Creed, correcting 1906, which lacked it. There follow the vows of the parents and the congregation. Again, to treat the questions as vows implies, if not a Methodist kind of Arminianism, at least a Melanchthonian kind of synergism. This may be okay for the Anglicans and even some Lutherans, but it doesn't sit with our confessions.

The administration is as simple as 1906, but this is followed by a declaration, an innovation which continues in 1987 and 1994. The declaration satisfies a felt need for saying something more at this point—one does not want to kiss and run (the modern Dutch approach is to pronounce the scripture verse which is given to the child for life). The declaration is a spoken confirmation, a dry chrismation, and a purely verbal signation. The problem with the declaration is that it takes back what it just gave. It says that the child is received into "the visible membership of the Holy Catholic Church." Why "visible"? The declaration conflicts with articles 29, 33, and 34 of the Belgic

Confession. I suggest this is an accommodation to popular doubts about the sacrament, by means of resorting to the old-Princeton sort of Calvinism, which makes much of distinguishing the visible from the invisible church. But, historically, we said that children ought to be baptized because they are members of the church already—and not the visible church, but simply the Church.

After the declaration comes a pleasing set of intercessory prayers. The intercessions treat baptism as a truly corporate event. They provide a transition to the general prayers of the usual Sunday service. And here it is manifest that baptism is expected to be celebrated in place of the Supper. What if you celebrate the Supper every week? The Reformed Church had not yet arrived at place of conceiving of Word, baptism, and Supper as a single dramatic flow, so deep as to structure the Sunday order of service even when the sacraments were not celebrated.

What shall we say about the 1987 form? It meant well. It's crabbed, it suffers from lousy layout, and the rubrics go overboard, as if the pastor can't be trusted to do it right. As for content, the authors forged a liturgy out of answers in the catechism. In our search for significance, we turned away from the covenant-people approach and headed back towards Heidelberg.

> Beloved in the Lord, the Sacrament of Baptism is a visible, holy sign and seal instituted by God so that he may the more fully reveal and seal to us the promise of the gospel, that because of the one sacrifice of Christ on the cross we are, through grace alone, granted the forgiveness of our sins and given new and eternal life.

This is a distillation of the catechism. Again, the motivation is apologetic, and this is reinforced by the rest of the meaning, which is scripture quotations and commentary. As a catechism lesson it's not bad, but it has no power as liturgy. It isn't context sensitive.

After this come the vows, and these really are vows. The third vow is patronizing: "Do you promise to show in your own person the joy of new life in Christ, by active participation in the life of the church...." Then the congregation is invited to "renew their own baptismal vows." But now we have gone too far from Abraham and made the covenant a covenant of works instead of a covenant of grace. Abraham never had to make any vows, and the gospel never requires believers to make vows.

One innovation is particularly noxious. In the administration, a rubric instructs the pastor to "use Christian names, omit surnames." Where did this come from? How did we let this into our Constitution?

If our Lord commands us to "baptize the nations," how can we exclude surnames? This was not thought out.[10] This rubric continues in 1994. It seems to me that this kind of thing only weakens the force of liturgy in our denomination.

The 1994 form is a huge improvement over 1987. The layout is elegant and clean. It is a decent and suitable version of the current ecumenical consensus of baptismal liturgy. This consensus is usually signaled by some use of the term "baptismal covenant." Our version of it looks a lot like the Presbyterian form in the 1993 *Book of Common Worship*, only ours is nicely simplified. It suffers from occasional sentimentality.

It opens with the institution, and the usual string of scripture quotations, followed by a very short statement of baptism's meaning. But this statement is so lacking that it's questionable whether it's even worth it. There's a rubric about pouring the water, which in itself is great, but the action is to be accompanied by these words: "Water cleanses; purifies; refreshes; sustains; Jesus Christ is living water." The last three are really for Holy Communion. What about "water drowns; kills, judges"? Why say anything at all? Why not let the sound of water speak for itself? After this come two short paragraphs that have endured from 1906. Then comes the presentation by the elders, which is great, though why say, "On behalf of the Board of Elders?" The profession opens with a renunciation. This is more medieval than biblical. Do we "renounce" sin or do we confess it? Indeed, do we renounce it or are we washed from it? And then to ask, "Who is your Lord and Savior?" begs the question. Who else would it be? In Caesar's day, perhaps, but in our day is this the point? Is this an accommodation to evangelicalism? It gets said better in the Creed, so why not trust the Creed liturgically? Why serve a hot dog when there's pot roast on the stove?

The Creed is offered in dialogue form, a salutary practice of the ancient church. The prayer of thanksgiving is thoroughly eucharistic, but it offers the best language in the form. After this is the administration, which is called, without explanation, the baptismal covenant.[11] The pastor asks for the name of the candidate, which is treated here as a Christening. Four times the rubric gets repeated to use only the Christian name, not the surname. Then we get an innovation

---

10 The *Directory's* explanation for the exclusion of the surname has nothing in it of theology, scripture, or the confessions. And what, really, is a "Christian name"?

11 The baptismal covenant is a very different thing in both the *Book of Common Prayer* and the *Book of Common Worship*.

by way of an address to the infant. Not only is it unnatural, but it's wrong.

> For you Jesus Christ came into the world;
> For you he died and for you he conquered death.
> All this he did for you, little one,
> Though you know nothing of it as yet.
> We love because God first loved us.

This gets John 3:16 exactly backward, and it shows how far we have gone from a theology of the kingdom of God. After this comes a laying on of hands, which is confirmation minus the oil, plus an optional signation. But these high church touches are cancelled by means of the declaration that this child is now received into only "the *visible* membership of the holy catholic church." This contradicts the last part of the Apostles' Creed. The usual prayer of blessing follows, plus a unison welcome by the congregation, and the Aaronic benediction.

What's the significance of baptism according to this form? It's unclear and it's dispersed among a multitude of signs. The Reformation approach is that the sign should be simple and should point clearly to something beyond itself. Baptism is certainly complex, but it needn't be foggy, and mystery doesn't mean misty. On the other hand, the Reformed Church is in good company, for this is what all the other denominations are doing in their recent liturgies. It means that we are out of touch with our own Reformation liturgical heritage. And if we've decided to depart from that, then why should we go with the ecumenical consensus of the mainline instead of the free-wheeling practices of the megachurches we are chasing after?

After so much criticism I suppose it's only fair to offer my own suggestions for the future. In terms of theology, needless to say, we have a lot of work to do, both in regard to baptism and the reign of God. In terms of liturgical form, we could remember that "the liturgical values of the Reformed tradition are simplicity and clarity, biblical fidelity, apostolic integrity, and congregational ownership."[12] I would return to the basics of water and the Trinity. I would return to a prayer of invocation and petition (with an epiclesis upon the action) instead of a eucharistic prayer or prayer of consecration. I would keep the dialogue format of the Creed, and have that be the only three questions we ask the candidates. Baptism is not about what you hope to do but what

---

[12] *New Westminster Dictionary of Liturgy and Worship*, 51-52.

you believe. The other questions can be asked in private by the board of elders. I would protect the sign of water and the symbol of washing by removing from our constitutional text such extra signs and rituals as the laying on of hands and signation, and leave these to the judgment and peril of local consistories. After the administration could come the Aaronic benediction or some other well-chosen scripture verse, followed by a prayer of thanksgiving and intercession. At the very end, the parents and congregation could be asked if they intend to instruct the child, etc., and this would be done as a response to the baptism and not as a condition.[13] If people want to heighten the ritual, then use a great deal more water and do a great deal more washing, and instead of adding words, add silence. And if you want to have all the truly wonderful drama of the Episcopal baptismal liturgy of 1979, then do it once a year at the Easter Vigil, where the congregation can take its time, do it thoroughly, and do it biblically and dramatically.

I close with the issue of where baptism should take place within the worship service as a whole. Remarkably, the 1906 form lacks any direction about this. We know that, since 1574, baptism was administered between the sermon and the long prayer. In 1906, however, the sermon was relocated to the end of the service, as the climax, and no doubt baptism will have been administered much earlier in the service. Everything changed in 1968, when we began to use the general scheme of Approach-Word-Response. We derived this scheme from Reformation liturgies, and it was a step in the right direction. Both sacraments were understood as responses to the Word, and thus baptism was to be "administered after the service of the Word." The 1987 form is silent on where it should be done. The 1987 *Directory* offers a rationale for either position—after the sermon, but as part of the Word of God, not as Response, or before the sermon, as part of the Approach, and I take this as further evidence of our uncertainty. There is a further complication in that the sacraments were reclassified in 1987 as Word instead of Response. In the 1994 form, the rubric states that it "may be administered as part of the Approach or as visible Proclamation of the Word." I think we can do better than this.

But first, it's time for the Reformed Church to move on from the scheme of Approach-Word-Response. It did help us think of the service organically, and it resonated with the guilt-grace-gratitude scheme of the catechism. We said we got this scheme from the Reformation, and we did, and we used it in 1968 to defend liturgical change against the

---

[13]   As in the old Palatinate Church Order and the new Scottish *Book of Common Order*.

charges of modernism or closet Romanism. But the scheme does not hold up when pushed (e.g., are sacraments under Response, or Word, or even Approach?). And we know too much about Patristic liturgy to continue with what we have been doing. In this case we are holding on to a Reformation heirloom when we could do better with the ecumenical consensus.[14] The ecumenical consensus is drawn from the models of the early Patristic church, which is where Calvin would instruct us to be looking anyway.

The Sunday service is basically twofold: Word and Table. It can be filled out in this way: Entrance-Word-Response-Table-Sending. I teach students to think of it as shaped like a suspension bridge, where the Gospel and the Great Thanksgiving are the towers. The long stretch in the middle—Sermon, Creed, Confession, Absolution, Intercession—is where the public gets converted to be the church each week. In this scheme, and as the Patristic sources reveal to us, baptism belongs right in the middle, as the heightened expression of Creed, Confession, Absolution, Peace, and Intercession.

We took a great step in 1968. We said that the Supper ought to be served every week. And we said, in the inspired words of Howard Hageman, that the Supper is a feast of remembrance, communion, and hope. This was a brilliant distillation of our Dutch Calvinistic heritage. But precisely because we were recovering our Calvinistic heritage, we missed something. Even more than remembrance, communion, and hope, the Supper is a feast of thanksgiving.[15] Most of all, we come in thanksgiving. Not just thanksgiving as the world can understand it, but in the Great Thanksgiving that requires faith and hope and love. It is our gift and obligation every week to exercise our royal priesthood and, on behalf of ourselves and the entire world, to offer the sacrifice of thanksgiving. That means that every Sunday morning service should climax in a eucharistic prayer, no matter if the Supper is served or not. If there is no Supper, than leave out the anamnesis and oblation and epiclesis and words of institution, but every Sunday the congregation should thank God for creation and salvation and then rise up to sing

---

[14] The current United Methodist Order of Sunday Worship is a good example.

[15] The Reformers generally missed this primary aspect of the Supper, as did the whole Western church. The Calvinistic Supper remained a reformation of the Roman sacrament. The recovery of the primacy of thanksgiving had to wait for the combined influence of the liturgical movement and the biblical theology movement.

the Sanctus and Benedictus together with the angels and the host of heaven.

It is at this place in the order of service that the eucharistic energy, if I may call it that, is properly expressed. And this is the final reason why I believe the baptismal prayer should not be eucharistic. To make it so is to miss the dynamic character of the service as a whole. Just as every service should be eucharistic, whether or not the Supper is served, so, too, every service should be baptismal, and it is baptismal when it passes through the sequence of creed, confession, absolution, peace, and intercession. The baptismal prayer should give voice and expression to this dynamic. And if it is creedal and confessional in narrative terms, as the flood prayer was in terms of flood and Pharaoh, then so much the better.

A RESPONSE TO CHAPTERS 1 AND 2

Dennis TeBeest

In the preceding chapters, Christopher Dorn and Daniel Meeter do important work for the church: they document the development of the Reformed Church in America's core liturgies for the Lord's Day (including the Lord's Supper) and baptism. Meeter and Dorn are liturgists of the first order—a rare breed in this denomination—whose writing on these pages will nurture the future of these orders and keep us liturgically vibrant.

The Reformed Church in America is a denomination which asks, over and over again, "Are we a liturgical church?" We are sufficiently bipolar to, on the one hand, insist that the *Liturgy* is at the core of our *Constitution*—the very essence of who we are; and, on the other hand, to refer to ourselves as "*semi*liturgical" (What does "*semi*liturgical mean?" Every now and then? Or just *laissez faire* about it all?).

What we mean by liturgy has always been a little slippery in the Reformed Church in America. Conducting the work of the church according to the *Liturgy*, for many, has not meant the careful shaping of Lord's Day worship. It has had more to do with using the proper form or order for baptism, the Lord's Supper, ordination and installation, and discipline in order to use the liturgy to teach right theology. Howard Hageman discusses this in his third 1966 lecture,[1] and defends this latter understanding of liturgy in our tradition.

The Reformed Church's "semiliturgical" stance yields a denomination famously—or perhaps infamously—didactic in our worship.[2] Ever since its birth in an era concerned to rescue the experience of God and of faith from deeply entrenched misunderstandings, Reformed worship has been largely an extension of Reformed apologetic: declaring God's worth by explaining the right understanding of God. Our worship motto has come very close to *Lex Credendi est Lex Orandi*—the law of belief sets the norm for our worship. Of course, that is not the church's classic understanding of worship, and such a motto is not sufficient to our day.

We would do well to accept Daniel Meeter's invitation to consider whether the development of our worship is driven by Reformation consensus or by liturgical consensus. Yet we need not come out on either side. There is nothing anti-Reformed about the venerable adage of *lex orandi, lex credendi*.[3] It *does* work both ways: the ways we worship can, will, and should influence the way we believe, as well as the converse. Worship that is simply vivid and celebrative does not betray our heritage. *Ecclesia reformata semper reformanda*; the church is reformed...and always reforming...and always about to be reformed.[4]

Christopher Dorn describes that vibrancy in his chronicle of the history of the reforming of our liturgy for the Lord's Day, as well as in his detailing of the intimate connection of our liturgy to our theology. That connection may be overstated: certainly, the Palatinate liturgy is intentionally and intimately intertwined with the Palatinate/Heidelberg Catechism. But to say that the *form* of that liturgy closely reflects the guilt-grace-gratitude structure of the catechism is a practical stretch; in reality, the Palatinate liturgy engages its most intense confession and absolution *after* the sermon and generally comingles the three

[1]   Mast, *In Remembrance and Hope*, 162.
[2]   James F. White, *Protestant Worship* (Louisville: Westminster John Knox, 1989), 60. Also see Howard Hageman, *Pulpit and Table* (Richmond: John Knox, 1962), 110-12.
[3]   For a multifaceted treatment of *lex orandi, lex credendi*, see Geoffrey Wainwright, *Doxology* (New York: Oxford Univ. Press, 1980), 218-83.
[4]   Joseph D. Small, "A Church of the Word and Sacrament," in *Christian Worship in Reformed Churches Past and Present*, Lukas Vischer, ed. (Grand Rapids: Eerdmans, 2003), 316-17.

components of the catechism. The form and movement of the 1968 liturgy actually comes far closer to the catechism structure than any previous liturgy for the Lord's Day.

Dorn recalls helpfully the liturgical discontent, experimentation, and revision of the mid and late 1800s. However, Howard Hageman himself debated, in his 1966 lectures, whether the Reformed Church's shifts in this period had as much to do with the eminently Reformed character of the Mercersburg movement as with the more socially motivated attempt to be more like the Episcopalians.[5] The 1870s engendered a liturgy often in want of a theology—or at least stretched away from the strengths of Reformed theology (witness how far the sermon had been removed from the reading of scripture in the "Order for Public Worship" at the end of the century). It may not be until the liturgy of 1968 that the Mercersburg movement actually shaped our liturgy.

Some complications in the denomination's liturgical development in the second half of the nineteenth century should also be noted. Two liturgical books were published, in 1857 and 1882. It is astonishing to note that the provisional liturgy of 1857 contained the first order for public worship in our history.[6] Yet, neither of these liturgical revisions were ever ratified by a sufficient number of classes and granted the final imprimatur of the General Synod.[7] What do we think about that? Neither 1857 or 1882 were ever constitutional liturgies, yet they circulated in, were used by, and shaped our worship life.

The development of the 1968 *Liturgy and Psalms* is arguably the most significant liturgical development in the history of the Reformed Church in America. Dorn notes this watershed development, then wonders if we have quickly deserted the 1968 liturgy for whatever is "wise in our own eyes." That may be true; surely worship in many Reformed Church congregations bears little resemblance to the 1968 Order of Worship. Yet, the reality of the order's partial disuse is not demonstrably different from the practice of the church at any point in the history of the Reformed Church in America. There has always been a significant percentage of Reformed ministers of Word and

---

[5] Mast, *In Remembrance and Hope*, 126-27.

[6] Mast, *In Remembrance and Hope*, 131.

[7] The Introductory Note to *The Liturgy of the Reformed Church in America (1907)* implies (pp. iii-iv) sanction of the 1868 revisions, along with General Synod recommendation of the 1882 publication for use in the churches. However, neither the 1868 revision, nor the 1882 publication was ever approved by two-thirds of the classes or finally declared effective by the General Synod.

sacrament—and of congregations—that has not paid heed to the *Liturgy*. We have no more cause to despair the use of our constitutional liturgy now than at any previous period in our denominational story.

The liturgy of 1968 deserves recognition as our tradition's most significant liturgical reflection of the Heidelberg Catechism, as well as of the Mercersburg movement. This is reflected in the liturgy for the Lord's Day, certainly; but more so in the liturgy for the Lord's Supper. The communion liturgy in *Liturgy and Psalms* was a massive change for the Reformed Church in America. The 1968 liturgy has done a stunning job of rediscovering eucharistic prayer, while maintaining a cogent presentation of a Reformed theological understanding of the Lord's Supper. It communicates wondrously an understanding of the Real Presence of Christ and the nature of the sacrifice, without becoming preachy. Dorn also notes the theological underpinnings of the *sursum corda*. This "Order for the Sacrament of the Lord's Supper" can likely be credited for increasing our frequency of celebration to a level closer to Calvin's longing.

What does the future hold for our use of the 1968 Order for the Sacrament of the Lord's Supper? In those congregations that *do* use the liturgy and *are* celebrating the Lord's Supper more frequently, the didactic "Meaning of the Sacrament" is infrequently, if ever, used. At what cost is it being set aside? Can it be simplified or shortened? Could its content be shifted into the eucharistic prayer itself? We do need to have a second communion prayer, or at least seasonal/variable prefaces. Could the evocative themes of remembrance, communion, and hope infuse those seasonal prefaces, so that we don't lose this classic text?

And what impact has the inclusion of baptized children at the Lord's Table had on the worship of the Reformed Church in America?

The celebration of the sacrament of baptism—both its theology and its practice—is examined evocatively in Daniel Meeter's chapter. Central to Meeter's thesis and presentation is a longing to return to the kingdom of God imagery that was the centerpiece of an earlier baptismal understanding in the Reformed Church.

Certainly, broad kingdom images are essential to Calvin, and to the 1906 liturgy.[8] Yet, those kingdom images in the "Office for the Administration of Baptism" are liberally accompanied by covenant images, initiation images, body of Christ images, and sin/redemption images. Kingdom may get first mention in 1906, but no more frequent mention than these other images.

---

[8]   The 1906 liturgies are nothing new; they just republish the old, plus abridged forms—adding nothing, dropping much.

I find Meeter's contention that kingdom imagery is gone from the current baptismal liturgy rather accurate. Kingdom/leaven in the world imagery is not in the 2005 "Order for the Sacrament of Baptism."[9] Yet it does now appear in related liturgies: in the welcome section of our "Order for Profession of Faith" (which effectively serves as our baptismal liturgy for adults), as well as in all the ordination liturgies. All these liturgies declare the truth of what baptism is: it is a commissioning to ministries in the world; it is being light and salt for the kingdom/realm of God.

Have we really deserted Calvin's theology of baptism? I think not. Calvin wished to return as closely as possible to the worship patterns of the early church. He just didn't have the information about the worship of the early church that the twentieth century liturgical movement has brought us. Shouldn't we honor those insights? It is true that there was not as much baptismal consensus in the early church as there was eucharistic consensus. But the variations are largely variations of order, not essence. Water was consistently central in the early church's liturgies, but the presence and coming of the Holy Spirit was also important. We need to recognize and celebrate the Spirit while staying focused on the centrality of the Trinitarian water baptism.

Meeter does make valid critiques:

- It is true that our "dry anointing" after the water baptism is a strange anomaly.
- Our need to hold on to our "visible" membership declaration should be reexamined.
- There are vestiges of our former liturgies that have become sticky encumbrances in our current baptismal liturgy.

On the other hand:

- Calling on the "given" name in the current baptismal liturgy can be traced to the early church, and it was used for good reason. The baptized are a "new creation," no longer given advantage or disadvantage by their family of birth.
- The liturgy's growing complexity from 1906 to 2005 (1994) is true, but significantly overstated. What Meeter's essay describes

---

9   Dating of liturgies has always been something of an imprecise enterprise. Meeter identifies the current baptismal liturgy as "2005," the year of the publication of the *Worship the Lord* book in which it appears. "The Order for the Sacrament of Baptism" was actually declared to have been approved by the classes for incorporation into the *Liturgy* in 1994.

as seventeen component parts to the 2005 liturgy are, upon closer observation, at most ten, at fewest six.

· It seems inaccurate to put the current liturgy at a comparative disadvantage to 1906. The 1906 liturgy may well be more accurately described as good sermon than good liturgy.

· In the development of our baptismal liturgy, the real glitch is 1987. The 1987 "Sacrament of Baptism" liturgy was an eccentric anomaly, ignoring many liturgical insights. The church quickly recognized its shortcomings; the liturgy was gone within seven years.

· One of the things Meeter longs for is actually delivered by the 2005 liturgy. Luther's wonderful "flood prayer" never made it into any of our earlier liturgies, including 1906, in any of its fullness. The current liturgy is more faithful to the flood prayer than any previous liturgy. Meeter does raise an interesting question of whether we "Reformed types" give thanks for water. However, this prayer is certainly more about the mighty acts of God than it is about water quality.

· Meeter critiques our current baptismal liturgy for its "ceremonial elaboration." "Vivid celebration" would be a more fitting description. Vivid components bring the congregation much more fully into the prayer and celebration of baptism. These components help get the message through. They unify and clarify.

The baptismal essay actually opens the church to a wealth of discussion. Are the vows really semi-Pelagian—do they imply that God's grace is waiting on our initiative rather than simply declare our response to that grace? Is it really un-Reformed for baptismal prayer to be eucharistic (to "give thanks")? Do variable placements for the Order of Baptism within the Order of Worship for the Lord's Day reflect doctrinal indecisiveness, or simply the doctrinal richness of a sacrament that defies singular placement? And, in Meeter's closing shift from baptismal issues to consideration of the very structure of the Order of Worship for the Lord's Day, just what revision would overcome our somewhat stilted Approach-Word-Response structure and give the sacraments a more natural placement? All of these are valid questions that we do not have space to answer adequately here.

What Meeter has done, of course, is to get our attention. He calls us to task to fulfill our Reformed mandate: to be conscious of what our actions and words in worship communicate at all times.

Are the core liturgies of the Reformed Church in America compelling, clear, consistent, and simple gospel? I think so. Are we enacting them in a way that speaks without mumbling? That question has a more mixed answer, the mixed answer that has been the bane and blessing of this "semiliturgical" church through all of its history.

ADDENDUM

Finding a Place for Children of All Ages

James Hart Brumm

As early as the Articles of Dort, the Dutch church order that formed the basis for the *Government* of the Reformed Church in America, baptism was said to be the seal of the covenant of God,[1] i.e., membership in the church; affirming Article 34 of the Belgic Confession[2] and Question and Answer 74 of the Heidelberg Catechism.[3] At the same time, Article 59 from Dort called for *adults*

[1] Article 56 of the Articles of Dort, as cited in Corwin, *Digest*, lxiv.
[2] "Having abolished circumcision, which was done with blood, Christ established in its place the sacrament of baptism. By it we are received into God's church and set apart from all other people and alien religions, that we may be dedicated entirely to the one whose mark and sign we bear....And truly, Christ has shed his blood no less for washing the little children of believers than he did for adults." Standard English edition of the *Belgic Confession* for the RCA as approved in 1991 and contained in *Liturgy and Confessions* (Grand Rapids: Reformed Church Press, 1990, rev. 1991), Part VI: Confessions.
[3] "Infants as well as adults are in God's covenant and belong to God's people. They, no less than adults, are promised the forgiveness of sins through Christ's blood and the Holy Spirit who gives faith. Therefore, by baptism,

77

who were baptized to be received into full communion, and the Dort order insisted that "[n]o person shall be admitted to the Lord's supper, but those who make a confession of their faith."[4] The order never said that one had to be an adult to make this confession of faith, yet, by the end of the nineteenth century, this was a customary interpretation of this dichotomous membership standing. Evolving understandings of children and nurture led, in the closing decades of the twentieth century, to an evolving awareness of the needs of children and their place in Reformed worship.

A Place at the Table

In 1972, the Classis of Albany overtured the General Synod "to instruct the Theological Commission to study the possibility of allowing baptized members of the church to partake of the Sacrament of the Lord's Supper before making a public profession of faith."[5] While this overture was denied, a similar overture from the Classis of Mid-Hudson the next year resulted in an instruction to the Commission on Theology to study the matter.[6]

The commission produced its first report on the subject in 1977, acknowledging that "[s]ince the sacrament of the Supper as well as that of baptism is a means of grace, the church throughout the ages has maintained that baptism needs to be followed by the sacrament of the supper, even as birth needs to be followed by care and nurture."[7] While examining the traditions and practices that led to what the Reformed Church has called "baptized non-communicant membership," the paper insisted that "we must acknowledge that the admission of children to the Lord's Supper, before public confession of their faith, is congruent with our theological tradition," and argued that "[i]f the church today is to encourage its children at an early age to be drawn to the table because of their love for the Saviour, we need to examine what it means for them to celebrate the Supper with the people of God."[8]

At the same time, the Commission cautions the church that the above judgments are not the whole of the matter. The

---

the sign of the covenant, infants should be received into the Christian church...." *Liturgy and Confessions*, Part VI: Confessions: Heidelberg Catechism, 1989.

4   Article 61 of the Articles of Dort, as cited in Corwin, *Digest*, lxviii.
5   *Acts and Proceedings,* 1972, 86.
6   *Acts and Proceedings,* 1973, 193.
7   *Acts and Proceedings,* 1977, 297.
8   *Acts and Proceedings,* 1977, 298-99.

implementing of the proposed change for the spiritual health and well-being of the Reformed Church in America will require that we be both vigilant and vigorous in our commitment to the doctrine of the sacraments common to our Reformed tradition. It will require our consent and resolve to give baptism a larger prominence both in our proclamation and our practice. Admission of children to the Table assumes that we are ready as a church to give renewed attention to the discipline of baptism, and that we are ready to stand together in our opposition to indiscriminate baptizing and anything that would lead to "cheap grace."...

The proposed change will lay heavier than usual demands upon the church to provide a continuing instruction, nurture, and a pastoral care that will open to the baptized more plainly the way of faith, and make clear also the obedience of faith which baptism involves.[9]

The 1977 paper was sent out to local congregations and classes for study and response. Two years later, the synod narrowly rejected adoption and implementation of the paper,[10] but that was not to be the end of the discussion. A new overture was brought by the Classis of California in 1981, calling on the synod "to allow our covenant children participation in the Lord's Supper."[11] An extensive discussion and another narrow rejection followed at the synod of 1982. Still, the Commission on Theology presented another major study, "Baptized Non-Communicants and the Celebration of the Lord's Supper," in 1984.[12] It was not adopted, but, in 1985, an overture from the Synod of New York called for a re-examination of that position and further study. Finally, in 1988, the commission made its case with the following points:

In baptism, God wills that baptized children shall be led by the Holy Spirit to appropriate all of God's promises and to affirm the knowledge of God's grace in their own public confessions of faith. Such is the faith expressed by the Apostle Paul: "I press on, to make it my own, because Jesus Christ has made me his own"

---

9   *Acts and Proceedings*, 1977, 305.
10   For a complete synopsis of synodical actions in this area, see *Acts and Proceedings*, 1988, 380-81.
11   *Acts and Proceedings*, 1981, 120.
12   This paper can be found in James I. Cook, ed., *The Church Speaks: Papers of the Commission on Theology* (Grand Rapids: Eerdman's, 1985).

(Phil. 3:12). Indeed, the church must provide the most sound and comprehensive program of nurture and education possible in order that the church's children will make public profession of faith in Jesus Christ as Savior and Lord.

However, nothing in the Scriptures, in reformed theology, or in the early history of the church requires such a confession of faith to be a prerequisite to participation in the Lord's Supper. Rather, the Lord's Supper is understood as a *means of grace* for nourishing and strengthening us to eternal life, righteousness, and glory. God gives to covenant children in the Supper the infinite goodness of our Savior and makes us all to be partakers in all God's blessings....As such, the Supper must surely not be considered as the *goal* for baptized children. It is not a reward for making confession of faith. Rather, the sacrament is a means of grace that properly leads one to public confession of faith. We do not withhold food and drink from our children until they are old enough to say they need it. On the contrary, the food and drink are among the means by which our children grow to maturity....

Throughout the early history of the church, the Holy Supper was understood as a means of grace to nurture the children of the church. After 1,200 years, and then only in the Latin West, the Roman Catholic Church excluded children from the Table. This was done for two reasons. First, the bishop alone, it was believed, could "confirm" a person making profession of faith, and the practice was declared to be a sacrament....Even after this action children were not immediately excluded. A second action combined with the first to change the practice gradually. The Fourth Lateran Council, A.D. 1215, defined the doctrine of transubstantiation in which the elements of the Holy Supper were regarded as too holy to be handled by any except a consecrated brother, priest, or bishop. So, children were excluded lest they "slaver" and desecrate the holy elements. For the same reason, the cup was withheld from lay Christians.

Reformed Christians do not believe in transubstantiation, but in the spiritual presence of Christ in the sacrament of the Table. Neither do we believe in confirmation as a sacrament. Nor is there any necessity for the individual's public confession of faith, essential though it be, to be a precondition for participation in the Lord's Supper....

The participation of children at the Lord's Table before public confession of their faith was a standard practice in the early church. Our own theological tradition nearly a hundred years ago demonstrates a congruence with the practice in the Children's Catechism approved by the General Synod of 1889:

What is the duty of the child?

It is the duty of a baptized child to worship God and to come to the Lord's Supper as soon as he is drawn to it by love for the Savior....

What is required of anyone to partake of the Lord's Supper is faith in and love for the Savior, ability to experience the Savior's love expressed in the bread and the cup, and the sense of belonging to the covenant community. The believing and discerning will be at the level appropriate to the child's age. Children can show the kind of love, trust, and thankfulness appropriate to their place in the family of God.[13]

This time, the arguments of the Commission on Theology led the synod "[t]o encourage boards of elders of RCA congregations to include baptized children at the Lord's Table." Still, this was not an easy decision; the advisory committee at that synod recommended rejecting all of the commission's recommendations in this regard, insisting that, among other things, "this new position would in practice virtually eliminate confession of faith and therefore deprive young people of this important point of commitment."[14] James I. Cook, a member of the Commission on Theology at the time, crystallized the challenge before the denomination in this sixteen-year discussion:

At the age of four, children demonstrate remarkable understanding of the stories of Scripture and of symbols in worship and sacraments. The awareness of love for Jesus, the feeling of belonging to the Christian family, and the desire to participate in the Lord's Supper are likely to emerge at this time. So it makes sense that this is also the age at which we should introduce the Lord's Supper, the third means of grace. The goal of the supper is precisely that of the Word and baptism, the other two means of grace: to move baptized children toward a personal affirmation of

---

[13] *Acts and Proceedings*, 1988, 383-84. The Commission on Theology acknowledged its indebtedness to Donald J. Bruggink's lecture, "The Lord's Supper for all God's Covenant Community," given at Western Theological Seminary's Fall Institute in 1979 in Holland, Michigan, for the historical material.

[14] *Acts and Proceedings*, 1988, 385.

James I. Cook

the baptismal covenant and a joyful participation in the full faith and life of the people of God.

When members of our denomination were struggling with this issue, we found the faith-development argument very convincing. But even to the almost-persuaded there remained the traditional biblical barrier of 1 Corinthians 11, with its sobering call to self-examination and its grim warning that those who eat and drink "without discerning the body" eat and drink judgment upon themselves. This passage appeared to establish an informed, adult faith in Christ as a necessary precondition for coming to the Lord's table.[15]

A Place for the Word

Growing understandings of faith development led to a new awareness not only of how Reformed children should be nurtured spiritually, but also of how they could be nourished through the proclamation of the Word. Sonja Stewart, professor of Christian education at Western Theological Seminary, rethought methods for teaching children based on the practices of Sofia Cavalletti, Italian author and educator.

[15] James I. Cook, "The Toughest Issue: Why the RCA Said Yes to Baptized Children at the Lord's Supper," in *Reformed Worship* number 12 (Grand Rapids: CRC Publications, 1989), 31.

Over a thirty-year period, Cavalletti brought preschool-aged children together for weekly two-hour sessions in a center filled with biblical and liturgical materials for telling Bible stories. She observed that children of that age were not just preparing to worship, but were worshiping, and that they could experience and integrate Bible stories into their understanding of themselves and their world.[16] Intrigued by her approach, Stewart partnered with Jerome Berryman to write *Young Children and Worship*.[17]

> The aim of "Children and Worship" is to create an environment that enables children to encounter and worship God: to abide in God's love as experienced in Bible stories, parables, and liturgical presentations; and to live as Christ's ministers in the world.
>
> The environment of the room serves as a channel for encounter with God. Through the religious imagination the worship leader helps the children transform the room into a special place to listen to and to talk with God. Ordinary, everyday time and place are transformed into liturgical time and space, the time and space of worship. In this new place we have all the time we need, so we don't have to hurry. We walk more slowly and talk more quietly, because someone might be talking to God and we don't want to disturb them.
>
> The language of worship is religious language, informed by Scripture. Since preschool children can't read but rather are learning through their bodies—particularly their hands—the Bible is translated into materials children can use in a sensorimotor way. These materials are placed on trays and kept in the same place on the shelves, week after week, so children can return to them as they wish, or work with one story in relation to another, thus engaging the rudiments of theology. In this room children have *appropriate* freedom to use the scriptural and liturgical materials that surround them.[18]

---

[16] Sonja M. Stewart, "Letting the Story Stand," in *Reformed Worship* number 12, 25-29.

[17] (Philadelphia: Westminster, 1989).

[18] Stewart, *Young Children and Worship*, 26.

Sonja Stewart

A Place to Grow

This changing understanding of the place of children in the life of the Reformed Church did leave a question about the status of confirmation. The General Synod of 1990 asked the Commission on Theology to "study, clarify, and define 'confirmation' as a concept and as RCA congregations practice it; and further, to pay particular attention to the relationship of confirmation to baptism, to membership in the body of Christ, and to membership in a congregation."[19] This was just two years after encouraging local boards of elders to welcome baptized children at the Lord's Table, and one year after the publication of *Young Children and Worship*. As if to emphasize the confusion, the Commission on Christian Worship introduced a new order for confirmation at that same synod. Even as the denomination was growing into a new understanding, it was trying to hang on to the old one.

In a paper presented to the 1992 General Synod, the Commission on Theology left little doubt as to its position: "The supplementary rite of initiation called 'confirmation,' which has recently come to be practiced in the RCA, is a mistaken direction which the RCA ought to reverse."[20] Yet the commission did not imagine this would be a simple matter:

[19]   *Acts and Proceedings*, 1990, 212.
[20]   *Acts and Proceedings*, 1992, 465.

If confirmation is not in keeping with the RCA's *Doctrinal Standards*, what should the RCA put in its place? It can hardly go back to the *status quoi ante* 1906.[21] Also, there are some good items that should be salvaged from the current forms. To guide future developments, some theological benchmarks are in order.

First, baptism itself must be protected from devaluation. The RCA *Doctrinal Standards* teach that baptism is the *sole* rite of initiation into the RCA. Baptism, not confirmation, is the ordination to the priesthood of all believers. Baptism, not confirmation, is the liturgical sign and seal of the Holy Spirit....

Second, baptism if the sufficient *sacramental* and *liturgical* qualification for Holy Communion—although in admitting someone to the Lord's Table, the board of elders is called to always take account of pastoral and disciplinary considerations....

The third benchmark is that, in the RCA, admittance to the Lord's Table belongs properly to the board of elders (with the pastor), and not to the congregation assembled. This act of admittance was originally meant to be an act of pastoral supervision, not of liturgical initiation....

Fourth, "conversion," which is an extremely important word for many Christians, must be understood in the full Reformation sense. Reformed theology sees conversion as both *subjective* and *objective*. Subjective conversion is the necessary decision for Christ as Lord and Savior. This decision, as the Reformation understood it, is never something once-for-all, but a process, something that is always continuing....

However Luther, when plagued by his subjective doubts and the survival of the old man in him, also said, "I am baptized." In this case he was referring to the objective side of conversion, which *is* once-for-all. This, too, is being born again, but it is signified and sealed by baptism, since it depends not on our decision for God but on God's decision for us....

Fifth, the RCA continues to value public profession of faith, especially of young people when they have reached the age of discretion and have been prepared through serious catechism. Admittance to the Lord's Table should not exempt children from preparing for this purely subjective act of identifying with the confession of the church.[22]

[21] The first time an order for confirmation as part of public worship appeared in the RCA *Liturgy*.
[22] *Acts and Proceedings*, 1992, 461-64.

While "confirmation" didn't have a place in the Commission on Theology's view of baptism and membership, profession of faith did, as did the idea that congregations recognize publicly the developmental passage toward adulthood: "Perhaps the RCA could devise an educational system that is directed toward a series of public professions of faith, keyed to the successive stages of fait development, continuing into adulthood."[23] That has not come to pass, but something else did. The very next year, the Commission on Worship looked for further definition.

> It has also become apparent that the church is struggling with the practical pastoral issue of nurturing young people in the Christian faith and in finding or developing programs and resources for guiding people to a more mature faith and in providing them with opportunity to witness to the faith in Jesus Christ. These concerns involve not only issues of theology and liturgy, but also have implications for Christian education, catechesis, pastoral practice, and church order.[24]

This led to the appointment of a task force which included in its membership representatives from the Commissions on Worship, Theology, and Church Order. After two years of work, this task force reported back to the synod with a three-pronged study. Under the portion excerpted here, "Recognizing Baptism and Professing Faith,"[25] the task force hit on the powerful biblical theme of "Ebenezer."

> The word "eben-ezer" means "stone of help," and it is the name given by Samuel to the stone he erected to commemorate the defeat of the Philistines, "for he said, 'Thus far the Lord has helped us'" (1 Sam. 7:12). Jacob erected such a stone at Bethel to commemorate his encounters with God (Gen. 28:10-22, 35:14-15), and Joshua erected a whole pile of stones to commemorate the crossing of the Jordan (Josh. 4). These stones were important markers in the history of God's dealing with Israel, even though they were not a part of the most central pattern of Israel's worship. Although the stones erected by Jacob and Joshua are not specifically named "Ebenezer," they fit a common pattern. What the RCA is looking for is a pattern of Ebenezers in the lives of its members....

[23]   *Acts and Proceedings*, 1992, 464.
[24]   *Acts and Proceedings*, 1993, 218.
[25]   *Acts and Proceedings*, 1995, 195-207.

The whole Reformed doctrine of the sacraments is based on an understanding of them as "covenantal signs" (as in the Old Testament) which are related to a single covenantal act, Christ's death and resurrection. Christ is the true covenant partner with God, and by means of the sacraments one shares in his or her status and what he or she has accomplished. This covenant is unilaterally enacted by a sovereign God, and it is God who extends the covenant to whom God wills by means of God's Word and Holy Spirit, creating faith, and gathering, protecting, and preserving a congregation for eternal life....

From the perspective of faith development theory, as we move through life we need both educational and liturgical opportunities which enable us to respond to God's grace in Jesus Christ—first given in our baptisms and nourished through Word and sacrament. Unique life issues, gifts, and capacities in childhood, adolescence, young adulthood, middle adulthood and older adulthood challenge individuals to deepen their self-understanding as people of God and to strengthen their commitment to the ministry of Jesus Christ. Both the RCA's educational offerings and liturgical celebrations for the raising of one's Ebenezer need to take account of the human life cycle.

What began as an examination of how children are welcomed into the worshiping congregation grew, in just under a quarter century, into an understanding of faith development and our relationship to God as a life-long process. With it came a renewed understanding of the sacraments within Reformed theology and of our covenant relationship with God and one another. While the most immediate changes when this report was presented were technical,[26] the influences of this report can be seen in the orders for baptism and profession of faith and ordination that appear in the 2005 *Worship the Lord*. Arguably, not all of the changes conceived in this period have been realized throughout the life of the Reformed Church, but it has the potential to become an outlook that both strengthens our covenant and helps us to welcome all the children of God—of whatever age—into fellowship with us.

[26]   They came in the form of changes to membership categories and definitions in the *Book of Church Order. Acts and Proceedings*, 1995, 224-31.

Part II

Becoming at Home with the Word: Congregational Song, Architecture, and Prayer

While the word "liturgy" means "work of the people," if one were to ask most people what they did during worship, they would probably not say "celebrate liturgy," but they would almost certainly say—after some discussion of the sermon they listened to—something about singing and praying. And when asked about the church, most people would not be as likely to speak of the local body of believers, the denomination, or what is described in answer 54 of the Heidelberg Catechism[1] as they would the building in which they sang those hymns and said those prayers and listened to the pastor doing whatever she was doing.

The second part of this book addresses these elements—architecture, congregational song, and prayer—that give human

---

[1] "I believe that the Son of God through his Spirit and Word, out of the entire human race, from the beginning of the world to its end, gathers, protects, and preserves for himself a community chosen for eternal life and united in true faith. Moreover, I believe that I am and forever will remain a living member of it."

context to worshipers' encounter with the Word. Chapter three presents Donald Bruggink's essay from the 2006 conference, a heavily illustrated discussion of architecture (which is, after all, best appreciated visually). James Hart Brumm's chapter on congregational song in the Reformed Church is the second-longest treatise ever published on the subject, which may explain some of the trends observed. Martin Tel's response to those two chapters makes some observations about the denomination's tendencies to forget its own heritage and to want to conform with others—more of the "thorns" amidst which worship grows—that should provoke many more discussions. Two addenda follow: the first, Jonathan Brownson's discussion of a powerful nineteenth-century prayer movement; the second, an examination of some of the Reformed Church people who have created congregational songs.

When Christians get together, they sing and they pray. In these next few entries, we seek to understand just a bit more about how the songs, the prayer, and the surroundings affect how we understand God, ourselves, and our worship.

CHAPTER 3

A Brief History of the Architecture of Reformed Churches in America

Donald J. Bruggink

A history of church architecture in the Dutch Church in America, which had its beginnings in 1628, is made up of fragments, the extrapolation of which may present a seriously skewed picture. But it is all we have, and anyone with additional or corrective knowledge is eagerly solicited to share it.

Word and Sacrament

The true marks of a Reformed church, Dutch or otherwise, are the right preaching of the Word and celebration of the sacraments. Architecturally, this meant that the pulpit had pride of place. Perhaps the earliest evidence of this is in our oldest extant church building, the Old Dutch Church of Sleepy Hollow (1685). There the most prominent and elegant piece of furniture is the pulpit, reputedly imported from the Netherlands.

One of the few other early churches of which we have an image, albeit of a restoration, is the Old Mud Meeting House of Harrodsburg, Kentucky (1800). While the structure of this Dutch Reformed outpost was mud and waddle, its liturgical accoutrements put many of our

Sleepy Hollow Church

contemporary multimillion dollar churches to shame. Both Word and sacrament receive impressive architectural acknowledgment with a table for Communion in the center aisle.

In the Reformed Church in Charlotte Amalie, St. Thomas, the Virgin Islands (1844), the front pews had narrow table-like attachments for use for communion Sundays. The pulpit was placed on a high platform, giving the congregation on the floor of the nave, as well as those in the balconies, equal access to the proclamation of the Word.

That the architectural provisions for Communion in these churches was not exceptional can be inferred from the fact that in the Reformed Church of the Netherlands, provision for partaking of Communion seated at table continued through the twentieth century.

Communion seating in the Oude Kerk, Amsterdam, 1784

Immanuelkerk, Gereformeerd, Delft, The Netherlands

The revivalism of the American frontier, which might be considered to have had its forerunner in our own Dominie Theodorus Jacobus Frelinghuysen,[1] by the nineteenth century had come to dominate and distort Reformed Church architecture. While Whitefield had been content to preach revival from hourglass, or box pulpits—or outdoors when required—by the nineteenth century the great organized revivals were frequently held in rented civic auditoriums or in specially built tabernacles, or for those of lesser fame, in tents. The architectural layout of the rented auditoria soon became the dominant revival architecture, and subsequently church architecture. The large auditorium platform was ideally suited to the physical movement of the revivalist. Unfortunately, while the platform was large, the pulpit was frequently reduced to a reading desk, giving prominence to the revivalist rather than pulpit and pulpit Bible as visual representations of the source of the message.

When the auditorium had an organ and raised seats behind the platform for choirs, this too fit in well with the needs of the evangelist to seat a choir to add direction and volume to the singing. Early, in the Cane Ridge revivals in Kentucky (circa 1810), days of evangelistic preaching were consummated in a "communion occasion" patterned after the Scottish custom of weekends of preaching climaxed by a Sunday Communion and Monday sermon to send folk on their away.

---

[1]   See *Forerunner of the Great Awakening: Sermons by Theodorus Frelinghuysen,* The Historical Series of the Reformed Church in America, no. 36 (Grand Rapids: Eerdman's, 2000).

A. C. Van Raalte Church, Thule, South Dakota

However, the affirmation of conversion soon became the revivalist's norm, rather than baptism or the celebration of the sacrament.

The result of revivalism can be seen in most of our churches built in the nineteenth and twentieth centuries, from the humble A.C. Van Raalte sod church near Thule, South Dakota, to the original liturgical arrangement of the great, lavish, Victorian Gothic St. Nicholas Collegiate Church in New York. In all, while not attaining its pre-revivalist splendor, the pulpit was nonetheless dominant, while the architectural presentation of the sacrament was confined to an inconspicuous table on the floor and a small bird-bath baptismal font similarly placed.

The latter half of the twentieth century enjoyed the revival of Reformed liturgy and architecture. In 1968, after decades of work, *Liturgy and Psalms* was published, with a Calvinian liturgy that in turn harked back to the early church. In 1965, *Christ and Architecture* was published,[2] relying heavily on post World War II Reformed church architecture in Switzerland, Germany, and the Netherlands to illustrate the cohesion of theology, liturgy, and architecture.

In some of the Reformed churches built in that period, pulpits became larger; some were given even further emphasis with sounding boards (such as those in Central Reformed, Grand Rapids, Michigan;

[2]   Donald J. Bruggink and Carl H. Droppers, *Christ and Architecture: Building Presbyterian/Reformed Churches* (Grand Rapids: Eerdmans, 1965).

St. Nicholas Collegiate
Church,
New York, New York

Central Reformed Church,
Grand Rapids, Michigan

and Second Reformed, Pella, Iowa). In others, greater prominence was given to the communion table (as at Lynwood Reformed, Schenectady, New York; and Church of the Saviour, Coopersville, Michigan).

Parma Park Reformed Church,
Cleveland, Ohio

Baptism received renewed emphasis (in places such as Parma Park Reformed Church, Cleveland, Ohio). Unfortunately, *Christ and Architecture* was published before the renewed emphasis on baptism with the accompanying running water baptismal fonts/pools allowing sprinkling or immersion.

Whether the return to our Reformed theological, liturgical, and architectural roots in the second half of the twentieth century will outlast the newest wave of revivalism/evangelism as modeled by Bill Hybels at Willow Creek and all of its contemporary variants is open to question. The impact of this new wave of evangelism can be seen in many newly constructed churches where the pulpit and table have been displaced by the praise band and the presentation of skits to illustrate real life situations (having been educated in an earlier age, I was under the impression that Holy Scripture spoke to real life situations). The prevalence of screens, the absence of hymnals, liturgies, and even Bibles in the pews, is further evidence of the devaluation of Word and sacrament in the attempt to beguile the unbeliever to come to God. H.J. Kuiper, longtime editor of the *Banner*,[3] once commented that the American church began to go astray when it made feeling transcendent to knowledge.

Word and sacrament, sometimes alone but at best together, have sustained the church for twenty centuries. Let us pray that there are those who will remain faithful in theology, liturgy, and architecture to our Reformed, biblical heritage.

[3]   Denominational magazine of the Christian Reformed Church in North America.

A Gathered Congregation

The very term *ekklysia tou theou* refers to a gathered people, and *leiturgia* is the work of the people. The congregation is not an audience, but God's people gathered together to do the work of worship. As such, the disposition of the seating should reflect this biblical/theological/ liturgical truth. It would be tempting to suppose that it was this truth which was intended by the early octagonal churches built in the Dutch Colonial period (such as Six Mile Run, New Jersey, and the Dutch Reformed Church of New Utrecht, New York). While it may have been simply a matter of structural economy, a South African architect has posited that newly built early Reformation churches took an octagonal form on the supposition that this was the form of the earliest churches, a conclusion reached from the still extant Church of the Holy Sepulcher in Jerusalem (with literary references to the famous Golden Octagon in Antioch, or the extant circular church of St. Stephano in Rome).

Often, churches were square, with the pulpit in one corner and seating gathered around. In other essentially square churches the pulpit was backed by choir and organ, with seating on a sloping floor wrapped around the pulpit in semicircular fashion—a gathered congregation. More common, however, was the rectangular church, with seating ranged front to back. The most notable early twentieth-century exceptions were churches build on the Akron plan (like the former Second Reformed Church in Pella, Iowa). In the Akron plan one side of the essentially square sanctuary was a movable wall to the church school unit with classrooms ranged on one or two levels on two or three sides around a central core that provided space for Sunday

Six Mile Run, New Jersey

Akron Plan Church and
classrooms,
former Second
Reformed Church,
Pella, Iowa

school assemblies and extra seating for the sanctuary when the movable wall disappeared.

In the liturgical/architectural renewal of the late twentieth century, the Resurrection Reformed Church in Flint, Michigan; the Lynwood Reformed Church in Schenectady, New York; and the Community Reformed Church of Colonie, New York, are exemplary exceptions to the front to back rule so architecturally unexpressive of a gathered people of God.

Style

Reformed churches came in all styles, from octagonal, square, or rectangular Dutch Colonial, to New England Colonial, Federal architecture, Greek revival (are there any Egyptian revival Reformed churches?), stone Gothic, Carpenter's Gothic, Victorian Gothic, High Dutch, and various modern and contemporary styles.

In all of the styles (which are unimportant as such), the dominant liturgical feature was until recently the pulpit, with a pulpit Bible visually proclaiming the importance of proclamation and the sacraments coming in a distant second. Tables were often minor, placed

Lynnwood Reformed Church,
Schenectady, New York

on the floor below the pulpit, while bird bath fonts were also relegated to the floor. The infrequency of the celebration of the Supper, together with the weak visual impact of table and font, has resulted in the relative unimportance of the sacraments in the mind and experience of the laity.

At Western Theological Seminary, a more frequent celebration of the Lord's Supper, begun under the leadership of Norman J. Kansfield, has now reached a weekly frequency under the aegis of Timothy Brown and is the best attended chapel service of the week. It is to be hoped that this practice will find its way into our churches attended by appropriate architecture and liturgical furnishings in order that our congregations may also visually enjoy a balanced diet of Word and sacrament.

Chapel communion,
Western Theological
Seminary

CHAPTER 4

Congregational Song in the Reformed Church: Praise, Subversion, Appreciation, and Glimmers of Understanding

James Hart Brumm

In his lectures at Western Seminary in 1966, Howard Hageman cited the origins of our hymnody in John Calvin's "Genevan" psalter. He then followed the thread through Peter Datheen's Dutch version of that book to the English translation commissioned by the consistory in New York City, and on through John Henry Livingston's work, *Psalms and Hymns*, beginning in 1787, a metrical psalter in English with a few hymns added, into the fuzziness of the mid-nineteenth century that was, by Hageman's description, resolved in *Hymns of the Church* in 1869. He insisted that final hymnal "was a volume of which the church could be and was proud."[1]

It's a wonderful story. Unfortunately, it probably didn't happen quite that way.

Not that this is Hageman's fault, for he was citing the minutes of the General Synod, the prefaces to several of the volumes attesting that they had done what they claimed to do, and the only Reformed Church hymnology published prior to 1989. That was presented to the General Synod of 1869 by John Bodine Thompson, chair of the committee

[1] Mast, *In Remembrance and Hope*, 137-43.

101

that produced *Hymns of the Church*, as part of the introduction of that book.[2] Thompson made every effort to portray his committee's work as the natural culmination of the evolution begun in Geneva, but with very little serious examination of exactly what each successive hymnal sought to accomplish, or why.

Here we run into a central problem. The hymnody of the Reformed Church in America has progressed without any serious self-examination of why we would choose certain songs to sing and order them in certain ways. Seeing only the what, but never the why, the church's song has been driven much more by a sociological desire to be like every other American congregation, but to do so on our own terms and by the individual political and theological viewpoints of a few individuals who showed an interest. This problem for the hymnody creates a corresponding problem for the hymnology; the absence of self-examination—public self-examination, at least—has resulted in the absence of a written record. Very little is left behind about what the committees and editors who prepared the hymnals were thinking.

Reformed Roots

John Calvin insisted that Christians ought to sing psalms. The Genevan dominie was trying to thread a fairly fine needle: Ulrich Zwingli, the reformer in Zurich, advocated no music in worship at all. This was because he had read not only the recovered Greek manuscripts of the New Testament but also the rediscovered works of Plato, who insisted that music had the power to excite the senses and distract the worshiper.

Calvin had also read Plato and knew full well the dangers of music. On the other hand, he believed that "the psalms can stimulate us to raise our hearts to God and arouse us to an ardor in evoking with praises the glory of his holy name."[3] He also thought that music could be controlled if one's mind was fixed upon God. Under such control, music could be an aid to prayer and worship. From this evolved his instruction that, during the Lord's Supper, "either psalms should be sung, or something should be read..." and at the conclusion of the sacrament "thanks should be given, and praises sung to God."[4]

---

[2]   That paper appears in the *Acts and Proceedings of the Reformed Church in America*, 1869, and is reprinted in Appendix F of James L.H. Brumm, *Singing the Lord's Song: A History of the English Language Hymnals of the Reformed Church in America* (New Brunswick, N.J.: Historical Society of the RCA, 1991).

[3]   John Calvin, *Works* (Brunswick: C.A. Schwetschke and Sons, 1863), X:1, 12.

[4]   Calvin, *Institutes*, IV:xvii:43.

Calvin moved beyond Plato to Augustine, accepting the latter's conclusion that "no one is able to sing things worthy of God unless he has received them from Him."[5] The psalms, for Calvin, are "replete with all the precepts which serve to frame our life to every part of holiness, piety, and righteousness, yet they will principally train us to bear the cross."[6]

And so Calvin said, "Let us sing psalms," and the people sang psalms—one of the few instances in church history where a hymnal was chosen based on mostly rational choices—psalms paraphrased in meter primarily by Clement Marot and Theodore de Béze, with tunes by Louis Bourgeois (the best-known of the musical editors); the final version was completed in 1562 and also included metrical settings of biblical canticles, the Lord's Prayer, the Apostles' Creed, and the Ten Commandments.[7] *Alcuns Psalms Mys et Chant*, which became known as the Genevan Psalter, benefited from Calvin's decision to allow his authors poetic freedom, all the while closely supervising their work to insure that scriptural integrity was maintained.[8] Bourgeois's tunes were in the style of lively popular dances of the day, but they were to be sung in unison and unaccompanied.[9] These standards were maintained for the German, Hungarian, and Dutch translations; the printings of the Genevan psalter are virtually identical in all four languages, except that the Dutch version by Peter Datheen interlined the text with the tune—very much like modern American hymnals, but practically unknown in sixteenth- or seventeenth-century Europe.[10]

It was Datheen's Dutch—along with some French, and possibly German—Genevan psalters which were brought along by Jonas Michaelius when he came to New Amsterdam to set up a church in 1628. Those were multilingual liturgies, with Walloons who spoke no

---

5   Charles Garside, *The Origins of Calvin's Theology of Music: 1536-1543* (Philadelphia: American Philosophical Society, 1979), 26-27.

6   John Calvin, trans. Henry Beveridge, *Commentary on the Book of Psalms* (Edinburgh: Calvin Translation Society, 1843), xxxvii.

7   The development of the Genevan Psalter is laid out wonderfully in Emily R. Brink's essay, "The Genevan Psalter." Bert Polman and Emily R. Brink, eds., *Psalter Hymnal Handbook* (Grand Rapids: CRC Publications, 1998), 28-39.

8   Erik Routley, *Panorama of Christian Hymnody* (Collegeville, Minn.: Litugical Training Publications, 1979), 5.

9   Ibid.

10   For more on this, see James H.L. Brumm, *Singing the Lord's Song: A History of the English Language Hymnals of the Reformed Church in America* (New Brunswick, N.J.: Historical Society of the Reformed Church in America, 1990).

Dutch singing in French alongside their Netherlander brothers and sisters, as per the instruction of the Dutch government and the Classis of Amsterdam.[11] As they stood shoulder-to-shoulder in the room above the mill, they sang, unaccompanied, what the *Articles of Dort* allowed them to sing:

> The 150 psalms of David; the ten commandments; the Lord's prayer; the twelve articles of the Christian faith; the songs of Mary, Zacharias, and Simeon, versified, only, shall be sung in worship.[12]

And so went the singing in Dutch Reformed churches in North America for most of the colonial period. There are indications that, in a few spots, such as the Catskills of New York and the Hackensack Valley of New Jersey, worship in Dutch was maintained until the 1840s.[13] While these were certainly the exception rather than the rule, the arrival of the next Dutch wave, settling in the U.S. Midwest about that time, would maintain at least some Genevan psalm-singing until the dawn of the twentieth century.

The First Subversion—the "Collegiate" Psalter

There were various social and traditional reasons that Dutch worship survived as long as it did in a British society and economy, but political concerns (about losing freedom of religion) were the overriding factor. By the middle of the century, however, these tensions had eased. The Dutch lived their weekday lives in English and were intermarrying into English families. The "Great Awakening" of the 1730s and '40s transcended denominational, cultural, and linguistic differences; in fact, Dutch Reformed dominies were among the leaders of the movement. The language issue was becoming a hindrance to the growth of the church, and it was being attacked. In 1727, a pipe organ was installed in one of the New York City churches, although it

---

[11] William Leverich Brower, et al., *Reformed Protestant Dutch Church of the City of New York, Her Organization and Development* (New York: The Consistory of the Collegiate Reformed Dutch Church, 1928),11-12.

[12] Article 69 from the Articles of Dort, 1619, cited by Edward Tanjore Corwin, *A Digest of the Constitutional and Synodical Legislation of the Reformed Church in America* (New York: Board of Publication of the Reformed Church in America, 1906), lxx.

[13] Firth Haring Fabend, *Zion on the Hudson: Dutch New York and New Jersey in the Age of Revivals* (New Brunswick: Rutgers Univ. Press, 2000), 70-72.

was not played on Sundays when the Lord's Supper was celebrated.[14] The custom of separating men and women during worship was being abandoned.[15] In 1763, the Reverend Archibald Laidlie was called to be the first English-speaking pastor of the Collegiate congregation in New York,[16] and he instituted English preaching the following April. Finally, on July 5, 1763, the Collegiate consistory proposed a metrical psalter "in English rime [sic] according to our music...."[17]

The consistory appointed a committee to see to the work and, at first, assigned elder Evert Byvanck to do the translating.[18] It was important that the new psalter be a musical match for the old, "so that Dutch and English Psalms could be sung to the same tune at the same time."[19] The consistory wanted to accommodate those who preferred the old style of worship even as they made way for the new. They believed it important to maintain their unique political situation as a Dutch worshiping community and so did not wish to borrow from existing English psalters. The consistory had also decided against Tate and Brady's *New Version*, as "the Consistory and other leading members of our Congregation have...thought it more Edifying [sic] to have the English Psalms sung in the same Tunes now used in our Churches."[20]

Byvanck was not up to the task of translating an entire metrical psalter by himself, so Francis Hopkinson, a lawyer and musician from Philadelphia, was hired to translate the work under Byvanck's supervision. Hopkinson (1737-1791) is remembered by history principally as a member of the New Jersey delegation to the Second Continental Congress and a signer of the Declaration of Independence. He was born in America, received his musical training in England, was organist at Christ Church, Philadelphia, and probable composer of *A Collection of Psalm Tunes...for the use of the United Churches of Christ Church*

---

[14] John P. Luidens, *The Americanization of the Dutch Reformed Church* (Ann Arbor: University of Mich. Microfilms, 1976), 127-28.

[15] Arie R. Brouwer, *Reformed Church Roots* (New York: Reformed Church Press, 1977), 46.

[16] Luidens, 154.

[17] Theodorus Van Wyk, "Minutes of the Consistory of the Reformed Protestant Dutch Church in the City of New York, 1700-1775," 241.

[18] Van Wyk, "Minutes of the Consistory," 241.

[19] Theodorus Van Wyk, "A Journal of the Consistory of the Reformed Dutch Church in the City of New York in Regard to the Petitions of their Congregation for Calling an English Preacher" (New York: unpubl. ms. in the collection of the New York Historical Society, 1762), 55.

[20] Van Wyk, "Journal," 67.

and St. Peter's Church in Philadelphia, 1763.[21] It is fair to assume, however, that facility with the Dutch language was not among Mr. Hopkinson's many talents—his writings make no reference to Dutch literature, and his library contained only one book in Dutch, which he, apparently, received from his father-in-law, Joseph Borden, a man whom Hopkinson didn't meet until 1768.[22] According to some correspondence with Benjamin Franklin, Hopkinson's primary motivation for taking the job was to make some ready cash for a planned trip to England.[23]

This could well explain why the end product of Hopkinson's labors did not match the book envisioned by the New York consistory. The title page read:

> *The Psalms of David with the 10 Commandments, Creed, Lord's Prayer, etc. in metre. Also the Catechism, Confession of Faith, Liturgy, etc., translated from the Dutch, for the use of the Reformed Protestant Dutch Church in the City of New York.*[24]

The contents, however, were not that at all. Very little of the material, if any at all, was actually translated from the Dutch (the catechism, confession of faith, and much of the liturgy were taken from the liturgy of the English-speaking Reformed congregation in Amsterdam[25]). The prefatory note, which acknowledged the psalter as "greatly indebted to that of Mr. Brady and Mr. Tate"[26] was much more honest, for this is what Hopkinson had used as a guide, taking Nicholas Tate and Nahum Brady's texts from their *New Version of the Psalms of David* and adding a word here and there or rearranging them ever so slightly to fit the Genevan tunes. This accounted for about 50 percent of the psalms, with another 15 percent being unadulterated Tate and Brady. The origin of the remaining fifty-two psalms is unknown; it is possible that they are the work Elder Byvanck completed before surrendering the task, Hopkinson's own work, or even the efforts of the

---

[21]   George Everett Hastings, *The Life and Works of Francis Hopkinson* (New York: Russell & Russell, 1968), 73.

[22]   Hastings, *Life and Works*, 76-77.

[23]   Hastings, *Life and Works*, 75.

[24]   Van Wyk, "Minutes of the Consistory," 312.

[25]   Daniel Meeter, lecture to the Standing Seminar on Reformed Church History, New Brunswick, New Jersey, March 14, 1989.

[26]   Francis Hopkinson, ed., The *Psalms of David... For the Use of the Reformed Protestant Dutch Church in the City of New York* (New York: James Parker, 1767), 1.

committee charged with receiving and revising his efforts.[27] Texts and tunes were interlined in the Dutch manner, but these tunes were only a small handful of the Genevan originals used over and again, often modified here and there, most likely at Hopkinson's hand.

The introduction of Tate and Brady sets the church's hymnody on a slightly different theological footing. English Puritans were stricter Calvinists than John Calvin: poets were to adhere rigidly to the King James translation in arranging the psalms in meter and were only allowed variation where rhythm or rhyme required it; in those cases, wherever possible, they were simply to rearrange the text, not paraphrase.[28] Poetic beauty was not to be a consideration, and that was obvious in the *Old Version* of Thomas Sternhold and John Hopkins, which Erik Routley called "on the whole a literary calamity."[29] Tate and Brady's *New Version*, like Pilgrims' *Ainsworth Psalter* of 1612 and Puritans' *Bay Psalm Book* of 1640, each sought to smooth out the problems associated with the *Old Version*—Tate and Brady were among the most successful—but the entire tradition was hobbled by the Puritan insistence on strict scriptural fidelity.

This would have been a bigger concern had the Collegiate Psalter caught on. In the eighteenth century, parishes did not provide hymnals in pew racks; every parishioner had her or his own, and brought it to worship each week. Thus, a committee was formed to attend to the sale of the book, both to members of the New York congregation and, potentially, to other parishes.[30] Sales were difficult, however, as the book was neither what the congregation expected nor wanted. It came back from the printers in December 1767, with the printing costs already £75 over budget;[31] by March 1769, only between six and seven hundred were sold, and the price was reduced to facilitate sales.[32] Finally, in February 1775, several unbound copies still remained, and the price was again reduced that they might be sold in bulk;[33] apocryphal stories claim that they were used as cannon fodder by the colonial army when the British invaded New York.

[27] See "Appendix B" in *Singing the Lord's Song* for a complete breakdown of authorship of the psalms.
[28] Routley, *Christian Hymns Observed*, 26.
[29] Ibid.
[30] Van Wyk, "Minutes of the Consistory," 278-79.
[31] Ibid., 312.
[32] Ibid., 319.
[33] Ibid., 410-11.

Our Own Hymnal, and the Personality Behind It

The U.S. War for Independence was the defining and transforming event of the next generation. When it was over, the Coetus-Conferentie schism that had plagued the Dutch Reformed churches, which revolved around English worship, pietism versus Dort Calvinism, and the general Americanization of the church, was also over. When the war had ended, the Dutch churches in North America were largely on their own, independent of the Classis of Amsterdam. In the same decade that the United States was establishing a federal government, albeit with some trial and error, our Reformed Church established classes and theological education and a constitution.

The church also created a denominational hymnal, the first such hymnal published anywhere in North America. It was begun in 1787, when the provisional synod formed a committee to prepare "another and better version of the Psalms of David, than the congregations as yet possess in the English language."[34] A year later, the synod, sensing the way in which the wind was blowing, instructed the committee to add "some well composed spiritual hymns...as a supplement" to the new psalmbook. The committee included David Romeyn, Jacob Hardenbergh, Solomon Froelich, Eilardus Westerlo, William Linn, Isaac Blauvelt, and John Henry Livingston. In the end, because it was exceedingly impractical in that day and age for much work to be done in committee by a group spread out from Kingston, New York, to Hackensack, New Jersey, Livingston did the actual editorial work, the committee reviewed it and passed it on to the synod, and Livingston's name was affixed to the title page as the editor.

Two things are important to note: first, the synod instructed the committee to create "a new versification out of other collections"— *plural*—"of English Psalms in repute and received in the Reformed churches," and they later amended that instruction, asking the committee to "limit themselves to the known Psalm-Books of the New York congregation, of Tate & Brady, and of Watts." Congregations were already worshiping in English, or at least singing in English, and choosing their own materials, despite the fact that Calvinism had, historically, found its middle ground in music between the Lutheran free acceptance of sacred song and the Zwinglian ban on all things musical by saying that people may sing in worship, but that they might only sing what the church approved. The Dutch Reformed Church in

---

[34] *Acts and Proceedings*, 1787, 167.

William Linn

North America had approved nothing to sing in the language in which everyone was singing, and a lot of their Protestant neighbors were singing these interesting metrical psalm settings by Isaac Watts, which were so much like hymns that it seemed no problem to sing hymns, too. The New York consistory had attempted, with the Collegiate Psalter, to create a hymnody like everyone else's (songs in English) but on their own terms (in the style of Datheen's Dutch Genevan Psalter), but it had failed. If the Calvinist ideal of prescribed hymnody, freedom with control, was to be restored, the church needed to get ahead of the wave.

The other important element was John Henry Livingston. Livingston, by 1787 already a professor of theology and a hero of the church, was also a consummate politician from a family of consummate politicians. His father, Henry, was a member of both the New York colonial and state legislatures and one of the authors of New York's constitution. His father's cousin, Phillip (also John Henry's father-in-law), was a signer of the Declaration of Independence. Young John Henry had, in 1770, celebrated his graduation from seminary by creating the *Articles of Union* that ended the Coetus-Conferentie schism and getting a job as a pastor of the Collegiate Church in New York.[35]

---

[35]   For a complete biography of John Henry Livingston, see Alexander Gunn, *Memoirs of the Rev. Dr. John Henry Livingston* (New York: Board of Publication of the Reformed Protestant Dutch Church, 1856).

The resulting book is a remarkably austere little volume. Whereas John Wesley began his hymnal with instructions for congregational singing, and Isaac Watts, in his introduction, waxed eloquent about his theology of hymnody, John Henry Livingston had no introduction save the extracts of the synod minutes that authorized the book and his imprimatur indicating that this was what he had done. On the surface, he had done exactly what the synod requested: metrical settings of the 150 psalms, and another 100 hymns. Closer examination, however, reveals that Livingston had done some creative interpretation of his instructions. It was common practice in English metrical psalmody to set psalms in several parts, usually to account for longer psalms with more than one distinct theme. Watts had expanded on that practice, using various "parts" of some psalms to present his own settings of the same psalm in different meters. Livingston broke several psalms into such parts, presenting different portions of a psalm, or different metrical settings by various authors. As a result, there are 287 metrical settings of the psalms or portions of them, from five different sources.

The organization of the hymns represented a stroke of brilliance on Livingston's part and allowed him to play the same little trick. The first 52 hymns are arranged to follow the 52-Sunday division of the Heidelberg Catechism; the next 21 are hymns on the Lord's Supper; and hymns 74 to 100 are on miscellaneous subjects. The little trick comes into play when he introduces "parts" to the Heidelberg hymns. For example, there are three "parts" to hymn 45, which are actually three distinct hymns, the last of which is a metrical setting of the Lord's Prayer. As a result, the 100 hymns are actually 133 hymns, from some 28 identified sources.

Isaac Watts's texts account for a little more than half of the book, but that is not unusual—Watts dominated most eighteenth-century English-language hymnals used outside of the Anglican communion. It is almost surprising that there is not more Watts, received less critically than what is here. Yet, by including so much of the work of this "Father of English hymnody," the man who would be known as the "Father of the Reformed Church in America" had, wittingly or unwittingly, opened the door for another shift in the theology of congregational song.

Watts was an English nonconformist preacher and a brilliant hymnwriter who sought to make the psalter more singable and more easily understood by the average worshiper. In that way, his practices seem actually to be very close to those of John Calvin. Where, for Calvin, the psalms clearly prefigured Christ, however, Watts saw them simply

John Henry Livingston

as unenlightened Old Testament writings, which needed to be made applicable to the Christian community.

> Where the psalmist uses sharp invectives against his personal enemies, I have endeavored to turn the edge of them against our spiritual adversaries, sin, satan [sic], and temptation. Where the flights of his faith and love are sublime, I have often sunk the expression within the reach of the ordinary Christian....Where the original runs in the form of prophecy concerning Christ and his salvation, I have given an historical turn to the sense: There is no necessity that we should always sing in an obscure and doubtful style of prediction, when the things foretold are brought into open light by a full accomplishment. When the writers of the New Testament have cited or alluded to any part of the psalms, I have often indulged the liberty of a paraphrase, according to the words of Christ, or his apostles....Where the psalmist describes religion by the fear of God, I have often joined faith and love to it: Where he speaks of the pardon of sin, through the mercies of God, I have added the blood and merits of a Saviour....When he attends the ark with shouting into Zion, I sing the ascension of my Saviour into heaven, or his presence in his church on earth.... [36]

---

[36] Isaac Watts, *Works* (Leeds, England: Edward Baines, 1813), in nine volumes, vol. IX, 32.

Now since it appears so plain, that the Hebrew psalter is very improper to the precise manner and style of our songs in a christian church [sic]; and since there is very good reason to believe that it is left us, not only as a most valuable part of the Word of God, for our faith and practice, but as an admirable and divine pattern of spiritual songs and hymns under the gospel; I have chosen to imitate rather than to translate; and thus to compose a psalm-book for Christians rather than the Jewish psalter.[37]

Once having decided to imitate rather than translate the psalms, Watts had opened the door for modern hymnody. "There is almost an infinite number of different occasions for praise and thanksgivings, as well as for prayer, in the life of a christian [sic] and there is not a set of Psalms already prepared that can answer all the varieties of the providence and the praise of God."[38] Thus we have a step beyond Calvin's own theology of music. Calvin had allowed for paraphrases in his psalter, but Watts argued that, if we must paraphrase the psalms in order to sing them, and they are still the Word of God, then we can also paraphrase other biblical texts in order to create Christian hymns. All the while, however, Watts insisted on a firm scriptural basis for hymns used in worship.

Livingston borrowed something besides inadvertent theology from Watts. He also attached a heading to each of the hymns, which was his interpretation of what the hymn was about. For example, hymn 21, part 2, "Blest be the tie that binds," was connected to the question in the catechism regarding the nature of the "Communion of Saints," which was the assigned heading. Livingston did something similar with the Lord's Supper hymns, attaching headings that correspond to the various sections of the liturgy.

To know why this is important, we have to remember why Zwingli banned hymns outright and Calvin put such tight controls on them. Both of those sixteenth-century reformers knew that what people sing has a much more profound effect on what they believe than do the sermons that they hear. Our favorite hymns imprint on our brains in a way that few, if any, sermons or theological treatises ever will. Livingston knew this, as well: by attaching specific hymns to the liturgy and the catechism, three years before the Constitution was even firmly in place, John Henry Livingston was making a public statement

---

[37]   Watts, *Works,* vol. IX, 14.
[38]   Ibid.

about Reformed theology, about what our best-known standard meant, and about the contents of our central liturgy. What we have here is a political document, dressed up as a hymnal.

The Explanatory Articles, which adapted the Articles of Dort to the governing of an American church, would pretty well seal the deal when they were adopted in 1792. Article 65 says that the only hymns to be used in English-language worship are "the Psalms and Hymns compiled by Professor Livingston, and published with the express approbation and recommendation of the General Synod."[39] These were the hymns that would be sung. These hymns would inform the interpretation of the rest of worship, and most of the Constitution. This book was, implicitly if not explicitly, the fourth leg of that Constitution.

Livingston's Influence Grows

In 1812, the General Synod asked for another addition of *Psalms and Hymns* to be prepared. This time, Livingston was to be the sole editor from the outset, and a committee of four of Livingston's former students was to review the finished product.[40] There are three pieces of evidence that suggest that John Henry himself instigated this request for a revision, and that he may already have had a nearly completed hymnal ready to go when the request was made. First, the overture to create a new edition with Livingston as the editor came from his own New York Classis. Second, only fifteen months passed from the time that the hymnal was requested until it had been completed, passed through the review process, and printed copies made available to the delegates at an extraordinary session of the synod in October 1813 (a land speed record for any hymnal).[41] Just three months later, printed copies were being distributed to congregations. Third, in the Dutch Church room of Gardner Sage Library at New Brunswick Seminary, there is a copy of the 1789 edition of *Psalms and Hymns* with the name "Sarah Livingston" inside the front cover (Sarah was the name of John Henry's wife), and copious margin notes for additions and alterations in Dr. Livingston's handwriting. I would argue that, sometime shortly after the first *Psalms and Hymns* was completed, Livingston began making notes on how to do it better, jotting them down in his spare time, and collecting, as he was able, other hymns and metrical psalms to include in a new edition.

---

39 Corwin, *Digest*, lxx.
40 *Acts and Proceedings*, 1812, 424.
41 *Acts and Proceedings*, 1813, 14-18.

The new book was significantly larger, with 324 metrical settings of psalms or portions of psalms, and 270 hymns. Also, where the metrical psalter of 1789 had stuck very conservatively to the original Hebrew text, the 1813 psalter Christianized the psalms much more freely and even used hymns that departed on the general themes of the psalms. Psalm 22 was a notable example, with its three parts being a meditation of Jesus' crucifixion, a catalogue of the blessings we receive from the crucifixion, and a hymn about the sufferings and exaltation of Christ. The headings attached to hymns in 1789 were now attached to psalms as well, to explain what each psalm or psalm portion was about (Livingston's theology again end-running the sermon). There were hymns prescribed for liturgical orders other than the Lord's Supper, including ten funeral hymns and a few funeral psalms; these are in keeping with a funeral liturgy that Livingston wrote in 1812, which called for no preaching, but the singing of hymns instead. The hymnal now seems to have a stronger ending, with a metrical setting of the Creed followed by nine metrical canticles, in canonical order. And it was successful; by 1819, 34,588 copies had been sold in a denomination with 11,269 communicants.[42]

There is something else we need to notice about the second edition of *Psalms and Hymns*: while there are 169 new psalm settings and 166 new hymns, no fewer than 132 psalm settings and 29 hymns have been removed. Given the limitation in the Explanatory Articles on what hymns would be sung—in fact, the synod of 1813 *instructed* all churches to replace the 1789 edition with the new book—this means that 161 hymns were removed from the approved repertoire of the church. This was the only time in the history of the Reformed Church in America when that has happened.

Psalms and Hymns after Livingston

The synod of 1830 created a small committee to meet and "report to Synod on the expediency of adopting such an additional number of

---

[42] The *Acts and Proceedings of the General Synod* for June 1813 record the synod's decision "that the copy right [sic] of the Book of Psalms and Hymns be vested in the Consistory of the Reformed Dutch Church in the City of New York, for the trust of the General Synod" and that "the said Consistory be directed to receive from every Printer who shall be permitted to publish an Edition not less than six cents for every copy." *Acts and Proceedings*, 1813, 18. The reports to the General Synod in the intervening years documented that a total of $2,057.31 had been collected by 1819, just a little more than would be required for 34,588 copies.

Hymns [sic], as the wants of our church may require, and, which, when approved by Synod, shall be printed in new editions, as a second Book of Hymns in our standard work."[43] Three ministers—Jacob Brodhead, John Hardenbergh Van Wagenen, and James Mathew—along with elders J.D. Keese and Peter Vroom reported back before the synod had even ended, with the following recommendation, which the synod approved:

> That the Rev. Thomas DeWitt, D.D., William McMurray, D.D., Isaac Ferris, and elders Peter D. Vroom and John D. Keese, be a Committee to select from different collections now published, Hymns on a variety of subjects, to the amount of say one hundred, to constitute the Second Book of Hymns, to be added to those now in use, in all future editions of our Psalm and Hymn Book, and that said Committee report such selection to the next General Synod for their approbation....
>
> *Resolved,* That the Committee on Psalmody communicate to the several Classes under the inspection of this General Synod, on or before the 1st of April next, a list of Hymns, their authors, the collections in which they are found, together with their number in said collection. [44]

This new study was undertaken just five years after John Henry Livingston's death, but almost a quarter of a century after the previous revision to *Psalms and Hymns*, and over four decades after the book's premiere. The Reformed Protestant Dutch Church had changed significantly, as had the nation; in many ways, Livingston, while highly revered, was seen by many to be somewhat of an anachronism.[45] Half of the ministers on the study committee—Brodhead, Mathew, and McMurray—were not students of Livingston's; Mathew and McMurray, in fact, both grew up in the Associate Reformed Church. One of Brodhead's teachers—Froeligh—had led the True Dutch Reformed schism and accused Livingston of Hopkinsianism. Brodhead was also the old man of the group, and even he, born in 1782, was thirty-six years younger than Livingston would have been. None of them knew of Coetus and Conferentie as anything more than a history lesson (and one wonders what sort of history lesson Brodhead would have

---

[43]   *Acts and Proceedings,* 1830, 300-301.
[44]   Ibid.
[45]   For more on this, see Corwin, *Manual,* 577.

Jacob Brodhead

received). Ferris and Van Wagenen had never known worship without *Psalms and Hymns*.

The final list of new hymns, "as a printed circular," was circulated to all Reformed Protestant Dutch Church ministers in March, a final report was ready for the synod in June, and the first copies of the book were printed by the end of the year.

> The committee have sought in their selection, to have respect to a diversity of subjects in connexion [sic] with the wants of our present collection, as well as the intrinsic merits of the hymns. The number to be selected was left by the resolution of the Synod somewhat indefinite.[46] On conversation with some brethren, the committee found a general opinion, that the additional hymns should be extended to at least one hundred and fifty. The subject of preparing a new index to the old collection was committed, at an early period, to Mr. Ferris. His ill health, and his journeying and residence to the south, have prevented the attention he would otherwise have paid. The committee afterward deemed it best to defer this matter until after the meeting of General Synod, as a complete index cannot be formed before the decision is made on the additional hymns. The alphabetical arrangement of the psalms and hymns, combined according to their subjects (as

---

46   The specific instruction from the 1830 synod was "the amount of say one hundred" *Acts and Proceedings*, 1830, 301.

adopted in Winchell and Rippon's Watts') would present some convenience and advantage; in such case there would of course be a reference at the heading of each psalm and hymn, referring to its place in the former collection, as also a tabular index prefixed, which would remove all difficulties in the use of the former books. It is left to the discretion of Synod whether this plan should be adopted, or the present arrangement should be preferred, which would then consist of the Psalms and two books of Hymns.[47]

In the spirit of Livingston, it would seem, the committee stretched the total number of hymns well beyond what the synod had envisioned. A more conservative committee could well have taken the 1830 synod at its word and sought only one hundred hymns. As it was, they went 50 percent beyond that instruction on the advice of "general opinion," and nearly another 50 percent beyond that overage, for a total of 172 hymns. Advice from the body also seems to have led to a suggestion that there no longer be separate psalms and hymns. The historical attachment to the psalter was clearly fading, something hinted at by even the 1813 edition, where metrical psalms were replaced by hymns without anyone taking much notice. It might also hint at a fading attachment to the Heidelberg Catechism. In fact, the very next item of business in the 1831 synod minutes was a request by the Glenville congregation on Long Island to be excused from the requirement to explain annually all of the questions and answers in preaching.[48]

The 172 hymns came from 75 sources, and 30 of the hymns (17 percent) are written by people who are not in vocational ministries (i.e., clergy, etc.) and 19 (11 percent) were written by women; this compares with only 6 percent of the hymns in 1789 being written by women, and 8 percent of the hymns in 1813 (none of the metrical psalm settings in either edition were written by women). It is difficult to say that Livingston deliberately shied away from women authors, as it was not always the custom of hymnal editors to credit authors' names—they weren't so credited in those editions of *Psalms and Hymns*.

Just over 60 percent of all the hymns in the *Additional Hymns* were old enough to have been included in the 1789 *Psalms and Hymns*, while only about 28 percent could be considered "new" (having been first published within the previous thirty years). This is a change from Livingston's work, especially with the hymns, which had brought in quite a bit of material as yet unused by the Reformed Protestant Dutch

---

[47] *Acts and Proceedings*, 1831, 312-13.
[48] *Acts and Proceedings*, 1831, 313-14. The request was denied.

Isaac Ferris

Church. It would seem that the desire was not so much for new hymns as it was for more hymns.

The combined list of the *Additional Hymns* and the 1813 *Psalms and Hymns* reveals a book with 772 hymns and metrical psalm paraphrases drawn on 118 sources. By 1831, 88 percent of all the texts in the books were written by evangelical and pietist authors, up from 56 percent in 1789. Given the sheer numbers involved and the fact that the average congregation probably sang no more than a couple of hundred hymns, if that, on a regular basis—not to mention the strong possibility that the metrical psalter was being largely ignored by this time—there is a high likelihood that the pietist hymns, focused largely on the worshipers rather than on God, were all that some congregations were singing.

While the ordering of the 1813 *Psalms and Hymns* remained unchanged, the *Additional Hymns* were arranged topically, grouped under "Perfections of God," "Advent of Christ," "Characters of Christ," "Praise to the Redeemer," "The Holy Spirit," "Alarming," "Inviting," "Penitential," "The Convert," "Salvation by Grace," "Graces of the Spirit," "The Christian Life," "Worship," "Revival," "Monthly Concert," "Occasional," "Seasons of Life," "Life and Death," "Resurrection," and "Heaven." If, as Erik Routley has suggested, the way we order our hymns both reflects and influences the way we understand our faith,[49]

---

[49]   Erik Routley, lecture to the Hymnody and Church History Class, Westminster Choir College, Princeton, New Jersey, Spring, 1982.

Eric Routley

then this small shift is profound. By itself, the *Additional Hymns* of 1831 constituted an evangelical revival hymnbook: forty-three of the texts in five sections are revival hymns, and the biggest section of the book deals with struggling faithfully against adversity.

A Step Further

In 1845, the subject of hymnody was again before the church. When the committee preparing the new *Sabbath School and Social Hymn Book* requested that nine new hymns—hymns not previously approved by the synod—be approved for use in Sunday schools to fill in nine blank pages that were going to be at the end of the book, the synod referred the entire subject of the church's hymnody to a special committee. This time Isaac Ferris—relegated to indexing the previous edition—would be the chair and would contribute a hymn. Thomas DeWitt and elder John Keese also returned from the 1831 committee. The new additions were elder William Woram and the Reverend Thomas M. Strong, pastor of the Flatbush Reformed Church in Brooklyn, a graduate of Princeton Theological Seminary who served his first parishes in the Presbyterian and Associate Reformed Churches.[50]

It should be noted that the only specific assignment before this committee was to recommend nine additional hymns for the *Sabbath School* book. They readily set that aside in favor of a much larger task.

---

[50]   *Acts and Proceedings*, 1845, 478-79.

After examination, it was found that it would be impracticable to add to the Hymn Book of the Synod's Board [the *Sabbath School* collection], what the wants of the Church required, without making it too unwieldy and costly for Sunday-school purposes, and it was felt that to place the new selection in such form would throw it out of the more public exercises, where additional hymns were needed, as well as in the social meeting.

It was agreed, accordingly, to leave the book of the Synod's Board for Sunday-school use, making such additions as would render it more complete for school use, and the various social meetings of Sunday-school teachers. In making such addition, they have met the views of a special committee of the Synod's Board, with whom they had a conference.

The committee herewith submit a selection of about 350 hymns to the Synod—having taken the lowest number suggested at the last meeting of Synod.

The committee have given special attention to the subject of a uniform arrangement of all the hymns in use, and give it as their judgment, that it should be carried into effect. It is believed that the real value of our present hymns is not seen, from the fact of their being separated as they are. They do not readily offer to the eye, and hence there is a feeling that there is a paucity of valuable hymns. After their labors, the committee are more ready than ever to say that some of the choicest productions of the kind in our language are found in our old hymns. This will be obvious to all, when such systematic arrangement is made; and if Synod approve the selection now offered, and the whole are made into one series, it is confidently believed that our hymn book may be favorably compared with any in the country.[51]

The report goes on to make it clear that several other hymnals in wide use have more than 1,000 hymns and psalm settings each in them, while the Reformed Protestant Dutch book languished with a mere 778 (the 1831 additions had brought that book to 772, not 778). Ever since the days of the "Collegiate Psalter," which was intended to present English psalms in a Dutch style, there was an aspiration in the church to be just like everybody else, even while remaining distinct. The result—340 new hymns, for a total of 1,112 hymns and metrical psalm settings—is an interesting interpretation of the classic Reformed

[51]   *Acts and Proceedings*, 1846, 93-94.

position on congregational song: since we are only to be allowed to sing within limits set by the church, lest we stray into heresy, those limits should be as wide as possible, to allow us to stray as much as possible.

Just over two-thirds of the book comes from clearly evangelical-pietist sources, but even more of the hymns would be identified as being in that style—with a strong personal piety—upon close inspection of the texts. In theory, the new hymns could have been blended with the old using Livingston's categories, with the Heidelberg Catechism and the Lord's Supper being the primary sections. In theory, all of the hymns could have been ordered alphabetically—or alphabetically within sections, as the committee advocated in its report. Yet none of that is what happened; instead, the 788 hymns were grouped as follows:

General Praise	17 hymns
The Scriptures	7 hymns
Perfection of God	19 hymns
The Trinity	7 hymns
Praise to Christ	21 hymns
Sonship of Christ	7 hymns
Names and Offices of Christ	30 hymns
Advent of Christ	9 hymns
Death of Christ	15 hymns
Resurrection of Christ	5 hymns
Exaltation of Christ	13 hymns
The Holy Spirit	17 hymns
The Decrees of God	5 hymns
Creation and Providence	11 hymns
Man's Ruin	17 hymns
The Law	39 hymns
The Gospel	25 hymns
Repentance	31 hymns
Conversion	29 hymns
Christian Character	12 hymns
Christian Experience	51 hymns
Love	17 hymns
Faith	6 hymns
Particular Duties	57 hymns
The Church	10 hymns
Prayer	9 hymns
Lord's Prayer	17 hymns
Ministry	10 hymns

Sacraments	1 hymn
Baptism	7 hymns
Lord's Supper	28 hymns
Missions	78 hymns
Dedication	7 hymns
Morning and Evening	10 hymns
The Year	14 hymns
Youth and Age	10 hymns
Mariners	4 hymns
National	10 hymns
Marriage	2 hymns
Miscellaneous	16 hymns
Death	51 hymns
Resurrection	4 hymns
Judgment	34 hymns

"Missions," "Death," "Particular Duties," "Christian Experience," and "Judgment" are the categories containing the most new hymns by far. The Reformed Protestant Dutch Church was about to embark on its greatest period of missionary endeavor, a mission emphasis that would define the church's self-identity for the next century and a half. Yet there is also the American evangelical perspective: most of these hymns, in the largest sections—even when one takes the older hymns into account—are focused on how we respond to our guilt and God's grace (rather than how God gives it to us), and then how we go forth in mission as partners with God; how we live daily life in a redeemed and revived state; how we face the horrors of death; and what judgment has in store for us.

While only three of the "National" hymns are from the new group, they are all hymns of thanksgiving for national life—though there are not yet any of the hymns modern readers would consider "patriotic" ("My Country, 'Tis of Thee," "O Beautiful, for Spacious Skies," etc.) in the corpus. The four hymns from earlier editions ask God's grace on the people and reflect on the horrors of war. Livingston would have edited the 1789 edition, of course, on the heels of the U.S. War for Independence, much of which was fought in Dutch Reformed communities, and the 1813 edition during the War of 1812. What's more, a worldview shaped by the Heidelberg Catechism would include a strong emphasis on social responsibility.

A Big Shift in a New Direction

In 1869, a new hymnal was created, aiming to be more thoroughly American. By this time, the denomination was officially called the Reformed Church in America—although the name "Dutch" still reared its head—and a number of social and Sabbath school hymnals had been approved to expand the repertoire available to the churches. In an attempt to create a hymnal that was "thoroughly American," the committee actually assembled a hymnal that was quite British, being closely modeled after *Hymns, Ancient and Modern for use in the services of the Church*, the most successful new hymnal of the day. *Hymns of the Church* quite nearly plagiarized the British book: the ordering and section headings are nearly identical—which meant it was an order based not on the Heidelberg Catechism, not on evangelical-pietist categories, but on the Anglican *Book of Common Prayer*—the tunes, with a few minor alterations, are harmonized in the American book as they are in the British (and are placed above the texts, in British style). Also, the texts and tunes taken wholesale from the mother book include the (then new) "Amens." The two leading contributors were still Isaac Watts (16.7 percent of the book), followed by Charles Wesley (7.6 percent), with other leaders including Philip Doddridge, James Montgomery, Augustus Toplady, William Cowper, Reginald Heber, and John Keble—all of them British, and most of them Anglican. There was but one American prominently represented: the Congregational church musician Lowell Mason. The Anglo-Reformed flavor was reinforced by the presence of Anglican chant settings of psalms (the chanting of prose had been recommended in an article in the *Christian Intelligencer* of June 4, 1863[52]).

All of these shifts over the years were largely unnoticed by John Thompson in his hymnology for the 1869 synod. No one really questioned how they had gone from a congregational corpus built solely around psalmody to a psalmody shared with a Heidelberg-based hymnody for a Reformed covenant community in an American context to a vestigial psalmody attached to an evangelical hymnal for American Christians, engaged in the American Christian endeavor, who happened to be Reformed. Because those questions weren't asked, those shifts weren't noticed, and nobody noticed that the new book was taking a significant swing in a new direction, a direction in which the denomination was not necessarily going.

[52] "Chanting in Public Worship," volume 34, number 23.

Entropy: Everything Falls Apart

This book met almost immediate resistance. During October of 1869, there was a brief debate in the *Intelligencer* between an E.E. and a T.W.C. regarding the merits and/or shortcomings of the new collection.[53] The synod of 1870 noted that *Hymns of the Church* was being used in fifty congregations and asked the committee to revise some of the tunes, over which there had been complaints.[54] In 1871, *Hymns of Prayer and Praise* was authorized, being a selection of about 325 hymns from the 1869 book, for private devotions and social worship.[55] This did nothing to stop the classes of Poughkeepsie and Hudson—and, eventually, North Long Island—to overture for permission to let classes and not the General Synod choose the hymnals; Poughkeepsie's second overture had announced that they had already done so. This was an era of classical activism and clashes over local versus denominational control. By 1876, the synod committee on the denomination's hymnody was so frustrated that it recommended that the constitutional requirement regarding hymns in worship be dropped. That motion was tabled and remains so to this day.[56]

The die, however, was cast. Beginning in the 1880s, the denomination approved a succession of hymnals—John Bodine Thompson's *Christian Praise* (1880), Charles Robinson's *Laudes Domini* (1884), Edwin Bedell's *Church Hymnary* (1891), and Hope Publishing's *Hymns of Worship and Service* (1906). There was no clear rhyme or reason for approving books, except that one group or another wished to use it. While the synod had previously approved the above-mentioned *Sabbath School and Social Hymns* (1843) and the *Fulton Street Hymnal* (1862) without making them constitutional, both were collections that contained sanctioned hymns. French and German editions of the Genevan Psalter had been made constitutional in 1792, and a German RCA hymnal had been published in 1853, but the new step was different.

Books not produced by the Reformed Church but simply endorsed for use in general worship represented a major shift in control of hymnody in the church. The warm pietist tendencies of the

---

[53]   Volume 40, numbers 41, 42, and 43; 14, 21, and 28 October 1869.
[54]   Corwin, *Digest*, 325.
[55]   Ibid. Complaints had been registered against the 1846 revision of *Psalms and Hymns*, but they were quickly dismissed. *Acts and Proceedings*, 1847, 200-205.
[56]   *Acts and Proceedings*, 1876, 501-502.

earlier hymnody—that found in *Psalms and Hymns*—continued, without the discipline of the Standards or other Reformed contextualization. Instead of one hymnody, there were several, with two main streams: a liturgical/rational tradition and a pietist tradition.

Ecumenical interests drove two hymnal projects in which the denomination cooperated. *The Hymnal of the Reformed Church* was prepared by a joint committee of Reformed Church in America members and members of the Reformed Church in the United States (the old German Reformed Church); it was a project begun in 1914,[57] when the two denominations were exploring merger, but delays related to World War I kept the book from appearing until 1929, after such plans for union had been abandoned.

The Hymnbook (1955), edited by David Hugh Jones, was prepared along with several Presbyterian groups, including the Presbyterian Church in the United States, with which the Reformed Church flirted over the matter of union until 1969. In some ways, it was an impressive book. Never before—and never since, in the United States—was there any example of so many denominations cooperating successfully (or cooperating at all) on one hymnal. And the book was indeed a success; despite the advent of Vatican II, Christian folk music, and the call for contemporary and inclusive language in worship, *The Hymnbook* remained a dominant force in the Presbyterian-Reformed world—or at least within the Reformed Church—for the next three decades (a 1987 survey would show 29 percent of RCA congregations polled to be using it[58]). But it was not an adventurous book. There are no tunes, and only one hymn, "Morning Has Broken," in the book written within the thirty-five years preceding its publication (though there are one or two tunes arranged in that time, most notably the four arranged by David Hugh Jones, the book's musical editor). Jones himself, when asked what

---

[57] *Acts and Proceeding,* 1914, 255-57. By 1929, new overtures were being received—though not approved—for other hymnals to be endorsed. In 1937, the Classis of Grand Rapids overtured General Synod to begin the process all over again, appointing a special committee to either prepare a new hymnal or endorse another book. When that committee reported in 1938, survey results were presented showing *The Reformed Church Hymnal* to be in use in eighty-four congregations, with fifty-seven of those dissatisfied. Of the fourteen other books reported in use, the *Church Hymnary*, approved before the turn of the century, was still the most popular.

[58] Gregg Mast, *Worship* newsletter (New York: Reformed Church in America Commission on Worship, 1987).

the greatest innovation of *The Hymnbook* was, replied that all of the hymn numbers were on the outer edges of the pages, for easier use.[59]

Both of these ecumenical efforts employed a hymn ordering which might be described as "Presbyterian hybrid"—a combination of the prayer book-liturgical ordering found in *Hymns of the Church* and the more evangelical-pietist topical ordering. This, in a sense, allowed for a common ground between the two hymnic streams presenting the Reformed Church. Still, the denomination did nothing of its own again until the 1980s.

A New Adventure

In 1978, as the Reformed Church was celebrating its 350th anniversary,[60] the Commission on Worship suggested that the time for a new official hymnal was approaching. *The Hymnbook* was nearly a quarter-century old and had been very conservative even for its day. The trends toward modern and nonsexist language had made the book seem even more outdated. A hymnic explosion, begun in Britain by the likes of Brian Wren, Fred Pratt Green, and Timothy Dudley-Smith, was becoming firmly established in the United States.[61] The new *Lutheran Book of Worship* and the Roman Catholic *Worship II* had been recently published, and the Episcopal Church was at work on *Hymnal, 1982*. Every new hymnal which was produced served to make *The Hymnbook* seem that much less adequate, as was pointed out by the then president of New Brunswick Theological Seminary, Howard Hageman, in an article in the *Church Herald*.[62] So the synod of 1978 appointed a committee to study the options for endorsing or creating a book.[63] The committee, consisting of Roger Rietberg of Hope College; Lawrence Van Wyk of Orange City, Iowa; Gloria Norton of Spring Valley, New York; and Howard Hageman as its chair, delivered this report to the 1979 synod:

> 1. The last hymnbook produced by the Reformed Church in America was that of 1869. Ever since that time we have endorsed the hymnbook of some commercial publishers or cooperated with another denomination in publishing a book, the last such being

---

[59]   David Hugh Jones, Lecture to the Church Music Forum, Westminster Choir College, Princeton, New Jersey, March, 1966.

[60]   Counting from Michaelius's arrival in New Amsterdam in 1628.

[61]   Erik Routley, *Christian Hymns Observed* (Princeton: Prestige Publications, 1982), 94-96.

[62]   Howard Hageman, "A Birthday Present," *Church Herald*, April 7, 1978, 30.

[63]   *Acts and Proceedings*, 1987, 241.

the *Hymnbook* which was produced in 1955 with a consortium of Presbyterian churches. It has, therefore, been 110 years since the Reformed Church in America has produced a hymnal for its own use.

2. A large variety of hymnals has been produced in the last decade, some by denominations, others by commercial publishing houses, but there is none of them which your committee feels able unreservedly to recommend as *the* hymnal for the Reformed Church in America.

3. It would, of course, be possible to endorse a number of hymnals as fitting the various needs and situations of our church, but it seems to us that following such a plan would be permanently to accept and even further the differences and divergencies that exist among us.

4. A survey of the most competent outside opinion which we could find strongly indicates that there would be interest in a *Reformed hymnal of excellence* beyond the bounds of our denomination. We define a Reformed hymnal of excellence as meaning a. a hymnal that recognizes our Calvinist heritage of psalmody as a central element in the praise of God; b. a hymnal that uses Biblical and theological integrity as a primary criterion in its selections; c. a hymnal which, while accepting the best in contemporary hymn-writing, strives to avoid the ephemeral and the *trendy*.

5. A preliminary survey of the cost factors leads us to believe that such a book could be produced at today's prices for a maximum of $75,000 to $100,000 as a capital outlay. A sale of 15,000 to 20,000 copies at $5 per copy would recover the investment. Our research indicates that in the past 24 years about 75,000 copies of the *Hymnbook* have been sold in the Reformed Church in America. To be sure, a necessary inflation figure has to be factored into any cost estimate, but we do not believe that the financial side of the enterprise should at this point be considered a deterrent.

6. While we are fully cognizant that no hymnal produced could ever satisfy the requirements of all our congregations, we believe that working on such a project could well prove to be a unifying factor in our denominational life, especially since it is a task we have not attempted in more than a century.[64]

From the outset, the new committee sought to answer certain historic questions: what will it cost, and is everyone expected to like it?

---

[64]   *Acts and Proceedings*, 1979, 164-65.

There was not even any illusion that the synod could think of requiring the use of this book in local churches (a power which had long since been surrendered). But there was an appeal to the thirst for identity: the criteria for a new book described it with the terms "Calvinist," "biblical," and "heritage of psalmody," and it was promised to be "a unifying factor in our denominational life." The synod quickly approved the notion,[65] and the committee was expanded by three members—Robert DeYoung, Norman Kansfield, and Merwin Van Doornik—so that all six particular synods were represented. The committee's first official action was to hire the Reverend Dr. Erik Routley to edit the new book.

The resulting work was *Rejoice in the Lord: a Hymn Companion to the Scriptures*. It used a biblical ordering that was truly unique and truly expressive of who we are, or at least who we aspire to be. It probably leaned too heavily toward the liturgical/rational stream of the church, and was too dour a hymnal for the modern Reformed Church. But the worst problem was that, as we did a new thing—or an old thing that we hadn't done for a very long time—we did it without any sort of education or introduction. The book was deposited into the laps of congregations without any way to help them appreciate it or appreciate why we should have some sort of a common hymnody. As a result, the book failed— being used by only 7 percent of Reformed Church congregations—even as it succeeded—going into six printings, sold largely outside of the denomination—with many elements being emulated by other, better-known hymnals.

Still Trying to Learn While We Sing

Still, the denomination faced the challenge of this disparate hymnody, its Calvinist discipline gone, and, with it, much potential creative tension. The latest attempt to facilitate the church's song, in which this author participated, was *Sing! A New Creation*, developed in cooperation with the Christian Reformed Church (CRC) and the Calvin Institute of Christian Worship. The committee included John Paarlberg, Barbara Boertje, Amy Van Gunst, and Alfred V. Fedak from the RCA, and Emily R. Brink, Bert Polman, Charsie Sawyer, Anetta Vander Lugt, and John D. Witvliet from the CRC. Only three of the members were ministers of the Word and sacrament, and all of them were from the RCA. Here, the task was to create a supplement of new hymnody; the problem was that, while the Christian Reformed Church was supplementing one book, the Reformed Church in America was supplementing seven or eight.

---

[65] *Acts and Proceedings*, 1979, 165.

Barbara Boertje

There was also the educational problem. Creating a hymnal is fun, and it sells well. Teaching materials aren't fun and, the committee was told, would be less cost effective. But it was the Reformed contingent in the committee that pushed hardest, from the very beginning, for a teaching tool, even though committee members were told they had to raise the money for it themselves. The resulting *Leaders' Edition*, which no one thought would sell, went into several printings, and other hymnal committees now look at it as the standard that they must meet.

Another problem was a huge amount of pressure toward niche marketing. Since some people wanted praise and worship music, some wanted world music, and some wanted traditional hymns, the committee was encouraged to survey congregations and to create a volume for whoever would buy the most, leaving out the rest. That notion was rejected, for reasons that Emily Brink, editor of the book, stated eloquently in the preface:

> *Sing! A New Creation* is a declaration that hymnals are important for encouraging Christians to sing songs that connect them to the larger body of Christ. It reveals a conviction that every congregation will be blessed by moving beyond its current repertoire. It is a testimony that the diversity of new worship songs from our various cultures is to be welcomed and embraced as a gift from God. God is calling many different people to live in community, to demonstrate to the world that our unity is found not in style or tradition, but in being members of one body, honoring one Lord, one faith, one baptism, one God of us all (Eph. 4:4-6). Therefore this is no homogeneous collection of songs marketed to one part of the church. *Sing! A New Creation* reflects the rich variety of the church today.[66]

Norman Kansfield

The resulting volume included a significant selection of "praise choruses" and contemporary songs—roughly a third of the book—that have become popular in the church of the late twentieth and early twenty-first century, from the "Praise and Worship" tradition, the ecumenical communities of Taizé in France and Iona in Scotland, and from Roman Catholic streams spawned by the Second Vatican Council. Another third of the book was formulated by various kinds of "world music," congregational songs primarily from Asia, Africa, and Latin America. The supplement also included the most psalm settings (55) of any RCA hymnal since *Psalms and Hymns*, with responsorial as well as metrical settings.

This author lacks appropriate historical distance to reflect on this latest step in Reformed hymnody impartially, but I would like to think that we achieved some of the central elements that Calvin sought in the Genevan Psalter: creativity and diversity bound by the discipline of scripture that will, in the end, "stimulate us to raise our hearts to God and arouse us to an ardor in evoking with praises the glory of his holy name." It could probably be considered another subversive hymnal, as well; once again, a group of people created a songbook that, to a certain extent, reflected where the church was, and yet, to a great extent, reflected where the compilers hoped it would go. If we are able to couple that impulse with an awareness of why the church has sung what it has sung before, this path could indeed make our praises reformed and ever reforming.

---

[66]   Emily R. Brink, ed., *Sing! A New Creation* (Grand Rapids: CRC Publications, 2001), 5.

A RESPONSE TO CHAPTERS 3 AND 4

Martin Tel

In the early 1990s, while I was a graduate student at the University of Kansas, my wife and I began attending Crossroads Church, a Reformed Church in America congregation in Overland Park, Kansas. It was a young church coming into its own. As the pastor and I considered ways in which we could instill in this congregation a sense of what it means to be Reformed, we took a look at our hymnal. Indeed, the hymnal did not reflect Reformed theology, especially with regard to the sacraments. Nor did it reflect a Reformed concern for the incorporation of scripture in song, particularly the psalms. How did a Reformed Church congregation come to acquire a hymnal that was incongruent with its liturgy and theology? For this congregation, the answer was simple: when the church was formed, a well-meaning congregation "donated" its old hymnals. It was agreed that the time had come for this growing congregation to determine its own hymnological path.

What hymnal should we use for worship at Crossroads Church? New to the Reformed Church, I had worked and worshiped previously in denominations that assumed the use of a denominational hymnal. I expected that the denominational office of worship would be able to direct me to the authorized hymnal for our church. Indeed, I did call the worship office in New York City. What I found was that the denomination was paralyzed by timidity when it came to the "hymnal" question. I was supplied with information about the wide array of hymnals used by RCA churches, many of which were not very different from the one we were replacing. The suitability of the hymnals of the Presbyterian (USA) and Christian Reformed denominations were noted. The Reformed Church's own publication, *Rejoice in the Lord*, was mentioned, but not without reservations. In the end I received no clear directives. Obviously, I had entered a minefield.

In a tradition that placed such high stakes upon defining the congregation's sung repertoire (à la Calvin's theology of congregational psalm singing), this is really troubling. What the worship office did not tell me was that the denomination has tabled since 1876 the question of the constitutional requirement regarding hymns in worship. I don't imagine that there is much nerve for taking this up again 130 years later.

At Princeton Theological Seminary, I regularly assign my Presbyterian students the task of studying the organization of their hymnal. It is my contention that the table of contents of a denominational hymnal offers a fairly accurate overview of that denomination's theological predilections and emphases. And so the seminary students track the shift of Presbyterian hymnals from the early psalters, through the nineteenth-century pietist collections, the theological recovery hymnals (what Brumm refers to as the "Presbyterian hybrids," like *The Hymnbook* of 1955), the apparent consternation of the *Worship Book* (1970), to the liturgical renewal thrust of the most recent *Presbyterian Hymnal* (1990).

With regard to this exercise, the Reformed Church has not given us much to go on in the twentieth century. We cooperated with the Presbyterians on *The Hymnbook* (1955) and finally, in 1985, produced *Rejoice in the Lord*. The fact that we have no functioning denominational hymnal is actually rather telling. It would suggest that we have no functional theological identity, that we are as fragmented as our choices of hymnals suggest that we are. It will be up to future generations to look back on the twentieth and twenty-first centuries to determine whether this is true. *Rejoice in the Lord* may indicate where some of the leadership of the denomination wishes we were rooted theologically, but the fact that it has never come close to functioning as a unifying denominational hymnal suggests that the wish remains unfulfilled in our churches.

For me, Brumm's paper has filled in the "table of contents" for the eighteenth and nineteenth centuries. This has been enlightening as I struggle to understand how we've gotten to where we are today. Brumm's study suggests why the hymnals in the pew racks are so out of step with the perceived theology of the church—and this divide seems to me most stark in the eastern segment of the denomination. Most of our churches are singing from "for-profit" hymnals that lean heavily toward Anabaptist and pietist interpretations of the sacraments. People learn their theology from their hymns. There are many reasons that Reformed Church members are woefully unaware of Reformed teaching on baptism and the Lord's Supper. I submit that the lyrical theology we have offered our churches has contributed to our corporate confusion.

Reflecting on Brumm's paper, I see two historical errors that the Reformed Church in America has repeated with regard to its psalmody and hymnody:

First, the Reformed Church has, in its lyrical theology, left its Calvinistic moorings without thinking through the alternatives clearly. Calvin had profound reasons for offering the church a rather rigid and small canon of congregational song. Denominationally, we have sloughed off Calvin's scruples about hymns, choirs, and instruments and have scarcely looked back. The brief history that Brumm has offered demonstrates that there is a price to pay for such theological-hymnological amnesia.

This is not to suggest that Calvin's rigid rules should be mindlessly promulgated. Particularly in North America, this is not what is called for. But Calvin and the Reformed tradition could have equipped us to make better judgments about the songs we sing. I'm thinking particularly of the nineteenth-century evolution of *Psalms and Hymns*. Rather than looking to our own tradition and theology for insights, we evidently were guided by expediency and a desire to be like everyone else.

The second error of our past was the introduction of major alterations that did not take into account the real milieu of the church. This was true even when these dramatic shifts were needed correctives. This occurred first in 1869 with *Hymns of the Church*, with its Anglo-Reformed flavor, and again more than a century later with *Rejoice in the Lord*. Brumm's paper helps us understand why these reactionary hymnals published. I for one have great sympathy with their editors. But the correctives found very little resonance in the church.

This poses the question: how can there be a correction that also resonates with the church? To be fair, one must admit that this may actually be impossible. In that case, choices must be made. But we should not play the "impossible" card too quickly.

Brumm mentions the newest hymnological resource put out by the Reformed Church (jointly with the Christian Reformed Church and the Calvin Institute of Christian Worship): *Sing! A New Creation* (2001). This hymnal seems to follow some similar use patterns as *Rejoice in the Lord*. At least in our area, it seems that there are more Presbyterian (USA) churches using *Sing! A New Creation* than Reformed churches.

Nevertheless, *Sing! A New Creation* does appear to take seriously Brumm's double concern for Reformed (Calvinist) fidelity and relevance to the current milieu of the church. Brumm seems to have the jitters when speaking about the hymnal (after hearing the history, one can understand his trepidation). He states that *Sing! A New Creation* could probably be considered another subversive hymnal, as well; once again, a group of people created a songbook that, to a certain extent, reflected where the church was, and yet, to a great extent, reflected where the compilers hoped it would go."

Brumm acknowledges rightly that we don't have the necessary historical distance to make judgments about *Sing! A New Creation*. Recalling my initial reaction to the hymnal, I confess that I was reticent to embrace it. Not having been in on the difficult work of compilation, I found much that seemed too culturally driven, including songs that were not really suited to congregational singing and aspects that seemed overly trendy. Though our seminary chapel committee was clamoring for a supplement, I resisted for over a year subscribing to this new book. But when I saw what the Presbyterians were preparing to put out, I quickly came to the conclusion that we had better get *Sing! A New Creation* into the pews as soon as possible!

The result at Princeton Seminary has been astonishing. The inclusion of the "praise songs" demonstrated that this collection is in a real way attempting to take the milieu seriously. Together we have discovered how to connect the contemporary praise song to the Psalms. And, for that matter, we have rediscovered the place of the psalm in worship, in every possible genre. In short, my initial criticisms have been tempered by my experience. And this is not because the vapid music has worked as magical enticement to get people to sing the "good stuff" (it rarely works that way; vapid music leads nowhere). Rather, my opinions have been challenged, and I have found good music where I had not expected it. Our worship is more rooted in scripture, particularly the Psalms, because of this book. This is truly a hallmark of Reformed worship and a gift to the ecumenical church.

Has history taught us anything? I think this most recent venture suggests that we have learned a thing or two along the way. Brumm and his cohorts are to be commended on this effort.

In response to Donald Bruggink's paper on architecture in the Reformed Church, I must lay out my biases as a musician. I suppose that when architects step into an unfamiliar worship space, they look at the structure. If they were concerned with worship and liturgy, one would hope that they would consider how the space supports the liturgical actions of worship. Church musicians, however, are a strange lot. When we enter an unfamiliar space, the first thing we do is clap our hands or sing a line and then listen to how the space responds. Will the architecture, furnishings, and surfaces support the voiced worship of God's people?

Despite my lack of expertise in architectural matters, I should spend more time getting us to think about architecture than hymnals. Perhaps we can steer the conversation somewhat in this direction. For it is my conviction that if the psalters and hymnals have largely determined what people sing in our churches (and by extension, what the people come to believe), the architectural spaces in which we worship largely determine whether our people sing at all. There is no greater hindrance to our congregational singing than the buildings in which we worship, and this needs to be explored further.

If we follow the trends of architectural space in the Reformed Church (very little different from the pragmatic building in most other denominations), we find that we are continuing down a road that erects worship spaces which place congregations in an increasingly passive role. Bruggink has traced this decline to the influences of revivalism and the emulation of the civic auditorium, and these observations are really helpful in analyzing the situation. Add to this the installation of sophisticated electronic media, and we have the equivalent of an acoustical rood screen which separates and elevates worship leaders from the congregation, to whom we can now accurately refer as the audience.

I concur wholeheartedly with Bruggink that the building teaches us a theology by where it places (or doesn't place) the table, font, pulpit and assembly. But when the space is visually theologically orthodox and aesthetically beautiful in every way but does not establish an acoustical environment that signals that the congregation is the bearer of the song, that the gathered community comprises the principal actors in the drama, then we are not being Reformed in our architecture.

Liturgical renewal has raised interest in the visual aspects of the church. As Bruggink suggests, perhaps the most significant visual symbol of worship is the gathered community. But it is not enough just to look at one another (as with any aspect of worship, this too can be turned toward idolatry, a misattribution of our worship). Worship needs to direct us toward God through proclamation, prayer, and praise. If the architecture doesn't enable us to do so this with our eyes, ears, voices—in effect, all of our bodies—our worship is diminished.

ADDENDUM

150 Years of Prayer in the Reformed Church in America

Jonathan Brownson

This is not a story about all prayer in the Reformed Church in America, anymore than Luke, even with the special inspiration of the Holy Spirit, could describe all the acts of the apostles. This essay focuses on only a very small part of the Reformed Church's prayer story: the Fulton Street Prayer Revival, which began at the North Dutch Church in New York City September 23, 1857.

Focusing on Fulton Street prayer will, I hope, be both historically faithful and denominationally fruitful. I believe the Fulton Street Prayer Revival to be a pivotal point in our prayer history, and that it holds within it some lessons for today. To the extent that history is cyclical, I believe the "it" of Fulton Street may be coming around the mountain again. This history might provide a ticket for a ride.

Who Is Praying?

They all joined together constantly in prayer... (Acts 1:14)

We know pastors are praying in the Reformed Church in America. We have almost four hundred years of liturgy to prove it. What we don't know as much about, however, is who else is praying. The story of the birth of the Fulton Street Noontime Prayer Meeting provides a historical record of prayer that was led not by an ordained pastor, but by a lay missionary named Jeremiah Calvin Lanphier.[1]

Jeremiah was born in Coxsackie, New York, September 3, 1809. He was the son of Samuel F. Lanphier, a farmer and currier, who moved from Connecticut to Coxsackie and for a while made his home there. The maiden name of his mother was Jane Ross. Her parents came from the Netherlands.

Jeremiah's early education was in schools which were, by his own admission, "not so well equipped." At the age of sixteen, he went to Albany to learn the tailor's trade, and he became an apprentice. After considerable travel and ongoing work in the tailoring business, he moved to New York to form a partnership with George Andrews in a clothing business located near the Old North Dutch Church. It was there that he met some of the church's consistory members, who eventually asked him to work for the church as a lay missionary. In June of 1857, he left his clothing business, and, on the first of July, began his work with the Old North Dutch Church on the corner of Fulton and William Streets in Manhattan.

Jeremiah was "tall, with a pleasant face, an affectionate manner, and indomitable energy and perseverance; a good singer, gifted in prayer and exhortation, a welcome guest to any house, shrewd and endowed with much tact, and common sense." In 1842, he had made a public confession of Christ in the Broadway Tabernacle Church, then under the pastoral care of the Reverend E.W. Andrews. After some years he transferred to a Presbyterian Church under the charge of the Reverend James W. Alexander.[2]

When it came to religious instruction, Jeremiah might be thought of as "uneducated and ordinary."[3] Yet he became an extraordinary prayer leader, perhaps the greatest prayer mobilizer in the history of the Reformed Church in America. His journey to his

---

[1]   Much of the biographical information which follows comes from Jeremiah Lanphier's obituary and other uncatalogued documents in the Collegiate Corporation Archives in New York. I am grateful to Rita Hollinga, archivist, for her assistance.

[2]   Minutes of the North Dutch Church Consistory, June 18, 1857. Hereafter, Minutes.

[3]   Acts 4:13.

knees began with the call of the consistory of the North Dutch Church. Here is how it was expressed in a flyer that was sent out to the local community:

> The Consistory, anxious that in the spiritual destitution of this part of the city, suitable investigations and labors may be employed, in order that the "poor may have the Gospel preached unto them," have obtained the services of a pious layman, Mr. J.C. Lanphier. He will devote his time and efforts to explore this lower part of the city, and, with all kindness and fidelity, to attract those whom he visits to the house of God, and to place parents and children under auspices favorable to their temporal and spiritual welfare. Although a number of pews are held by individuals and families, yet far the larger number of those in the body of the church, as well as all in the gallery, are entirely free, and all who are willing are cordially invited to occupy them "without money and without price." Where families may signify their purpose to be stated worshippers in this house, the sexton, on application, will designate pews which they may regularly occupy. In the CONSISTORY BUILDING, immediately behind the church, there are very convenient rooms for Sabbath-school, Prayer-meetings, etc. It is very desirable that an effort to fill up largely the Sabbath-school would be made. It is an important field for such an effort. May we not hope that there are many thoughtful or pious young men in this vicinity, who will unite to bear a combined influence to accomplish such an end? Transient visitors in the city, and sojourning in this part, are cordially invited to worship in the Old and venerable North church. The Consistory commend Mr. Lanphier to the confidence, and kind regard of all whom he may visit, with the prayer that he may be the instrument of blessing to them for time and eternity.[4]

The leaders of the North Dutch Church looked for a pious layman to "preach good news to the poor." More specifically, they looked for someone to reverse the trend of people (parishioners) moving out of the city (church) and businesses moving in. The consistory wanted to send someone out calling in the community during the week so that the pews would be full on the weekends. During Jeremiah's first couple of months at the church, the consistory asked that he provide for them carefully documented visits to neighborhood residents. Calling and

---

[4]   Flyer found in the Collegiate Corporation Archives.

outreach were their chief concern, rather than prayer.[5] For Jeremiah, however, the call to prayer became so personal and powerful that he could not ignore it. So, on September 23, 1857, he led his first prayer meeting, which he described like this:

> I do not like to speak about myself, but I cannot give you an account of the origin of this meeting otherwise. But let me first say that no two meetings can be started or carried on exactly alike. Many noonday meetings for prayer have been started throughout the country since the beginning of this one, and in many cases copied after it, but wherever they were successful they developed some characteristics that were peculiar to themselves. Of course our work here may move others to do something and may suggest methods for carrying on this kind of work. But it must never be forgotten that the first condition of success is the presence of the Holy Spirit.[6]

In 1857, the total communicant membership of the Reformed Church in America numbered 46,197. Those members were spread out over 393 congregations,[7] meaning there was approximately one senior pastor for every 118 members.[8] If pastors were the primary leaders of corporate prayer in 1857, prayer was being led by less than one percent—actually about 0.82 percent—of Reformed Church members. However, as other gatherings emerged where parishioners actively led and participated, the percentage of RCA members involved in prayer leadership increased dramatically.

The *Liturgy* provided for prayers from the congregation only when invited by and written by ministers of the Word. Out of the legacy of Fulton Street Prayer emerged instead a "liturgy" made up of thousands of prayer requests submitted by men and women in the pews and lifted up to God by other people in the pews. This was, for the Reformed Church, prayer on a different level.

While the roster of ministers of the Word was exclusively male in 1857, opening up the leadership of the prayer meetings to parishioners opened the door to women. Women in 1857 could not yet

5   Minutes, various entries from the year 1857.
6   Lamphier [sic], J.C., "The Origin and Methods of the Fulton Street Prayer-Meeting: an Interview with the Founder and Manager," *Preacher and Homiletic Monthly*, no. 3, October, 1878 to September, 1879, 224-26.
7   Statistics gleaned from *Acts and Proceedings*, 1858.
8   Statistics from *Acts and Proceedings*, 2005 indicate that there is now an average of 184 members for every senior pastor.

stand behind the pulpit in the Reformed Church. They could, however, get down on their knees. Prayer requests sent in to the initial prayer meetings indicate that there were many women involved in this prayer movement.

> Three sisters who humbly hope, and believe in the savior, desire the prayers of their Christian sisters for their Father who is aged and infirm often tender and interested but still uninterested.
>
> A widow mother who believes in the efficacy of prayer desires the prayers of the Christians of Fulton Street meeting for her 4 children, 3 sons and 1 daughter who are out of the ark of safety. The 11th of this month is the birth day of one of the sons. Will you that evening make the precious children a special subject of prayer for their conversion. Rochester, October 7, 1858.
>
> Ye men of Israel help Ye daughters of Israel help for he has no mother to pray for him for where 2 or three are agreed, the Lord will help.[9]

Apparently, the involvement of women in the prayer movement was not something that Jeremiah intended:

> The noon of the day of our first meeting arrived; I opened the room but no one came. I waited; I went to the window and I saw a woman reading the notice. I hurried down stairs; I told her: "madam, this is a workingmen's meeting; it is not intended for women. If women come, men will hesitate to come in their working clothes; and that I would prefer that she would not come in." That is the reason we do not allow women to participate in the meeting. Of course, we now allow them to attend.[10]

Women's participation in prayer was not intentional. It was, however, inevitable. Women did contribute. Not only did they participate in these gatherings, they started some of their own. Just a few short years after Jeremiah began the prayer meeting in the North Dutch Church, Sarah Doremus started praying for missionaries in the South Dutch Church. In November of 1860, she began the Women's

---

9   From *Requests: Fulton Street Union Prayer Meeting,* housed in the Collegiate Corporation Archives. This album contains over one thousand handwritten prayer requests from all over the United States.

10   Lamphier [sic], "Origin and Methods," 224.

Union Missionary Society.[11] Doremus set up a watershed for women's involvement in prayer. For years to follow, missionaries around the world would, literally, be prayed into place by women in the Reformed Church in America.

The leadership of businessmen in prayer and the involvement of women represented a huge shift in the manner and politics of prayer. How did it come about?

Jeremiah believed that "the first condition of success (for the prayer meeting) is the presence of the Holy Spirit."[12] For Jeremiah, the most important person in prayer is the person of the Holy Spirit. In Acts 2:17-18, Luke the historian seems to suggest that you can't invite the Spirit, without getting the Spirit's women coming along. Jeremiah's decision to make the Spirit central made it very difficult for him to keep women on the periphery.

The story of prayer in the Reformed Church doesn't end with Dutch men and women. Chris Moore, research coordinator at the Schomburg Center for Research in Black Culture at the New York Public Library, recently uncovered The Farmers' Cabinet, March 3, 1858. He believes it to be a "pretty good snapshot of the [Fulton Street] meeting spreading throughout the city, and being put to use by the antislavery and abolitionist community."[13]

THE REVIVAL IN NEW YORK

...About twenty-five large prayer-meetings are held every day, at which the attendance seems to be daily increasing; — not to mention the regular or the extra meetings held in various churches. The establishment of the noon-day meeting in the "Old North Dutch Church," in October last, was the beginning of these, yet that meeting, though still continued, and filled every day in its three rooms to overflowing, is no longer called a large gathering. One thousand persons, assembling during business hours, in a business quarter of the city, to spend an hour in prayer, is no longer a large number. Two thousand attend the meeting in the Methodist Church on John Street, while even a

---

[11]   Women's Union Missionary Society: 1860-1974. In Collection 379 [September 6, 2003], Records: 1860-1983, in the Billy Graham Center Archives.

[12]   Lamphier [sic], "Origin and Methods," 224.

[13]   Email correspondence from Christopher Moore, June 22, 2006.

greater meeting numbering nearly three thousand, is now held in a still more unusual place.

Last week the old theater in Chambers Street was thrown open, and filled, on the first day, from pit to dome, with a congregation such as never before faced its foot-lights. Some merchants in that vicinity, finding themselves inconveniently distant from Fulton and John Streets, leased the building from Mr. Burton, the celebrated manager and actor, and issued a general invitation to business men to attend. The meeting, thus far, has been conducted, alternately, by ministers of different denominations – and on Saturday last, by the Rev. Henry Ward Beecher. The gathering on that day was the largest that has assembled since the commencement of the revival in this city....

Another of the most encouraging prayer meetings in the city – though in point of size not to be compared with this – is held near "the Tombs," in Centre Street. A very marked religious interest has been for some time past developing itself in that locality, and among the daily congregations at the meeting, are many persons of previously vicious characters, some whom have been converted and reformed, while every day others asking for prayers. Men go into these meetings from their daily occupations, with their sleeves rolled up, and with grime and dust on their faces, who have just dropped their tools in the neighboring factories, to spend part or all of their noon recess at the union chapel.

The neighborhood has a large colored population, many of whom attend; and who, to the astonishment of some very Christian church-members, take seats among their white neighbors, and are treated with equal respect and attention. In fact, such is the cordiality and catholicity of the managers of the meeting, that even the lowest classes of society are freely welcomed...A general awakening, like that which now exists, has never occurred in this city, and its progress is watched with increasing interest every day.[14]

People of color engaged in an act of social transformation by taking their seats "to the astonishment of some very Christian church-members...among their white neighbors." We might even say that this

---

[14] "Correspondence of the Congregationalist," *Farmer's Cabinet*, vol. 56, Issue 35, March 22, 1858, 2. From the Early American Newspapers Collection of the New York Public Library.

"civil prayer" helped precipitate the Civil War. New social gatherings astonished the church and eventually helped transform the nation. In 1857, in some remarkable ways, the Reformed Church shared in some of this transformation.

What Do They Pray about?

...devoted themselves to prayer and a ministry of the word (Acts 6:4)

I consulted with no one but God. I drew up the plan. It was to be a business men's meeting for prayer; to begin at the hour of noon; to last just one hour; people to be permitted to come in and go out at any time. There was to be no constraint. It was to be understood that coming in and going out would disturb no one, so that business men, who had but ten minutes to spare, could run in, in the shirtsleeves for that matter, join in a single prayer and one hymn and then go Back to business. It was to be wholly informal. It was to avoid all things that were controversial, to be based on the points on which all Christians were agreed. Episcopalian and Methodist, Presbyterian and Baptist, Lutherans, all were to find this a prayer meeting home.[15]

We have an important part of our history already documented in our liturgy. We know what is on the hearts of church members by looking at what is in our habits. We know that "our help is in the name of the Lord...." We see in life a rhythm of approaching, hearing, and responding in the name of Father, Son, and Spirit. For the most part, however, it prescribes more than it describes.

To discern the prayer of the average person requires other resources. In 1857 one of those resources was the Fulton Street Union Prayer Meeting Request Book. We have no way of determining how many of the prayer requests contained in the book came exclusively or even primarily from Reformed Church members (most are not signed). We can verify, however, that they all came to the North Dutch Reformed Church in a period of roughly eighteen months from the fall of 1857 to the spring of 1859. The following requests came from one day in the life of the prayer meeting.

---

[15]   Lamphier [sic], "Origin and Methods," 224.

Feb. 11, 1859

Fulton St. Prayer Meeting

Dear Bretheren for years I have been praying for the conversion of my husband and two brothers, one in California. Pray God for Christ' sake that they may be brought to the knowledge of the truth as it is in Jesus

A sister desires the prayer of God's people for a sister, who is entirely given up to the world. She is a mother. O! may she be turned to the knowledge of Christ and be enabled to bring up her children in the nurture and admonition of the Lord.

A young man residing in this City who came a few years since from England where his parents are now residing, he being the only member of his family unconverted is presented by a Christian friend who desires his immediate conversion as a subject of special prayer.

A young lady in this on some weeks, a very serious and deeply interested in her [?] so much so, as to seek God in prayer before a recent conversation, the writer learnt that it impossible to rest his mind on Religion been all her life, amidst the world's pleasure very moment she attempted to pray and the very moment she attempted to pray and [?] all sorts of foolish and worldly thoughts in her mind. Can not special prayer, be offered for this cause, one who desires to become a believer but is too weak to resist the snares of Satan.[16]

What were people praying about at Fulton Street? What was on their hearts? On February 11, 1859, they were praying about people and not problems. These prayers came out of a time of great economic hardship. Banks were closing, people were out of work. There were pressing challenges. Still, at least in the prayers captured in the request book, there was no mention of the larger social issues of the day. Instead, there was an ongoing parade of people: young women and men, wayward children, and resistant spouses. These were ordinary people praying for ordinary people.

Prayer happened person to person, prodigal son by persistent mother. The earnestness, the passion of the prayers was personal. This was prayer not only in the name of the Father, Son, and Holy Spirit. This was prayer in the name of Jeremiah and Jonathan, Susan, and

---

[16]   From *Requests*.

Sharon. People were praying for friends and family. More specifically still, people were praying for the conversion of friends and family.

How is it that so many requests came in to Fulton Street? Why was there such a focus on personal and community-wide revival? We get a clue from the Jacksonville letter above: "We have heard of the efficacy and power of your prayer meetings...."

People prayed about what others wrote about. The Fulton Street Prayer Requests were a responsive reading to newspapers like the New York *Observer*. The prayer meetings received extensive coverage through books and articles. This visibility in turn informed and directed the prayer. There was a liturgy to this legacy which involves a ministry of the Word *and* prayer (Acts 6:4). Business people like Jeremiah are the pray-ers. Writers like Samuel Prime, editor of the New York *Observer*, ministered.

T.W. Chambers, in "Prayers of a Generation," summarized the process:

> During the course of thirty years the press has been more or less used in connection with the services. The following named books owe their appearance in whole or in part to its existence:
> 1. "The Noon Prayer-Meeting." By T.W. Chambers, #.#. 308 pages. 12 mo. Board of Publication Reformed Dutch Church, 1858. This for many years has been out of print.
> 2. "The Power of Prayer." By S. Irenaeus Prime, D.D. 300 pages. 12 mo. Scribner & Co. This volume has had a wonderful circulation. Seventy editions were issued in English in this country and in Great Britain, and the work was translated into the French, Dutch, and several other languages.
> 3. "The Fulton Street Hymn-Book." This little volume, prepared for the use of the meeting under the direction of the Committee, contains a number of the evangelical lyrics in general use among the various churches that day.
> 4. "Five Years of Prayer," by S. Irenaeus Prime, D.D., a duodecimo volume issued by the Scribners in 1862, detailed the results of the meeting during the period mentioned in the title.
> 5. During the first ten years of the meeting's existence a number of small volumes were issued by the Board of Publication of the Reformed Dutch Church, each of which bore a relation, more or less distinctly marked, to what had occurred or been recounted in the Noon Meeting. These are "The Little Syracuse Boy," "The Drummer Boy," "Living Words," "The Young

Quartermaster," "Christ ever with You," Hospital Life," "Out of Darkness into Light," "The High Mountain Apart."

6. "Hours of Prayer," edited by T.W. Chambers, D.D. was issued by the same Board in 1868. The little volume classified and annotated some of the incidents of the meeting.

7. "Fifteen Years of Prayer." By S. Irenaeus Prime, D.D. This volume, published by the Scribers in 1872, continued the series of narratives given in the author's previous volumes.

8. "Prayer and Its Answer." By the same author and publisher. This volume, the last on the subject prepared by the lamented Dr. S.I. Prime, was issued in 1882. It treated them "as illustrated in the First Twenty-five Years of the Fulton Street Prayer-Meeting."

These various publications did very much to extend the knowledge of the meeting, not only in this country, but in various places in the four quarters of the globe. It is a singular fact in the gracious providence of Almighty God that a meeting so simple and unpretending in its character, whose origin and aims were only local, should yet have become familiar to multitudes all over the world. This result was due to the press, partly through reports in the secular and the religious journals, but still more through the volumes issued, especially those prepared by Dr. Prime, the genial and accomplished editor of the "New York Observer." Christians everywhere were encouraged or stimulated by the marvels of grace wrought in answer to believing supplication, and others were often awakened or guided by the varied experiences of conversion which were incidentally mentioned."[17]

A generation of publicizing worked hand-in-glove with a generation of praying. There were liturgists and congregants, but now their roles and responsibilities reached far beyond Sunday morning. Their books, along with several periodicals, including the *Christian Intelligencer*, provided Lukan accounts to the Acts of the apostolic at Fulton Street. They ministered in ways that encouraged prayer.

Jeremiah Lanphier could be said to have a twentieth-century counterpart in Norman Vincent Peale. The North Dutch Church building—where the Fulton Street Prayer Meetings began—was torn down, replaced in ministry by the Marble Collegiate Church. Peale, as pastor at Marble, became, perhaps, a successor to Samuel Prime. Peale's

---

[17] Talbot W. Chambers, "Prayers of a Generation," sermon delivered on the thirtieth anniversary of the Fulton Street Prayer meeting, appendix.

paper was not the New York *Observer*, but *Guideposts* magazine. The pray-ers are the subscribers. Today, via the Internet, hundreds of prayer requests pour in to *Guideposts*, not at Fulton Street, but at Seminary Hill Road. Even though Peale is dead, these requests are very much alive, held not in a request book but on a web site. They are received not in a geographical place, but in cyberspace.

What does that book of requests look like today? Here is a portion of what appeared on the *Guideposts* web site September 8, 2006 (deleting the names):

> Please pray for my 17 yr. old son....He is currently in AA but I'm not sure he's serious about it. Please pray that he will see that I love him and I've been trying to help him have a better life (right now he isn't speaking to me). I ask that you pray for his recovery from all drugs and help him find Jesus Christ, whom he believes in, but is not leaning on for strength. I miss my wonderful son and I pray for him everyday. Thank you and God bless
>
> Lord, I humbly ask that you touch my best friend who is in ICU after having surgery for colon cancer. Lord, strengthen her so that she may have a speedy recovery and no recurrence of her cancer. I also pray for a mighty increase in peace, love, happiness, health, financial means and wisdom for me and my children. Lord, bind all hurt, harm and danger. Strengthen us where we are weak and forgive us for our wrongs. Thank you for your grace and mercy. In holy name of our Lord and Saviour...AMEN.
>
> please pray that I find a job close to home, with good benefits, holidays and good pay.
>
> Please pray for my finances. Thank you!
>
> I'm very concerned for my parents' health. Please pray that they will be well!
>
> Please pray for my friend who is traveling to India to be married next week. Please pray that God will protect them and bless their marriage. Pray that she will be joyfully accepted into the family. Please also pray for her mother who can't be there due to her health. Thank you!
>
> PLEASE PRAY THAT I GET A JOB WITH GOOD PAY, GOOD BENEFITS, HOLIDAYS, AND THAT THE JOB IS CLOSE TO MY HOME. THANK YOU
>
> Please pray that I'll do what God wants me to do. Please pray for strength and wisdom for me, and great health for all of my loved ones and myself. Thank you!

Please pray for our son....to be strong and have courage to defeat the obsessive thoughts in his brain. Pray that his brain will be filled with serotonin and he can manage his OCD with little discomfort and that he can be reunited with his wife. In Jesus name, Thank you,

Please pray for my parents' health. Please pray that they are completely well and that the test results show that. Thank you![18]

Prayer requests are still coming to New York to a ministry birthed in the Reformed Church in America. Only now the prayers shift from spiritual health to physical health. Practical rather than eternal concerns are more on people's minds today. Healing ministries are replacing revival ministries as the cutting edge of Reformed Church prayer.

Where Were They Praying?

"...they were all together in one place . . ." (Acts 2:1)

The original Fulton Street Prayer meetings were held in the consistory room of the Old North Dutch Church at 151 William Street. A shoemaker named John Haverdink (1644-1724) gave seventeen acres of land to the North Dutch Church. The building itself stood on that property from 1769-1875. When the building was torn down, the prayer meeting moved to 113 Fulton Street.[19]

What was the importance of this place to the prayer in 1857? Whereas Church accommodation in the lower part of the City has become seriously diminished by the recent removal of the Brick Presbyterian and the Broadway Tabernacle Churches, leaving the North Church almost alone in the midst of a large population stationary as well as floating, therefore, Resolved, That it be referred to a Committee of three to devise such measures as may seem most conducive to an increased interest in and attendance upon the Divine Word and ordinances, as dispensed in that Church, by individuals and families residing in that vicinity, and also to any other ends connected with the spiritual growth and prosperity of that portion of our Zion....[20]

[18] http://www.dailyguideposts.com/prayer/pray for others.asp
[19] Information provided by Rita Hollenga, Collegiate Corporation archivist.
[20] Minutes, May 7, 1857.

...at the next regular meeting of the Consistory, held June 4, this Committee reported a series of resolutions contemplating the appointment of one minister and several lay missionaries to be employed as auxiliaries to the pastors, in making the North Church a centre of religious influence upon the surrounding vicinity....[21]

...to employ a suitable person or persons to be engaged in visiting the families in the vicinity, and inducing them to attend the services in that church; and also to bring children into the Sabbath School, and to use such other means as may be deemed advisable for extending our Redeemer's kingdom in that port of our city....[22]

Prayer started in a place that had become "seriously diminished." The North Dutch Church stood "almost alone in the midst of a large population stationary as well as floating." This lower part of Manhattan seems an unlikely location for a prayer movement. We would not expect the Reformed Church in America to be strong in prayer in the midst of the kind of social upheaval that would continue in metropolitan areas for the next 150 years.

Members of the Reformed Church eventually moved out to the suburbs to live. In 1857, however, they came into the city to pray. The story of Fulton Street Prayer began as an account of one church with European roots trying to maintain its membership in the midst of changing urban demographics. The consistory of the North Dutch Church sought a missionary in Jeremiah. They looked for someone to fill the sanctuary pews on Sunday. What they found instead was a person who filled their consistory room with pray-ers every day of the week.

Fulton Street Prayer in 1857 was a metropolitan movement that spread from city to city more than from church to church. Major media outlets in metropolitan areas in part fueled the growth. However, there was also a change in paradigm: no longer were people seeking simply to bring people to church buildings, they were praying instead for entire cities come to Christ.

To the Fulton Street Prayer Meeting
    Brothers in Christ—I have written to you before-some two or three weeks ago I wrote saying a small church and a cold one

---

[21]   Minutes, June 4, 1857.
[22]   Minutes, June 18, 1857.

seeming to have had but little reviving in several years. God in great mercy has heard our pleadings. Our communion was Sabbath before last—we had one addition by letter. The church has been roused, our meetings still continue, since the communion, five have been added to the church. Others are anxious the Holy Spirit seems to be moving in our midst. There is no excitement—a quiet gentle moving reigns.

Dear Brethren

A minister in the western part of Penn asks an interest in your prayers for himself and congregation. I have been ministering to the people for many a year and there appears to be a little life; although for the last 30 years the cause of God has been on the decline. Do pray that God may have again the captivity of this position of his vineyard and that he may give out a salvation blessing upon us at our communion season who is to L. the 1st Sunday of March. You may expect to hear from me again.

A Pastor

Near Jacksonville, FL

To the Members of the Fulton Street Prayer Meeting

We have heard of the efficacy and power of your prayer meetings, the result of your self denying love for the good of others and hope you will be rewarded with his love to ask an interest in your prayers for a community in central Illinois. It is chiefly in the backwood where there is more drunkenness and revelry carried on than refined civilization. One man left a church which he had once before been a member and commenced drinking till he quit the church altogether. Now he has commenced again and he is expected dying almost every day. It may be too late by the time this reaches you but we will pray and hope that he can yet be reclaimed again. He has a wife and four interesting children. Can you spend a little time in prayer for them and the whole community. The Holy Spirit is making some progress among them but not fast enough because we are such a wicked people. We do not wrestle and pray enough. One of them has been converted and has started preaching the gospel to his fellow men in by a bus or any place where they will let him. They have no meeting or school house any house in the neighborhood will you give them an interest in your prayers that not one single

soul of them be lost but all be gathered in the power of the Lord is the prayer of some of your brother and sister travelers to Zion.
A Sabbath School Student[23]

People were praying in and for cities in 1857. They were more conscious of geography than ecclesiology. There were few requests for God to grow individual churches. There were many requests for God to revive entire communities. People were weeping over cities, rather than whining over churches.

Still, we must recognize that much of this movement, like the inclusion of women and minorities in prayer, happened not because of, but in spite of, the efforts of church leaders. The consistory of the North Dutch Church in the early years of the movement continued to measure Jeremiah's ministry primarily by the number of people he called upon rather than the number of people with whom he prayed. The North Dutch Church remained a site for prayer but did not necessarily share a deep sentiment for prayer. For them there remained a tension between practical and prayerful concerns, between the spiritual and the social.

Prayer also happened in the marketplace. The prayer meeting was specifically "designed to give merchants, mechanics, clerks, strangers, and business men generally an opportunity to stop and call upon God amid the daily perplexities incident to their respective avocations."[24]

The prayer meeting was designed for business people. More importantly, it was designed to change business people.

> If this revival of religion exerts no permanent power on the conduct of men in their daily walk and conversation making them more sober, godly, and heavenly-minded; if it does not reach the intercourse of man with his fellow man in the social and commercial relationships of life, making merchants more honest, mechanics more truthful, tradesman of every name more upright, conscientious and punctual in their engagements; if it does not elevate Christianity in the estimation of the world...it will have accomplished far less than we anticipated for the honor of Christ and the good of men.[25]

---

23   From *Requests*.
24   Chambers, "Prayers of a Generation," 5.
25   S. Irenaeus Prime, *The Power of Prayer* (New York: Charles Scribner and Company, 1859), 125.

The goal seems to have been achieved: "It was often remarked, during the winter of 1857-8 that there was a diminution of vice, even under circumstances that might have been expected to increase it."[26]

Prayer moved from city to city and from workplace to workplace. It happened in meeting places, in marketplaces and even in mission places.

But the narratives of what was said and done here [Fulton Street] have gone much farther. Like the heavens,

"Their line has gone out through all the earth and their words to the end of the world."

The echo has come back from Australia and China and Japan and India and Cape Colony and Central Africa and the islands of the sea. In these far-off regions many an inquirer has been stimulated and guided by learning of the doings of God's Spirit here, and many a faithful laborer in the fields white unto the harvest has been encouraged and refreshed by the knowledge that at home his brethren of different names were pleasing with God on behalf of him and his work.[27]

After 1857, prayer continued in places we might not expect. In 1874 the Old North Dutch Church building surrendered to the wrecking ball. We might assume that, without a place to pray, the Fulton Street Prayer meeting stopped. Instead, it simply moved down the street to 113 Fulton and continued to pray daily until 1960. Buildings were torn down, but the prayers still rose up.

When Did They Pray?

"About noon...Peter went up to the roof to pray." (Acts 10:9)

My early education was neglected. I learned the tailor trade in Albany, this state. Afterward I started into business in this city. I was not a Christian, but was a strict moral man. Finally, I was made to see that I was a sinner and needed to be born again. One day at the hour of noon I found peace by believing in Christ.

Ever after the hour of noon was sacred. It was to me a sweet hour of prayer. In 1857 an elder of this church—it was known as the Old Dutch Church—persuaded me that it was my duty

---

26   Prime, *Power of Prayer*, 174.
27   Chambers, "Prayers of a Generation," 6.

to be its lay missionary. I drew back. I could not feel that I had qualifications for this work, my education had been so neglected; but he would not let me go. I made it a matter of prayer. Finally I felt myself called to the work and gave up my business, to the disgust of my partner, who pronounced me a fool. The salary given me was 800 dollars. I visited from house to house, engaged in prayer if opportunity offered, talked to business men and invited children to the Sabbath-school. Soon the work began to tell in an increased attendance at our regular Friday evening prayer meeting and Sabbath services.

The summer of '57, as you know, was a time of great business depression. I met Christian business men on the street. We talked on religion. I asked them to come in here and pray with me a few moments. During that summer almost any hour you could have found two or more Christians in our old meeting room in prayer. In September of that year I felt that it would be well to have a prayer meeting for business men at the hour of noon. I chose that hour, I suppose, because it was so precious an hour to me.[28]

Robert Bakke points out that, several years before Jeremiah Lanphier started his prayer meetings in New York City, there were people praying in Boston with a very similar format.[29] What seems to be distinctive about the prayers of 1857 is not just the content of the prayers, but the clock, not only the what, but the when. Timing is not everything, but it is something of what makes Fulton Street Prayer unique.

Fulton Street Prayer happened daily at noontime. It was a midday movement. When the meetings first began, they were generally called union prayer meetings, putting the emphasis on who was attending. Hence, the title of the prayer album of 1858 was the Fulton Street Union Prayer Meeting. As the meeting continued, however, the name changed. Talbot W. Chambers, at the thirtieth anniversary, referred to the prayer meeting as the "Daily Noon Prayer-meeting, Fulton Street."[30]

The name changed because the prayer changed. Prayer moved during this period from being intermittent to persistent. God's people joined together *constantly* in prayer. Even though churches continued to seek Sunday worshipers, Jeremiah looked for daily prayers.

---

[28] Lamphier [sic], "Origin and Methods," 225.
[29] Robert O. Bakke, *The Power of Extraordinary Prayer* (Wheaton: Crossway Books, 2000), 123.
[30] Chambers, "Prayers of a Generation," 1.

The move from weekly to daily corporate prayer was an extraordinary shift in the Fulton Street Prayer movement. Before Jeremiah, there were many prayer meetings being held midweek, Sunday night, etc. There was a monthly prayer meeting "of the New York-Brooklyn foreign missionary society" publicized in the *Christian Intelligencer*. There were even other prayer meetings being held during the week at the North Dutch Church. Starting in October of 1857, however, people prayed together at the North Dutch Church every working day of the week.[31] Even more remarkably, these daily prayers continued, not just for a season, nor just while a certain program was being launched. There was a daily corporate prayer meeting in New York City sponsored and organized by leaders in the Reformed Church in America for 103 years.[32]

The prayer meetings were every day *and* they were at midday. There were practical reasons to hold the prayer meetings at lunch time. The church was a downtown church. There were thousands working downtown within walking distance. Most of those workers were already planning to take a lunch break. Choosing the noontime hour was convenient for those who worked downtown.

Time of day was important to the prayers of 1857. So also was the time in history.

> The year of 1857 was a year of financial embarrassment, culminating in the suspension of specie payments in the month of October. The whole horizon was covered with clouds and men moved with fear and trembling, not knowing what a day would bring forth. The apprehension of disaster was almost as trying as its reality, sometimes more so, since imagination always exaggerates the evils it forecasts.[33]

Without the financial collapse, it is questionable whether the prayer meetings would have grown so rapidly. Men who had lost their jobs suddenly had time to pray. More importantly, a whole society had lost confidence in the almighty dollar and now sensed its need for prayer.

---

[31] Information from various issues of the *Christian Intelligencer* during the year 1857.

[32] Uncatalogued financial records in the Collegiate Corporation archives indicate that leaders of the prayer meeting leased Room #103 in building 93-99 Nassau Street, New York, until July 1, 1960.

[33] Chambers, "Prayers of a Generation," 6.

What about today? There is a growing interest throughout the Reformed Church in daily prayer. For the first time ever, round-the-clock[34] prayer persisted the entire week of the General Synod in 2006. It started with a youth movement of prayer around the clock at Central College in Pella, Iowa. Hope College in Holland, Michigan, ended its spring semester in 2005 with constant prayer. Christ Memorial Church in the same city celebrated "24-7" prayer with the help of more than two hundred volunteers from July, 2005, through July, 2006.

Daily prayer is spreading throughout the Reformed Church today. So is noontime prayer. In Zeeland, Michigan, a group of pastors pray weekly at noon. At Trinity Reformed Church in Rotterdam, New York, there is "Noontime Prayer for Revival and Salvation" happening weekly.

How Did They Pray?

> "*...decently and in order...*" (*1 Corinthians 14:40*)

The leadership of the prayer meeting varied, but the time and format did not. Leaders were given a "Bill of Direction" and required to strictly observe it:

Please observe the following rule:

Be prompt, commencing precisely at twelve o'clock.

The leader is not expected to exceed ten minutes in opening the meeting.

1st. Open the meeting by reading and singing three to five verses of a hymn.

2nd. Prayer

3rd. Read a portion of Scripture

4th. Say the meeting is now open for prayers and exhortations, observing particularly the rules overhead, inviting the brethren from abroad to take part in the services.

5th. Read but one request at a time—requiring a prayer to follow—such prayer to have special reference to same.

6th. In case of any suggestion or proposition by any person, say this is simply a prayer-meeting, and that they are out of order, and call on some brother to pray.

7th. Give out the closing hymn five minutes before one o'clock. Request the benediction from a clergyman, if one be present.[35]

---

[34] Twenty-four hours a day, seven days a week; i.e., constant.

[35] J. Edwin Orr, *The Second Evangelical Awakening* (London: Marshall, Morgan, and Scott, 1949), from chapter three, "Typical Prayer Meetings."

In addition to what each leader had in hand, there was a placard hung on the wall—in a prominent place—commanding the attention of the whole meeting:

> Brethren are earnestly requested to adhere to the five-minute rule.
> Prayers and exhortations not to exceed five minutes in order to give all an opportunity.
> No more than two consecutive prayers of exhortations.
> No controversial points discussed.[36]

What was it about the liturgy of Fulton Street that was so contagious? What in the format fueled such a far-reaching movement? There is a mystery about the appeal of Fulton Street: not addition, but multiplication. I cannot ultimately explain why the style of prayer was so popular in 1857. I can only make some educated guesses.

First, singing enhances prayer. The psalmist invites us to "come into God's presence with singing...." That phrase seems to suggest that there is something about music that is attractive to God's presence and our prayer. In corporate prayer we need music and God loves it. For Fulton Street to insist on beginning with hymns invited God's presence and corporate participation.

Second, scripture focuses prayer. Music gives us the tune of prayer and scripture gives us the words. Music takes the focus off the person leading and puts it on the person of the Spirit. Scripture then allows us to hear the Spirit speak. Our *Liturgy* puts scripture at the center of our worship, and Jeremiah Lanphier learned from that.

Third, sharing multiplies prayer. The bill of direction was simple and accessible. It was liturgy for the laity. It allowed for creativity and spontaneity. It invited people to bring something to prayer, rather than simply to take something from it. It was participatory. Anyone and everyone had an opportunity to offer a prayer request.

Fourth, structure sustains prayer. How does one prayer meeting last for 103 years? Promptness, punctuality, and purpose. The more time we have, the less we sometimes say. Promptness precipitates more prayer. People can take five without taking over. Punctuality assures that the prayers are to the point. An overarching purpose helps measure the answers and motivate more prayer.

The most interesting of all the rules, however, may be the rule that no controversial issues may be discussed. How can it be, we might

---

[36] Ibid.

ask, that they could be praying on the eve of the civil war and never mention the issue of slavery? Part of the answer, I believe, lay not just in what they were praying for, but who they were praying with and to. When they insisted that there be no controversial issues, they gave no one an excuse to stay home. When they invited the Holy Spirit, they gave no one the opportunity to stay the same.

Avoiding controversy, for Fulton Street anyway, was not a political decision, but a theological one. It was not a statement about the importance of the specific issues. It was instead a statement about how to address the issues most effectively. Lanphier decided it would be "not by might or by power but by God's Spirit" (Zech. 4:6). He sided with Paul in the conviction that the meetings must be characterized not by "wise and persuasive words, but demonstrations of the Spirit's power" (1 Cor. 2:4). Lanphier's leadership represented an investment in the power of prayer over the power of preaching. It was a choice to ask for a Comforter, rather than to be a convincer.

Why is it that we in the Reformed Church in America continue to be at the forefront of bringing people together in prayer? Our general secretary presently serves as steering committee chair of Christian Churches together with this stated purpose:

> The purpose of Christian Churches Together is to enable churches and national Christian organizations to grow closer together in Christ in order to strengthen our Christian witness in the world....To fulfill its purpose of growing closer to Christ and to each other, Christian Churches Together focuses, in its annual meeting, on praying together, discerning the guidance of the Holy Spirit through prayer and theological dialogues, and providing fellowship and mutual support. Out of this process, participants discern how and when to take action together in common witness to our society.[37]

Perhaps it is an insistence on avoiding division due to controversy that serves our ecumenism so well. In our refusal to be separated from others because of arguments, we may have found ourselves in a better position to pray with others. Perhaps it accounts for some of the reason we, through groups like Christian Churches Together, have been able to host modern day "union prayer meetings."

---

[37]   http://christianchurchestogether.org

ADDENDUM

Hymnodists of the
Reformed Church in America

James Hart Brumm

In his 1966 lectures at Western Seminary, Howard Hageman suggested a monograph on Reformed Church members who have written hymns:

> They were not great, but then, few hymnwriters [sic] are. But they represent a side of our tradition too little known and certainly too little valued.[1]

This is not that monograph, although it may be a taste of things to come if ever the Historical Series were to publish a thorough history of hymnody in this denomination. What follows is a set of brief sketches of ten of the most prominent creators of congregational song from the Reformed Church in America. Each sketch is followed by an example of that writer's work, which may give the lie to Hageman's estimation of their abilities.

---

[1]   Mast, *In Remembrance and Hope*, 142.

John Henry Livingston or Henry Livingston, Jr. —or Both

The first Livingston, editor of the first two editions of *Psalms and Hymns,* was profiled in the previous chapter. There is an oral tradition in the Reformed Church that credits our first professor of theology with the authorship of several of the metrical psalm texts in those volumes. Among Livingston's surviving letters and papers, however, no such poetic work is mentioned. The one written record comes from the 1859 and 1860 printings of *Psalms and Hymns,* where authors were credited for the first time and the name "Livingston" was attached to eight metrical psalm texts; there were no first names used, however, and at least some of the author assignments were incorrect (for example, Joel Barlow is credited with a portion of Psalm 21 that is a modified text of Isaac Watts's, a text which does not appear in Barlow's psalter). Norman Kansfield, who was a member of the committee that produced *Rejoice in the Lord*—where the text "Searcher and Savior of my soul" is credited to Livingston—made an argument for Livingston's creation of that text:

> At the same time that he [Livingston] was moving in Watts' direction (relative to having the Psalms sing the praise of Christ) he was also taking some strong steps toward Hebraicizing the Psalms. And it is at this point that "Searcher and Savior" becomes interesting datum. When one looks at the last four parts of Psalm 119 in the [1813] edition one is struck with the fact that J.H.L. as editor was attempting to restore the acrostic character of the Psalm. Part 19 is, in Hebrew, q, and each line of that section begins with the letter q. Livingston transliterated the letter *Koph* and has each of the three stanzas of his part 19 begin with a "K." Part 20 is r. All three stanzas of "Searcher and Savior" begin with "S." Part 22 is t and all seven stanzas begin with "T."
>
> "Searcher and Savior" is also, I believe, the only Psalm or hymn included within the [1813] *P & H* which is written in blank verse. That does not immediately feel like an argument for J.H.L.'s authorship. It is difficult to envision a sixty-eight year old, conservative theologian bravely opting for so untraditional a form. Still, it is even more difficult to envision Tate, Brady, Watts, Newton, the Wesleys, or even . . . Dwight using that format. The text begins to feel like the kind of piece an editor would create to fulfill a need.[2]

---

[2]   Norman J. Kansfield, letter to James Hart Brumm, March 15, 1988.

Yet there is another possibility. Mary S. Van Deusen, a Livingston family descendant, has uncovered a modest but significant poetic career by John Henry's younger brother, Henry Livingston, Jr. (1748-1828). The younger Livingston was a farmer, surveyor, politician, and a major in the Continental army during the War for Independence.[3] He may also have been the true author of *A Visit from Saint Nicholas*, the classic Christmas poem commonly attributed to Clement Moore.[4] Henry only published a small number of his poems, and always anonymously or under a pseudonym—"R," "L," and "Banks of the Hudson" seemed to be particular favorites. These published works reflect many of the qualities of the texts credited to "Livingston" in *Psalms and Hymns*.

This evidence suggests that Henry Livingston, on a smaller scale, could have served the same role for his older brother that the Methodist Charles Wesley served for his (who was coincidentally, also named John). While "Searcher and Savior" is still unique and probably the older Livingston's work, it is possible that the other psalms associated with Livingston are actually Henry's work, perhaps with John's theological guidance. Or perhaps John Henry drafted texts which his brother edited and polished.

> Searcher and Savior of my soul,
> my Sun, my Shield, my sovereign Judge,
> all things are naked to thy view,
> my heart, my thoughts, my words, my ways.
>
> Sinners of state with power arrayed,
> who fear not God, nor man regard,
> have persecuted without cause;
> but all their hatred I decry.
>
> Still to thy Word my soul repairs;
> thence I my highest comforts draw;
> though foes may fight and devils rage,
> if God be for me, all is well.

---

[3]   Mary S. Van Deusen, *A Mouse in Henry Livingston's House*, website chronicling her ongoing research into Henry Livingston's poetic work. www.iment.com/maida/familytree/henry.

[4]   See Don Foster, *Author Unknown: On the Trail of Anonymous* (New York: Henry Holt, 2000).

Sustain me with thy promised grace,
revive my heart, increase my faith:
I hate to lie, I love the truth;
Oh! Make me be what I profess!

Seven times a day my prayers ascend
with mingled praises to thy throne:
'tis good to seek my Father's face,
and plead in my Redeemer's name.

Strong peace have they, who love thy law;
firm on a rock their hopes are built;
their faith looks up to nobler scenes,
and nothing can detain them here.

Seal to my soul thy pardoning love,
let strength be equal to my day;
then will I run with great delight,
and eager press, to seize the prize.

Supremely wise, and good, and great;
Oh! search my heart, and try my ways
thy word I love, thy judgments fear,
and tremble, while I pray and praise.
—*attr. John Henry Livingston, 1813*

The memory of Christ's glorious name
  through endless years shall run;
his spotless fame shall shine as bright
  and lasting as the sun.

In him the nations of the world
  shall be completely blessed;
and his imputed righteousness
  by every tongue confessed.

Then blessed be God, the mighty Lord,
  the God whom Israel fears;
who only wondrous in his works,
  beyond compare, appears.

Let earth be with his glory filled;
   for ever bless his name;
whilst to his praise, the listening world
   their glad assent proclaim.
          —*attr. Henry Livingston, Jr., 1813*

George Washington Bethune

One of only three Reformed Church in America ministers to be mentioned in John Julian's landmark work *Dictionary of Hymnology*, and the first to be published in hymnals in Great Britain,[5] Bethune's long and varied career included missionary work in Savannah, Georgia; church planting in the Saint Lawrence Seaway; serving as a pastor in New York City, Philadelphia, and rural upstate New York; and even supply preaching in Rome, Italy.

Bethune was born in 1805 in New York, studied at Dickinson College in Carlisle, Pennsylvania, and graduated from Princeton Theological Seminary in 1826. After his missionary year in Savannah, he served churches in Rhinebeck and Utica, New York, before settling into Philadelphia (at First and then Third Reformed Church) for fifteen years. Then, after nine years in Brooklyn and three in Manhattan, he retired to Florence, Italy, for his health and died there in 1862. Before he retired, he turned down offers to be chancellor of New York University and provost of the University of Pennsylvania.[6] Along the way he gained national renown as a public speaker and a scholar of English literature and poetry; his volume, *The British Female Poets*, published in 1848, was considered a definitive work in the latter half of the nineteenth century. He also published two volumes of poetry: *The Fruits of the Spirit* in 1839 and *Lays of Love and Faith* in 1847.[7] Some of his hymns are actually excerpted from these volumes, but there were also translations and paraphrases of ancient Greek hymns, children's hymns, Christmas carols, and metrical psalm settings included in his canon. Like other Reformed hymnodists, his work faded from hymnals after World War I,

---

[5]   John Julian, ed. *Dictionary of Hymnology: Origin and History of Christian Hymns and Hymnwriters of all Ages and Nations, Second and last Revised Edition with new supplement,* 1907, reprinted in two volumes (Grand Rapids: Kregel, 1985), 138-39.

[6]   Corwin, *Manual,* 318-19.

[7]   Julian, *Dictionary of Hymnology,* 138.

though he has appeared in some Baptist books in since 1950, and two of his hymns are in *Rejoice in the Lord.*

But what about the church planting? Bethune was an avid angler and regularly spent summers fishing in the Thousand Islands. He lobbied for a new church start in Alexandria Bay to bring the gospel to the locals whom he had met, and so that there would be someplace he could worship while he was there.

> Joy and gladness! Joy and gladness!
>   O happy day!
> Every thought of sin and sadness
>   chase, chase away.
> Heard we not the angels telling,
> Christ, the Lord of might, excelling
> on the earth with us is dwelling,
>   clad in our clay?
>
> Son of Mary (blessed mother!),
>   thy love we claim;
> Son of God, our elder brother
>   (O gentle name!),
> to thy Father's throne ascended,
> with thine own his glory blended,
> thou art, all thy trials ended,
>   ever the same.
>
> In thy holy footsteps treading,
>   guide, lest we stray;
> from thy word of promise shedding
>   light on our way,
> never leave us nor forsake us;
> like thyself in mercy make us,
> and, at last, to glory take us,
>   Jesus, we pray.
>
> *—George Washington Bethune, 1847*

Sarah Emily York

    Julian's *Dictionary*[8] associates Sarah York (née Waldo) with the Reformed Protestant Dutch Church, because of a hymn of hers that was first published in the 1847 edition of *Psalms and Hymns* before it was widely circulated among hymnals of various denominations through the rest of the nineteenth century. Her *Memoir*, which Julian says was published in 1853, might verify her membership in the denomination. She lived just thirty-two years, dying in 1851.

> I am weary of straying; Oh! Fain would I rest
> in the far-distant land of the pure and the blessed,
> where sin can no longer her blandishments spread,
> and tears and temptations for ever have fled.
>
> I am weary of hoping; where hope is untrue,
> as fair, but as fleeting, as morning's bright dew:
> I long for that land, whose blessed promise alone
> is changeless, and sure, as Eternity's throne.
>
> I am weary of sighing o'er sorrows of earth,
> o'er joys glowing visions, that fade at their birth;
> o'er the pangs of the loved, which we cannot assuage,
> o'er the blightings of youth, and the weakness of age.
>
> I am weary of loving what passes away;
> the sweetest, the dearest, alas! May not stay;
> I long for that land, where these partings are o'er,
> and death and the tomb can divide hearts no more.
>
> I am weary, my Savior, of grieving thy love;
> Oh! when shall I rest in thy presence above?
> I am weary; but Oh! let me never repine,
> while thy word, and thy love, and thy promise are mine.
>   —*Sarah Emily York, 1847*

---

[8]   Julian, *Dictionary of Hymnology*, 1597.

Hervey Doddridge Ganse

Born in 1822, Ganse could be said to have been on loan to the Reformed Protestant Dutch Church from the Presbyterians, who raised him up in Fishkill, New York, and helped educate him at Columbia University before he came to New Brunswick Seminary, where he was a member of the class of 1843. He returned to the Presbyterians in 1876 to pastor a congregation in St. Louis and to serve on the Presbyterian Board for Colleges and Academies, but, during his thirty-three years among us, he served as founding pastor of what is now the Freehold, New Jersey, Reformed Church, and spent another two decades as pastor of the West 23rd Street Church in New York City, which moved to Madison Avenue under his tenure. While he was in New York, he served as president of the General Synod (1866), was a member of the committee which, in 1867, recommended dropping "Dutch" from the name of the denomination—Ganse wrote the report—and, from 1871-1875, edited the *Christian Intelligencer*, precursor to the *Church Herald*. Edward Tanjore Corwin, in the fourth edition of his *Manual of the RCA*, called Ganse "a reasoner of exceptional dialectical power" and "a poet of singular sweetness." He died in 1891.[9]

He began writing hymns while in New York, as well, but he wrote one of his first back in Freehold. The story of one of his first is told in John Julian's *Dictionary of Hymnology*:[10]

> "Lord, I know Thy grace is nigh me"...was composed on a winter's night in his bedroom, in a farmhouse near Freehold, New Jersey, while on a visit of consolation to former parishioners. The first couplet came into his head without thought, and he adds, "I composed on my pillow in the darkness; completing the verses with no little feeling, before I slept."

That hymn—which is reprinted below—was included in *Hymns of the Church*; Ganse also contributed to *Hymns and Songs of Praise* in 1874 and *The Church Hymnary* in 1890, as well as other late nineteenth-century hymnals. The *Reformed Church Hymnal* of 1929 was the last RCA volume to include any of his work. As late as 1972, however, *The Christian Hymnary*, published jointly by the Church of God in Christ and the Mennonites, included his hymn, "Eternal Father, when to thee."

[9]   Corwin, *Manual*, 482-84.
[10]   P. 404.

Hervey Doddridge Ganse

Lord, I know thy grace is nigh me,
   though thyself I cannot see;
Jesus, master, pass not by me;
   Son of David, pity me.

While I sit in weary blindness,
   longing for thy blessed light,
many taste thy loving kindness;
   "Lord, I would receive my sight."

I would see thee and adore thee,
   and thy word the power can give;
hear the sightless soul implore thee;
   let me see thy face and live.

Ah, what touch is this that thrills me?
   What this burst of strange delight?
Lo, the rapturous vision fills me!
   This is Jesus! This is sight!
                    —*Hervey Doddridge Ganse, 1869*

Alexander Ramsay Thompson

The third Reformed Church minister—with Ganse and Bethune—mentioned in Julian's *Dictionary*,[11] Thompson was born in New York in 1822 and reared in the Presbyterian Church, graduating from Princeton in 1845. After service in Presbyterian congregations in Brooklyn, Manhattan, and Morristown, New Jersey, he came into the Reformed Church as a missionary in the Bedford section of Brooklyn. Once he became part of our family, according to Corwin's *Manual*, "[h]is attachment to the Reformed Church was sincere and strong." Thompson served congregations in the Reformed Church for thirty-seven years. In 1873, he began a twenty-two-year association with Roosevelt Hospital in New York City as its chaplain, where he worked during his entire pastorate at North Church in Brooklyn and through his retirement, the loss of his wife and family to death, and an illness that left him in profound physical pain during the last year of his life. Despite all of that, he continued to serve until just a few weeks before his death in 1895.

Corwin reports that Alexander Thompson "thought in poetry," and he was the author of a number of hymns. Yet his larger contribution to congregational song was as a translator of ancient Greek and Latin hymns.[12] This was work he began while on the editorial committee for *Hymns of the Church*, published in 1869, following in the footsteps of John Mason Neale, the Oxford Movement hymnodist who gained notoriety with the classic English hymnal, *Hymns, Ancient and Modern*, in 1861. In this work, Thompson was considered to be second only to Neale. His daughter published a volume of his hymns and translations posthumously, and his hymns have appeared in seventy-two North American hymnals, though no RCA hymnals since 1900.

> Wayfarers in the wilderness,
>   by morn, and noon, and even,
> day after day, we journey on
>   with weary feet towards heaven.
> *Oh land above! oh land of love!*
>   *thy glory shineth o'er thee;*
> *O Christ our King, in mercy bring*
>   *us thither, we implore thee!*

---

[11] P. 1168.
[12] Corwin, *Manual*, 794.

By day the cloud before us goes,
   by night the cloud of fire,
to guide us over trackless waste,
   to Canaan ever nigher.
Oh land above! oh land of love!
   thy glory shineth o'er thee;
O Christ our King, in mercy bring
   us thither, we implore thee!

Each morning find we, as he said,
   the dew of early manna;
and ever when a foe appears,
   confronts him, Christ our Banner.
Oh land above! oh land of love!
   thy glory shineth o'er thee;
O Christ our King, in mercy bring
   us thither, we implore thee!

The sea was riven for our feet,
   and so shall be the river;
And, by the King's highway brought home,
   we'll praise his name forever.
Oh land above! oh land of love!
   thy glory shineth o'er thee;
O Christ our King, in mercy bring
   us thither, we implore thee!
          —Alexander Ramsay Thompson, 1869

Edward Augustus Collier

Edward Collier's two older brothers graduated from New Brunswick Theological Seminary in 1852 and 54,[13] which may be why Edward broke the mold, graduating from Princeton Theological Seminary in 1860 and serving Congregational and Presbyterian parishes in New York's Hudson Valley before returning to the Reformed Church as pastor of Kinderhook in 1864. After that, he remained, and even spent thirty-four years as stated clerk of the Classis of Rensselaer.[14] Like

---

13   Corwin, *Manual*, 381, 383.
14   Ibid., 381.

Bethune, Collier had the rare honor of being published in hymnals on both sides of the Atlantic; his "Thou, Lord, art God alone" was part of the Church of Scotland's *Church Hymnary*, published in 1898. He held on in RCA hymnals until *The Reformed Church Hymnal* in 1929, and then made a reappearance in *Rejoice in the Lord*. In other denominations, he last appeared in 1961's *Trinity Hymnal* of the Orthodox Presbyterian Church.

> Thou, Lord, art God alone,
> veiling thy burning throne
>   from mortal sight;
> yet thou our Father art,
> from whose all pitying heart
> nor life nor death can part,
>   nor depth nor height.
>
> We praise thee, Holy One,
> thy Father's only Son,
>   his image bright;
> our Prophet, Priest and King,
> who dost redemption bring,
> thy matchless grace we sing,
>   thy saving sight.
>
> We praise thee, Heavenly Guest,
> thou great and last bequest
>   of love to man;
> O blessed Paraclete,
> guide thou our pilgrim feet,
> 'til glory shall complete
>   what grace began.
>
> We praise thee, Father, Son,
> and Spirit, Three-in-One,
>   God of all grace;
> angels and cherubim,
> with flaming seraphim,
> thy name, thrice holy, hymn
>   with veil-ed face.
>
> —*Edward Augustus Collier, 1898*

Denis Wortman

This best-known Reformed Church hymnodist was not much known as a hymnodist in his lifetime (1835-1922). He was a child of the Hopewell, New York, Reformed Church and graduated from New Brunswick Seminary in 1860.[15] Fairly well-known during his own life as a poet—he published two large works, *Reliques of Christ* in 1888 and *The Divine Processional* in 1903, as well as many shorter poems[16]—he actually authored "God of the prophets, bless the prophets' sons" as part of a greeting from his graduating class for the New Brunswick centennial in 1884. It had seven stanzas and was not sung at all, much less to the quasi-Genevan tune TOULON,[17] until much later; its first inclusion in a collection was for the *Church Hymnary* of 1891. Since then, it has appeared in some fifty hymnals of various denominations, and attempts to improve and update it have been made by the Presbyterians (for *The Hymnbook*, 1955), noted Episcopal hymnodist Carl P. Daw, Jr. (for *Hymnal, 1982*), the Christian Reformed Church (for the 1989 *Psalter Hymnal*), and Norman Kansfield (for *Rejoice in the Lord*).

Most of Wortman's half-dozen hymns were actually pieces of his poetry reworked for hymnals. One of the very few texts he actually wrote as a hymn, for the dedication of Jay Gould Memorial Reformed Church in Roxbury, New York, in 1893, was not sung, but read at the occasion.

Wortman served several short pastorates over forty-one years, as well as serving as president of the General Synod in 1901, before retiring to full-time writing. He doesn't seem to have thought too highly of hymnody: in an article for the *Homiletical Review* for March and April, 1896, he wrote: "As a matter of record, it will be seen that comparatively few hymns of the church are by the master-poets in other lines."

> There is a city great and strong,
>   twelve gates of precious stones,
> with turrets high and battlements,
>   not needing light of suns;
> the streets aglow with fire of gold,
>   it hath no sound of strife;

---

[15] Russell L. Gasero, *Historical Directory of the Reformed Church in America, 1628-2000* (Grand Rapids: Eerdman's, 2001), 473.

[16] Corwin, *Manual*, 918-19.

[17] TOULON is actually a later abridgment (circa 1861) of Psalm 124, from the Genevan Psalter.

Denis Wortman

in glory all its own it stands
   beside the stream of Life.

A joy is there that knows no cloy,
   a light that ne'er grows dim,
a multitude that never cease
   from grateful praise and hymn;
lo, all the sainted sons of earth,
   and angels there I view;
and there, O vision glorious!
   There standeth Jesus, too!

Jesus, I know 'tis he; I see
   the mark of nail and spear;
and on his face I catch the trace
   of earth-time smile and tear;
but on his brow a crown shines now,
   and bending hosts adore!
'Tis he, 'tis he who on the tree
   the thorn-crown meekly wore!

O wondrous, fair Jerusalem,
  shall I thy gates pass through?
Thy jubilations surely join,
  thy lordly splendors view?
O Crucified, O Glorified,
  may I thy face behold,
and join the ransomed as they sing
  along the streets of gold.

      —*Denis Wortman, from* Reliques of Christ, *1888*

Daniel James Meeter

The author of one of the articles in this volume, Daniel Meeter (b. 1953) is, as of this writing, senior pastor of the Old First Reformed Church in Brooklyn, New York, and one of the Reformed Church's leading liturgical scholars. A 1980 graduate of New Brunswick Theological Seminary, he has served congregations in South River and Hoboken, New Jersey; Wainfleet, Ontario; and Grand Rapids, Michigan.[18] Several of his hymns were written while in South River, a historically Hungarian immigrant parish, where he created English paraphrases of some of the hymns that the original members brought over with them to sing the liturgy.[19] The example below, however, is an original text for Pentecost.

Pentecost morning came:
humble band, weak and tame,
heard the wind, saw the flame
of the Holy Spirit.
Jesus' Holy Spirit
filled them from on high,
made them prophesy
with the Word of the Lord.
Praise the Holy Spirit.

Pentecost festival:
thousands there heard the call
of the band, preaching all
by the Holy Spirit,

---

[18] Gasero, *Historical Directory*, 263.

[19] Emily R. Brink, ed., *Sing! A New Creation Leaders' Edition* (Grand Rapids: CRC Publications, 2002), notes to selection 73.

Jesus' Holy Spirit
poured out on all flesh;
Jesus' holiness,
glorious, comes to us.
Praise the Holy Spirit.

Jesus Christ, crucified,
reigns on high, glorified;
to his Church, to his bride
gives the Holy Spirit.
Roaring, burning Spirit,
lift our voices high,
come and sanctify,
testify, prophesy.
Come, Lord Holy Spirit.
   ©Daniel James Meeter, 1983. Used by permission.

Barbara Boertje

Barbara Boertje grew up in the Reformed Church in Iowa, where she got a music degree from Central College in Pella before earning a master's degree in church music from Westminster Choir College in Princeton, New Jersey. She has served as a congregational musician at two Presbyterian churches in California and at the First Reformed Church in Grandville, Michigan, and taught for a year in Tokyo, Japan. She also served as a member of the committee that prepared *Sing! A New Creation*.[20] As a pastoral musician, Boertje has primarily paraphrased scriptural passages, for which she has composed tunes.

---

[20] Brink, *Sing! A New Creation Leaders' Edition*, notes to selection 70.

Barbara Boertje, based on Psalm 133

How ver-y good and pleas-ant when we live in u-ni-ty.

It is like pre-cious oil, like fresh morn-ing dew.

We gath-er here to-geth-er with our hearts and voi-ces raised

to God, who's the cen-ter of our u-ni-ty in praise!

Copyright © 1997, Barbara Boertje. Used by permission.

Part III

Where We Might Go with All This:
Our Present and Possibilities

The very purpose of the Historical Series of the Reformed Church in America is to foster scholarship that helps us reflect on our identity and mission in a way that informs both the church and the academy (see the series title page of this very book). The bulk of this book has reflected on various aspects of how our Sunday morning worship has become what it is. Now we look at our worship mission as we move forward with the identity formed by our history.

Paul Janssen's chapter examines the most recent denominational worship survey—published in 2004—for clues to where we are as a collected church. Kathleen Hart Brumm's chapter discusses ways in which congregations might go about creating contemporary worship within a Reformed framework.

Some would argue that she is actually advocating creative "traditional" worship. Both are true, in a very real sense, and so it is a false dichotomy. All Christian worship is traditional in some sense; it arises out of the tradition. And all worship is contemporary, in that it occurs in the here and now. What Brumm calls for is worship that allows congregations to adopt many elements of what is called "contemporary" worship, marry them to useful older elements, and use them to reinforce and build on Reformed theological values. Indeed, the thorns addressed and confronted in this final section are similar to those we have always had: desires to be like our neighbors and reluctance to do the hard work of continual reformation.

Norman Kansfield, in his response, is optimistic about the possibilities for the future of Reformed worship and suggests paths for those who want to build on the history we've been reading. A list of suggestions for further reading follows, so that liturgical creativity might continue and flourish. The thorns will always be with us, and that may even be a good thing, for in the thorns we are reminded of our full humanity, and we are called to look for the divinity growing among us.

CHAPTER 5

Worship among the Thorns: Observations from the 2004 Survey on Worship

Paul Janssen

Thorns? What Thorns?

To use the phrase, "liturgy among the thorns," gives the appearance that there is something pristine, something even lily-white (to make further reference to the passage from the Song of Solomon) about liturgy. Liturgical worship is pure; it is the heart exerting its highest and best use; it is the restless soul finding its rest in God. Indeed, worship, we might say, is what we're made for; it is the purpose that drives the fevered lives of men and women of the cloth, and one of the several habits of highly effective otherwise-vocationed people. I recall one of the sayings of Richard Feynman, the Cal Tech theoretical physicist (he who dunked Morton Thiokol's O-rings in a glass of ice water to show that it was too cold in Florida for the space shuttle *Challenger* to take off), to the effect that the wildest fancies of physics had to have real-world correlatives. The corollary of that statement is that real-world events can be accounted for by a textbook-type way of describing them. We tend to say something similar about the relationship between the church at worship and the church at work. Worship must find expression in what are these days called "missional"

179

activities, on the one hand; and on the other hand, the program, the evangelistic efforts, the pastoral care, the education (all these other things congregations do) must feed into the life of worship. Worship thus exerts both a centrifugal, outward force as well as a centripetal, inward force in the life of a congregation. Either way, worship is at the center. In addition to all that, a gathering of mostly clerical folks would be less than honest if we failed to admit that we identify worship with the lily because we fancy we're fairly good at it. In other words, it feeds our own egos to claim the highest ground for worship, because that is precisely where we tend to find ourselves the queens and kings of the hill.

But as for those thorns—"boo!" the thorns! Whatever they are, they are not quite up to the beauty of the beloved. If the thorns are the daily mill of pastoral work, then the thorns are mere distractions. If we were to say, "Reformed worship among the thorns," then we'd fall straight into the pit of self-congratulatory pretense and allow how the way we do it is just a bit better than the pomp and circumstance of some, the howling passion of others, the dry conservatism of still others, and the corrupt and degraded theology of, well, really, all the others but us. Devotees of traditional forms may name Power Point presentations, phantasmagoric projected spectacles, even aisle-wandering preachers as "thorns" to be avoided at all costs;[1] in which case, the thorns are among us. If "thorns" means the image-based consumer culture,[2] then, of course, worship is a lily: we don't change camera-angles every seven seconds, we are not hawking a product, we are not sexing up our liturgies to please the vulgar tastes of the masses, et cetera, et cetera. We delight in the differentness of worship, its sheer nonutility, its odd habits of singing en masse and of oral transmission.

The above musings may seem to avoid the topic, but I'm not intending that at all. For when the question is asked, "What is going on in Reformed worship today?" one must find a foothold, because the question is too broad. If you want a snapshot of customs and usages, I can refer you to the 2004 report commissioned by the Commission on Christian Worship. Indeed, I will make reference to it at some length in

---

[1]   Richard Lischer, in *The End of Words* (Grand Rapids: Eerdmans, 2005) offers an insightful critique of the ways that mass-communication culture is on the ascendant in the church; see specifically, "The Gospel of Technology," 24-27.

[2]   Elizabeth Thoman, web article at http://www.medialit.org/reading_room/article12.html.

just a few moments. But I find a foothold from another source, which some of you may recognize as I quote snippets from it:

> Throughout the Reformed Church one notes a "prevailing unseemly diversity" as regards liturgical observances. Not even the treasured forms for baptism and the Lord's Supper..."receive that uniform marked observance that may be claimed for them."[3]

These comments appear in a report of a committee of the General Synod convened in regular session in the year of our Lord 1848, barely two generations past the Explanatory Articles of 1792, but, one might guess, well more than a world away from the liturgy that accompanied those articles, translated from the original Dutch of the 1619 liturgy of Dort. Well more than a world away, because (as any high-school sophomore knows) the first fifty years of the nineteenth century found the American children of European children in the thrall of American pietism and the Second Great Awakening. In other words, in its worship, the church was engaged, willingly or not, in a long-term dialogue with the culture.

What was happening then is what is happening now. The dialogue continues as both church and culture change, for well or ill. What is happening in worship in the Reformed Church today? What isn't? It's changing, that's what's happening.

Snapshots, Not Cinema Verité

The precise nature of the change will begin to become evident as we look together at the results of the 2004 worship survey. The survey has three main sections.

The first is a snapshot section. The snapshot has two major limitations. First, it's like a family photo that captures a moment in time. It shows what is happening on the day the photographer stood behind the camera and said, "Look at the birdie." It does not say how much agony it took for mom to get her teenage son to put on a tie, or how many attempts were made before the three-year-old stopped pulling up her dress. Thus the snapshot is instructive, but limited. So, too, a survey of congregational worship practices in 2004 gives no indication of the blood, toil, tears, or sweat that are being exerted in

---

3   *Acts and Proceedings*, 1848, quoted by Howard Hageman in "Three Lectures," Mast, *In Remembrance and Hope*, 123.

knock-down battles over worship in the local congregation. It does not answer why some congregations do this and others do that.

Second, the snapshot is limited because it's such a large picture, perhaps so large that a single congregation would never be able to identify itself in it. The 2004 survey might be compared to those old black-and-white photos of men in funny hats sitting around tables at a convention. The pictures showed a wide shot of hundreds of men, mostly indistinguishable blotches. A conventioneer showing the photo to his wife could say, "I was over at that table somewhere," but, without powerful magnification or higher resolution, could not really say what seat he was in when the picture was taken. So as one wades through the text and graphs of the worship survey, where precisely does any one congregation fit in? Sort of "over there" or "back in the left-hand corner."

We can, however, say at least this. A sizeable number of the conventioneers who were called to pose for the picture actually showed up. The overall response rate for the survey was 60.2 percent, which is a rather impressive return. And despite the fact that the snapshot can only capture a brief moment in time, it can at least do that; and that is what the survey has accomplished.

The second section of the survey divvies up the data by regional synod. The practical utility of this data is limited. For the most part it will confirm some suspicions, but it will not offer much insight into the fact that in a single synod—or classis, or town, for that matter—one can find Reformed churches with the slickest of high-tech production values on the one hand and on the other hand a classical, traditional service that owes more to Dort than to Willow Creek.

The third section is far more instructive, because it offers a comparison among surveys taken in 1987, 1994, and 2004. Three snapshots, taken over time, provide a more accurate picture of what is happening (although the "why" is still inaccessible to the lens). Putting the three pictures side by side can be compared to looking at class pictures of the preschooler, the middle-schooler, and the college graduate. What has changed? Where are the obvious continuities? And what might the next picture reveal about the subject? How will he change in the next ten years?

Although some will complain loudly that worship in the Reformed Church has come to parallel the historical situation regarding which the prophet Isaiah lamented: "The shepherds also have no understanding; they have all turned to their own way" (Isa. 56: 11), one can find a fairly broad and recognizable middle. The worship life of the Reformed Church in America may be like Forrest Gump's box of chocolates, but for the most part, when one takes a bite, one will get the flavor of chocolate.

At Least It Tastes Like Chocolate

Thus, the survey says, if you scan the yellow pages for your local Reformed church, you are likely to land on a congregation that begins worship between 9:00 and 11:00 on a Sunday morning. When you arrive there, you are likely to be greeted by somewhere between 75 and 275 fellow worshipers, and you'll all be going to one service. When you sit down in the pew (the survey didn't ask whether our churches had pews, so I'm assuming here), you are likely to pick up a mildly evangelical, non-church press hymnbook. Next to the hymnbook you're likely to find the New International Version of the Bible; it may be the New Revised Standard version, but in any case you are likely to find a Bible in the pew rack. You can look up the day's scripture passages if you wish. They may be the same as the ones read at the Congregational church up the street or the Roman Catholic church across the street, but it's equally likely that the worship committee paid no attention to the lectionary. You may or may not use that hymnbook for all your singing, however; you'll have a 50/50 chance of seeing a screen in front of the congregation. When you do sing, you're most likely to be led by a paid musician, and, at least occasionally, you are going to go well beyond singing the psalter or the traditional German linear chorale; you'll be singing that American invention, the praise chorus (the more worshipers you meet at the door, the more likely you're going to be singing praise choruses to a screen). At some point in the service, a choir will lead worship. The old standby instrument, the organ, will most likely accompany your singing, although you shouldn't be surprised to be led by piano or praise band or some combination of all three.

If worship begins at 10:00, you should plan to receive the benediction right around 11:05. You should be able to mark off the service in three moments: Approach to God; Word of God; Response to God. Somewhere in there the minister or someone else will have a few words for the children. You're not likely to recognize the minister by his or her dress. She may be wearing a cross, but she won't be wearing a robe. At some point in the service, perhaps during the scripture reading (there will probably be only one) or the call to worship or the prayers, someone other than the minister will be leading you from the font or a lectern or the Lord's Table or the head of the aisle. Prepare to hear a sermon lasting between a quarter and a half of the service. You might want to brush up on the Apostle's Creed, because if any creed is used, that's likely to be the one. When you gather to pray, the minister will offer an extemporaneous prayer.

Chances are you won't be there on a Sunday when one of the sacraments is celebrated, but, on the other hand, you're not likely to have to wait three months for Communion, either. Within the next month the congregation will most likely gather at the Lord's Table. If you do happen to attend on a Sunday when one of the sacraments is celebrated, you're likely to get a dose of Reformed didacticism along with celebration. You will be able to observe "house rules" and clergy-chosen modifications to the orders for the Lord's Supper and baptism, but, for the most part, the congregation will be speaking and hearing the same words as the Reformed church three states over.[4]

Some may say that the picture just painted is a fiction. There is no "typical" Reformed Church congregation any more than there is a "typical" Reformed Church member. Indeed, the results may be skewed because only 71 of the 593 congregations represented in the survey (out of a total of 985 RCA congregations at the time) are from Canada or the Far West, a disproportionately small number. Nevertheless, despite what many would claim as a prevailing unseemly diversity, there does seem to be a rather broadly shared pattern of customs and usages in worship.

That is not to say that regions do not have their tendencies. Worship is more likely to begin earlier in the Midwest. One is likely to be singing in a larger crowd west of the Alleghenies. Congregations in the East are more likely to use denominationally provided hymnbooks and resources and to opt for hymnbooks rather than projection. The farther west one goes the more likely one is to be accompanied exclusively by a praise band; the farther east, exclusively by an organ, while the middle synods have developed a middle way, using a broader variety of instruments. If one prefers short sermons, one would do well to stay in the Albany, New York, and Mid-Atlantic synods, where the sermons are more likely to be (at least loosely) based on the readings from the Revised Common Lectionary. Generally speaking, the eastern synods are also most likely to observe liturgical days and seasons.

More notable differences arise in sacramental life. Generally speaking, the farther west one goes, the less likely one will be celebrating the Lord's Supper on any given Sunday, and if the Supper is celebrated,

---

[4]   Reformed Church in America 2004 Worship Survey (Holland, Mich.: Hope College, 2004), 9-18.

the less likely a worshiper is to hear that "the holy supper we are about to celebrate is a feast of remembrance, of communion, and of hope." Children are more likely to be welcomed at the Lord's Table in the three eastern synods, although the practice is also fairly common in the synods of the Far West and the Great Lakes. What was indicated regarding the liturgy for the Lord's Supper holds true for baptism as well: the use of an RCA-approved liturgy was lowest in Canada and the Far West. A number of methods are used for baptism, with sprinkling by far the most common. Nearly half the responding congregations in the Far West, however, reported using immersion for baptism (respondents could choose more than one answer, so it is impossible to comment on the frequency of immersion or whether it is becoming normative).[5]

Having first examined a snapshot of a mythical "typical" Reformed Church congregation, and, second, examining selected details in different sectors of the photograph, it is now time to turn to comparing current photographs with earlier ones. What is changing? And what seems to be remaining fairly constant?

Change Happens, More Or Less

A number of shifts seem to be occurring, although as any financial advisor will tell you, future results cannot be guaranteed from past performance. What will be offered is descriptive of the past, not predictive about the future. Further, what will be noted are shifts that seem to be statistically significant. But, since significance may be in the eye of the beholder, every person should consult the results of the worship survey to make an individual judgment concerning which changes matter and which ones don't. One last warning: some of this reportage will appear simply to repeat what was said earlier. Keep in mind the image of the photographs: as we compare three photographs this time, we will notice some ways that worship in 2004 looks the same as in 1987. In some ways, however, the faces will have changed. The intent of this section is to note how the faces seem to be changing over time. With those provisos in mind, a few observations are in order.

First, as to the sort of information you'll hear on an answering machine if no one is in the church office: Worship is getting earlier. Half as many churches in 2004 were beginning worship at 11:00 as began at that sacred hour in 1987. You're more likely now than you were then to have only one worship item on the menu; over seventeen years the percentage of churches with one service rose by 15 percent. While you're

5   RCA 2004 Worship Survey, 39-49.

in worship, you should be prepared to sit a bit longer than you did in 1987. Services are getting longer, though sermons aren't getting that much wordier. Apparently, other things are going on to expand the worship time.

Second, as to the sorts of items you'll have to actually darken the church doors to discover: More and more, congregations are singing praise choruses, and it is probably all to the good that if a congregation is going to sing, "Jesus, We Just Came to Thank You," at least they're less and less likely to be singing it to a pipe organ. Congregations across the denomination are far more likely to be lifting their heads to sing words that are projected onto a screen, a fact that this observer believes is closely related to the ever- increasing relationship between congregations and copyright licensing organizations. What the survey calls "lay people" are appearing far more frequently on the scene in worship, both in the planning process and in the public performance. Finally, when you are led in prayer, you are far more likely now than you were in 1987 to be led by someone (not necessarily an ordained pastor) who is praying extemporaneously. You are also three times more likely to encounter a prayer culled from some other source: from an anthology of prayers, perhaps, or from a denominational source book.

What about the sacraments? Is the Reformed Church any farther along in recognizing a "uniform marked observance" of our "treasured forms"? It's hard to say. A significant trend seems to be occurring when it comes to the frequency of celebrating the Lord's Supper. The number of congregations who celebrate more than twelve times a year has almost tripled in seventeen years, and although, as we have seen, where one celebrates the Supper is a strong determinant of how one celebrates, nevertheless the slippage in use of an approved liturgy for the Supper is slight. I'm quite certain, however, that one would have to do significantly deeper research to find out what's actually happening on the ground. The survey did not ask whether other liturgies are also in use, nor did it probe the depths of just how many liberties are being taken with the text of the 1968 order. Likewise, with regard to baptism, regardless of whether one finds the current liturgy for baptism to be up to snuff, a remarkable number of congregations still use one of the approved liturgies for the sacrament. Pollsters are not given to ask questions like, "Do you pretty much use the liturgy, except for the parts you can't bring yourself to say?"—which might give us a more accurate read of how completely the forms are being used. Also not asked by the survey was whether congregations are also, or alternatively, practicing dedications of infants, or are developing policies and services for the rebaptism of the already baptized. How often either of those practices occurs, no one knows, but it is known that they are indeed happening— in some cases even with the knowledge and blessing of a classis.

What is changing in regard to whom you are likely to encounter in worship? On average, attendance hasn't changed much, but that of course doesn't mean that it hasn't changed much in an individual congregation. The bigness of the big seems to be offsetting the smallness of the small, and vice versa. What is noticeable is that increasingly children are present for only part of the service, not all; whereas in 1987 less than half of the congregations welcomed children for part of the service, now two-thirds of congregations now report partial participation by children (three choices were given: all, part, and none).

In the Pipeline

So, what is happening in worship in the Reformed Church today? Up to this point I've indicated what the worship survey has told us and indicated the limitations of a survey approach. But there is more happening in worship than simply what is occurring at the local level. It would hardly be accurate to say that worship has been at the core of the agenda of recent General Synods, but they have been thinking about worship.

First, I'll point to something tangible. In 2005, after a considerable number of fits and starts, the Reformed Church published *Worship the Lord: the Liturgy of the Reformed Church in America*. It has its strengths and it has its weaknesses. But it was published and is receiving a fair amount of distribution throughout the church. Combined with a number of the results of the worship survey, that indicates that there are a good many folk throughout the denomination who still care what the greater church says we ought to be doing in worship. Whether they are motivated by loyalty or by an enclave mentality or by inertia or by a sense of catholicity or by the beauty of a common language for prayer, most want to be together, at the very least, at the table and at the font.

Second, the Commission on Christian Worship has been given the task of developing new forms for the celebration of the Lord's Supper. That it has been given the task is further confirmation that there are those in the church who believe it important to use an approved liturgy. Within the charge to the commission lies a curious echo of a century-old desire. The General Synod of 1902 appointed a committee to deal with the entire liturgy, requesting that it "seek simplicity, dignity, and brevity." In its turn, the General Synod of 2005 adopted the following recommendation:

> To affirm the Commission on Christian Worship's work to create additional liturgies of the Lord's Supper, and to ensure that these liturgies are briefer than those currently available; and further, to request that the commission define the essential components and expectations of the liturgy, for report to the General Synod of 2007.[6]

Historians will thus be left with the impression that the commission had been working to create additional liturgies prior to the synod of 2005. That is not quite the case. What was happening was that the commission was working to offer resources that would assist the church's gathering at the Lord's Table by offering "spoken and musical responses, resources for personal preparation, and other items."[7] That is a far cry from creating additional liturgies or even from creating one new additional liturgy.

Although those congregations that celebrate more frequently have requested a variety of forms, the loudest hew and cry today harks back to the desire for brevity expressed a century ago. The expressed desire for brevity presses the question about what, precisely, constitutes the Order for the Administration of the Lord's Supper. Does the entire order consist of every section, from meaning to communion prayer to thanksgiving to intercessions? Does it begin with meaning and end with the communion prayer? Is it the communion prayer only? We don't have very hot fights about this, but it is safe to say that there is a rather broad diversity of opinion on this matter. Indeed, if the order consisted only of the communion prayer, one would be hard pressed to find anything briefer within the broad spectrum of liturgies for the Supper.

Perhaps that is why the General Synod of 2005 also instructed the commission to define essential components and expectations. Performing exegesis on the desires of General Synods is a never-ending task for its commissions; this instruction is particularly slippery. In this case, this commission assumes that the General Synod is not asking it to say what the church expects to happen when it gathers around the table; that is a matter for the Holy Spirit to determine. "Expectation"

---

[6]   *Acts and Proceedings*, 2005, 373.
[7]   *Acts and Proceedings*, 2005, 310.

seems to have more the flavor of *compliance*, as in, "Does the church expect us to use exactly these words, or can we try to maintain the spirit of the words?" That understanding would appear to coincide with the desire that the commission define "essential components." Essence, like beauty, is in the eye of the beholder. Is bread essential? And wine? Who could argue? Indeed, who could, except perhaps those who have delivered Coke and Triscuits to hungering teens at a retreat and called that Communion? Liturgical scholars debate on a higher playing field, but the questions remain similar: What is necessary? Two epicleses, or only one? And where? And where do the intercessions belong? Why? Some would contend that the Reformed Church should pay no attention at all to what other communions say when they gather at the table. Others view that question as essential. I could go on: Is it necessary that we repeat the ephapax, "offered once on the cross," in order to echo the Heidelberg's assertion that "the Mass teaches that the living and the dead do not have their sins forgiven through the suffering of Christ unless Christ is still offered for them daily by the priests"?[8] Suffice it to say that the commission has been given a tangled knot of questions that are not proving easy to untie.

These concerns illustrate that questions about the status of the *Directory for Worship* are still active. The preamble to the *Government* indicates that the *Liturgy with the Directory* is part of our *Constitution*. Not the *Liturgy and* the *Directory*. The nuance, well known to those who shed blood over it, is that the *Liturgy* and the *Directory* are related to one another in much the same way as the Heidelberg Catechism and its Compendium. One would never throw out the Heidelberg in favor of its explanatory notes. Neither ought one toss out the *Liturgy* in order to reconstruct a personally palatable series of services based on the definitions offered in the *Directory*. Yet those who desire a definition of what is essential at the table seem to be looking for a directory so they can make up their own services. Again, what the commission will do with these questions remains to be seen.

About those Thorns Again . . .

What is happening in worship in the Reformed Church today? Because the birth of the Reformed Church in America ought to be dated to the *Explanatory Articles* of 1792 (not to the Church in the Fort in lower Manhattan), its history is roughly coterminous with the history of the United States. That sounds rather bland, but the intent

---

8   Heidelberg Catechism, Question and Answer 80.

of that rather obvious statement is that, since the beginning of the Reformed Church in America, our ancestors have been Americans at worship. True, we may have been transplanted Dutchmen and women or Germans or Italians; we may be the descendants of the middle passage; we may be the children of immigrants from various parts of Latin America; and, increasingly, we may be the one-and-a-half and two-and-a-half generations from Korea, China, and Japan. Nevertheless, we have worshiped here as Americans, and that has had and continues to have a profound impact on how we worship. And I'm not talking about the nearly ubiquitous American flags in our sanctuaries. The matter goes much deeper than that.

It has become a commonplace for those who study the history of missions to comment on what happens when a sending culture exports missionaries to a receiving culture. Roughly stated, the story goes like this: the sending culture unintentionally and subconsciously believes that both the formulation of the gospel and the forms in which it is carried are pure, unchangeable. These treasures are brought to foreign lands and shared with the natives, who may or may not receive what the sending culture intends to be good news. Because the vessels (here, meaning liturgical practices, from orders of worship to prayers to hymns to clothing to symbols) are deemed to be just as treasured as what they carry (the message of reconciliation through Christ), the vessels take on a quality that pleases both sending and receiving cultures. Thus, one will find Protestant Filipinas singing the tunes and words of the Wesley brothers in an assembly hall that could be picked up and transported to Maurice, Iowa, without much need for remodeling. Those Filipinas will sing very different songs to their children, and by "different" I don't just mean different words to different tunes. By different I mean tunes that may not be linear, and words that may well not rhyme or have any kind of meter that is discernable to the western ear. As the critique of western mission goes, the mind of the recipients of mission is thus split in two, a confusion of idioms is introduced, which ultimately softens up the recipients of the receiving culture for that greater product of the sending culture: western capitalism. Chinua Achebe's *Things Fall Apart* is probably the most masterful novelization of that saga, but it is by no means the only representative of a genre of critique.

The question at hand is if, as the gospel goes forth from place to place, the forms in which it is carried are deemed most appropriate to that gospel (i.e., if *lex orandi, lex credendi* is most visibly in play on the mission field), then what has happened, and what is happening, when the sending culture not only sends missionaries but whole communities of people into what is (to that sending culture) a "new world"? Does the critique of imperialist missions apply? To what extent could it apply, since the folk who came to settle here came precisely as settlers, not as messengers? And what happens as people gather to worship in a land that intends quite self-consciously to be a new kind of thing on earth? Would it not be appropriate, as enclave settles next to enclave, for the Dutch to sing in Dutch, and the Swedes to sing in Swedish, etc.? To put it bluntly: The European founding parents of the Reformed Church in America had no interest in Christianizing the Native Americans and going back home. They came to stay, and they brought their *dienstboeken*, and their church order, and their *dominies* with them. So, what happens in worship when these old world cultures rub up against an emerging new world culture?

What does it mean to be an American? Numerous commentators have offered sweeping visions, and this observer does not have the breadth of historical background to offer a wise critique of competing visions. Nevertheless, I find the voice of one far wiser than I am to be instructive. In his *Freedom Just Around the Corner*, Walter A. McDougall draws on the observations of Herman Melville to name the quintessential American as the "hustler: self-promoter, scofflaw, occasional fraud, and peripatetic self-reinventer. But...[the hustlers are also the] builders, doers, go-getters, dreamers, hard workers, inventors, organizers, engineers, and a people extremely generous."[9] As hustler types, Americans are free to pursue, to go after, to track down, to develop, to make up, to do whatever it takes to...well, to do exactly what?

To pursue happiness. That is the essential obligation of the American character. Not to obey or glorify God, but to grab the brass ring. That may well sound too crass, too worldly a vision for those who follow the Christ of the poor. Indeed, McDougall claims, "how to feel good about doing well was a central psychological concern of British Protestants and their American offspring."[10] Avoiding either an "Essene" approach (opting out) or a "Sadduccean" mindset (worship God on Sunday and mammon the other six days), Americans have always been about the business of designing "a uniquely American brand of Protestantism that make[s] the pursuit of happiness sacred, that commercialize[s] religion and sanctifie[s] commerce."[11]

9   (New York: Harper Collins, 2004), p. 7.
10   McDougall, *Freedom*, 124.
11   McDougall, *Freedom*, 507.

But since the topic for today is worship, we must ask what specific forms does a uniquely American congregation adopt when it gathers to worship? What appeals to the American character? Would sermons that conform to the careful and precise language of the academic disputation excite the faith of the movers and shakers of American society? Would prayers written be understood as a genuine expression of the soul's desire to a transcendent God? Would psalms sung somewhat haltingly from the Genevan psalter (those 6/4, 4/4 numbers that make it impossible to tap your toes) capture the American imagination?

McDougall again gives us an indication of what may be reckoned as "liturgical" manifestations of the desire to appeal to the American character. In the first place, "observant religious leaders recognized from the moment of independence they must adjust their doctrine, ecclesiastical governance, and evangelical style to Americans' civic religions and rollicking freedom of movement and choice."[12] Thus they "scorned lofty seminarian disquisitions...[and] cried from the pulpit or stump in the idioms of the people, addressing their real-life concerns and appealing to emotion rather than reason." Further, the American evangelists "were on the cutting edge of technological and cultural change....A busy, commercial, consumer culture needed quicker, more entertaining spiritual sustenance."[13] In the words of Charles Grandison Finney, "To expect to promote religion without excitements is unphilosophical and absurd. The great political, and other worldly excitements that agitate Christendom, are all unfriendly to religion, and divert the mind from the interests of the soul. Now these excitements can only be counteracted by religious excitements."[14] In other words, the prevailing methods—the language, the style, the heart-moving, behavior-transforming techniques—that motivate the populace in the public square need to be baptized and put to use in the temple.

Why Are They Doing those Funny Things in the Church Next Door?

Whether you like him or not, one of the leading influences on the direction of worship in the Reformed Church is the Reverend Dr. Leonard Sweet. Sweet, the author of *Soul Tsunami* and *Aqua Church*, describes waves of change occurring in the culture and offers prescriptions for what the church ought to do about it. With regard

[12] McDougall, *Freedom*, 508.
[13] McDougall, *Freedom*, 510-11.
[14] Ibid.

to the church at worship, Sweet most specifically calls the church to develop practices that have an epic shape about them. Commenting on the popularity of the television show, "Who Wants to Be a Millionaire?" Sweet claims that it was successful because it "made the transition from rational to Experiential, from representative to Participative, from word-based to Image-based, and from individual to Connected. In other words, it is EPIC programming. The recovery of Christianity in the next millennium is likely to be based on whether or not the church can carve (not cast) its ministries into more EPIC shape."[15]

EPIC: E is for Experiential, P is for Participative, I is for Image-based, and C is for Connected. It is not hard to hear echoes of Finney in Sweet's vision for the supposedly postmodern church. The evangelists of the Second Great Awakening saw their entire project as a redemption of the church from intellectual morbidity into vivid experience. Their method (looking sinners in the eyes, grabbing their arms, challenging them "man to man")[16] was nothing if not participative. A true believer grew into the image of the perfect, masculine, courageous Christ, in much the same way that true believers today are unashamed, clean-living promise-keepers. Even the value of connectedness is connection-by-choice, not connection-by-inheritance; hence, connection is a product of the individual will, not a "given" commodity.

The point here is that Sweet has become an opinion leader in the tribes of many who go about the weekly task of planning for worship. He will often be misunderstood, as happens when committees woodenly apply his insights. But his influence is evident. It is not in the least uncommon to hear talk, not of worship, but of a "worship experience." The once-taciturn worshipers who would no sooner leave their pews than dance the hula in worship are encouraged to "get into it," to raise their hands, to say amen (out loud!), in other words, to participate. Not that they weren't participating before, of course, but to participate visibly. Images abound, and I'm not talking about screens. Yes, they are becoming more prevalent, but insofar as most of them have only words projected onto them, they do not yet signal a significant shift from a word culture to an image culture. By "images" I mean the highly intentional use of everything from pop culture icons to film clips to dancing men and women to banners and paraments—even to metaphors that capture the American mind. "Image" has to do with picture (as opposed to text), but it is broader than flashing a picture of a mountain on a screen as a worship leader is reciting "I lift my eyes to

15   http://www.next-wave.org/may00/sweet.htm
16   McDougall, *Freedom*, 510.

the hills." Finally, worshipers are urged to connect with one another, most visibly through prayer, as the old form of pastoral prayer evolves into a congregation divided into multiples of six, with holy huddles discussing their personal needs and buzzing until the buzz dies down.

Worship in Sweet's EPIC mode may or may not appeal to those here gathered. That is not at all the point. It is not meant to appeal to graduates of eastern theological schools. It is meant to appeal to the ordinary American. Such worship is based on the idea that worship has at the very least an evangelistic aspect to it. It is, in other words, a local, public expression of American Reformed evangelicalism. And, while some will argue with the congregational manifestations of Sweet's thinking, one ought at least do him the intellectual courtesy of reading him.

What is happening in worship in the Reformed Church today? When we gather, we do all sorts of things that our ancestors would find foreign and misguided and that our descendants will consider quaint— and misguided. Still, we are trying our best to proclaim the gospel in forms that are adequate to its goodness. We may not articulate our purpose as "helping people feel good about doing well," but we do seem to be adopting many of the customs and usages of the culture that enables the prosperity of our gathered congregations. To put it in terms I mentioned earlier, one could ask the question whether the evolving patterns in our worship serve to "soften us up" for the aggressive influence of western capitalism (the medium being the message.) If I am not mistaken, the average income of a Reformed Church family is still pretty high, compared to the averages of families in other American denominations. In any case, worship in this denomination continues to be both a Reformed and an American experiment. Its history is the history of interplay between a highly word-based liturgical culture whose intent was to glorify God and an increasingly image-based culture whose intent is to secure happiness. In its current form, those steeped in the word are hanging on for dear life, while those educated in image are running at full speed. Whether the hangers on or the speed runners will ultimately prevail is an open question. In any case, of this alone can we Reformed folk be assured as we look toward tomorrow: Whether it happens in our own sanctuaries or elsewhere, God will be glorified.

CHAPTER 6

Creative and Contemporary Worship in a Reformed Context

Kathleen Hart Brumm

When all is said and done (and we have certainly said quite a bit, if we haven't yet done much about it), there remains the question of what this discussion means for the practice of liturgy. What implications does it have for the actions we do and the words we speak and how we do what we do during the time we are assembled as the body of Christ to worship God?

Coming near to the subject, my underlying assumption is that liturgy is very much like theater. Public worship is where we act out, participate in, and learn about who God is and who we are in relationship to divinity. It usually takes place in a public arena where preparations are set up for the adequate comfort of participants. It uses sets and costumes and even has a script and actors. Since it is the locus of interaction between humanity and divinity, it is by its very nature a creative act, just as the work of lighting technicians, costumers, directors, stage hands, and actors combine in the creative act of presenting a play.

Using the theater as a metaphor for worship, then, we will survey the various divisions of labor and what each of those divisions requires in order to be useful to the whole experience of worship. We will look at what already exists at our command and also imagine what is yet needed to make the most of the short time we have while assembled as the body of Christ. We will also catalogue the requirements for the best possible outcome from those who participate in the drama of God interacting with humanity. In addition, I hope to set forth the argument that our Reformed order is sufficient to the task, burden, and joy of true worship.

If liturgy can be seen as drama, then it requires three things: a stage for the scenes, a script with the plot and dialogue, and actors who know what they are doing. In addition, it would be good to have an idea of who the audience is and what the actors need to give a successful performance. Contrary to widespread belief, the minister/liturgist/celebrant need not—*must not*—be the solo actor, spouting a monologue to the audience sitting in the pews. Much closer to true worship is the inclusion of the entire congregation in the work of the people, with God being the audience. It is no big secret that this takes work and planning. It is in large part the responsibility of the celebrant to set the tone for worship and to model for the congregation an appropriate attitude toward the work we undertake together. Larger still is the community's responsibility to take its cues and do its part in worship.

Assaying the Roles

In order to do well at leading worship, celebrants have to be, at least in part, actors. Not that any of us are expected to be Julie Andrews or Sir John Gielgud any more than we are asked to chew the scenery, but there is call and space for the leader to be sensitive to what is going on not only in the moment, but to have thought about it and worked on it previous to the time of service. No actor goes on stage without having studied his lines, figured out what motivates his character, and rehearsed with other actors to make meaning from the written word on the script. In large part, this detailed preparation is the job of the celebrant: understanding what is happening in the large picture and knowing how to get from the beginning to the end while engaging the heart, soul, mind, and strength of the gathered people to derive meaning from their experience.

Thus it is incumbent upon the celebrant to be prepared to lead worship. What does preparation entail? First, a humble heart that seeks God and strives to share that knowledge with other people. Second, the courtesy to plan ahead so that the rest of the actors have adequate time to do their share of preparation well. Third, a close knowledge of the Word and the world, so that both can find connection during the service. Fourth, physical preparation: enough sleep the night before, perhaps speech coaching and voice lessons, training in poise and presentation, having in hand all the necessary materials including an outline or manuscript of the sermon (even if it's memorized) for use during the service. This advance work frees the celebrant to be truly present in the moment, an attractive quality that draws other worshipers into consciousness of the nearer presence of God.

The congregation, too, needs to be prepared for the work of worship. Publishing the readings of the day at least a week previous to the service allows people to read them before entering the sanctuary. Inclusion in the service leaflet of an introductory welcome paragraph indicating your congregation's customs during worship, such as directions for sitting and standing, what to do with young children, where the rest room and changing facilities are, and a brief explanation of the season of the year, is in order. A note about helps for people who have trouble seeing, hearing, or getting around is also a good idea, even if you have nobody who needs them; if people know you make concessions for these folks, they will be more prone to invite them to church. The people in the pews do well to take seriously their part in preparing for worship: reading and meditating on the indicated passages, praying for the preacher, and perusing the worship leaflet and texts of the hymns to be sung, and, if possible, reading their part of the score of the hymn/song tunes. This preparation, like that of the celebrant, is the warm-up for the "production's" success.

The Read-Through

Central to the preparation of both the celebrant and the congregation is the "script" that is used; in other words, the form and words the liturgy demands. I confess a strong bias for leaving the details and their places in our prescribed order of worship pretty much alone. One need not throw the baby out with the bathwater while trying to be creative, fresh, and relevant in worship. If there is a change to be made in the order, let there be a solid theological or pastoral reason for it. Otherwise, why try to fix what is not broken? A quick review of those details follows, as well as a short explanation of what they are, giving a clue as to why they are put in this place in the service.

Act I: APPROACH
We prepare to worship and hear God

VOTUM
> We express our desire to worship God.

SENTENCES
> Scripture sets the tone of the service.

SALUTATION
> We are greeted in the name of Christ.

HYMN
> We ascribe praise to God.

RITE OF CONFESSION
  Prayer of confession
> We admit our guilt and wrongdoing.

  Kyrie
> We ask for mercy.

  Assurance of pardon
> We accept forgiveness and grace.

  The law of God
> We rehearse God's prescription for good.

PSALTER AND GLORIA PATRI
> We remember what God has done in the lives of people before us.

Act II: WORD
> God speaks to us

LESSONS
> We read from scripture to hear what God has done.

SERMON
> Through the preacher, God explains and we apply the lessons of the day.

PRAYER FOR BLESSING
> We request that the Word bear fruit in us.

Act III: RESPONSE
> We show that we have heard and will act.

HYMN
> We respond to the Word.

CONFESSION OF FAITH
> We profess belief.

PEACE
> We share God's blessing with each other.

OFFERING
> We show gratitude for God's gifts by returning a portion of them, with ourselves, to God through the church.

DOXOLOGY
> We give praise to the Trinity.

PRAYERS OF INTERCESSION
> We offer our concerns for each other and the world.

HYMN
> We are reminded of the Word or ascribe praise to God.

BENEDICTION
> God gives a parting good word to God's people.

There are things that do well to be variable in the service and things that are best left as they have been. The one thing best left alone is the scaffolding of the service, the "skeleton," if you will. In its simplest form it comprises what we in the Reformed Church have labeled "Approach, Word, and Response." Since the point of worship is to listen for God's Word and respond to it both verbally and actively, this formula is the most logical and most Reformed. To take these three events in any other order makes very little sense, and doing anything else is not worship. Making very little sense is a grave infraction against reason, an important tenet in our Reformed tradition, and if it is not worship when we gather, we are deluding ourselves and may as well be playing mumblety peg.

It is not only reason that makes this scaffolding nonnegotiable. Again, as Reformed people, we are in covenant with one another as well as with God in this endeavor. That covenant includes being able to understand what we are about together, and this basic form makes it clear. If the covenant consists of, "Obey my voice and I will be your God and you will be my people," then it is essential that we gather—both to be a "we" and to hear that voice of God and respond to it. It is a collective body, then, that assembles, not just one individual standing next to another individual standing next to another individual. What is done in worship is done by that gathered body. What is done in worship is done to glorify God, not to indulge individuals. What is done in worship is done to remember and refresh the covenant among us and sustain God's people as God's people. This order constitutes us as the body of Christ. There is no reason to ask, "Why are we here?" (a question used in opening sentences once popular with a Presbyterian pastor I used to work with) if this underlying assumption is as reliable and strong as the floorboards on which we walk.

If it is true that approach, Word, and response are steady and solid as floorboards, the smaller elements, too, do well to stay where they are in the order of service. Having said that, how is there to be innovation, a chance at freshly breaking open the Word? Is the implication that nothing may ever change in the order of worship? Are we doomed to learn nothing from the past, but only repeat its mistakes? I believe the answer lies in taking a close look at the righthand column above rather than confining ourselves to the left. If the word/action in each of the scenes is accomplished—by whatever means—we have woven both a connection to the church universal and the church in specific.

There is a great debate going on among those who prefer "contemporary" worship and those who are more comfortable in "traditional" worship. In point of fact, these labels are misnomers. Every service is contemporary; if it were not, we would not be able to participate in it since we would not be temporally present for it. On the other hand, in some sense, each service is also "traditional" in that it is aimed at the praise of God and the edification of the worshiper, something the people of God have been doing for millennia. Rather than using these somewhat misleading caricatures, it may be more helpful to cast this debate in different terms: what is the constitution of the gathered body, and how is it best for this particular gathering to hear, internalize, and respond to the enduring Word of God? What will most energize the body of Christ for ministry in the world?

Not only are the labels misnomers, but the reasons for insisting on one flavor or another for what the community does is inconsistent with the message of the gospel. What more are we called to do than to love one another? If we cannot share space and make allowances for one another during worship, we have missed the mark. And if we cannot do it in the relatively safe and rarefied atmosphere of worship, what chance is there that we attempt it outside the sanctuary? In addition to adoring God by our words and movements in worship, it is also the place where we practice living in the new creation. Love does not insist on its own way.

There are churches who have found it expedient to abandon "liturgy" altogether, that is, liturgy as a formal set of things that must be done in a particular order. Pastors and worship committees have felt free to concoct a service with whatever elements fit their purpose and without those that do not. Some might go so far as to say that they have no liturgy, in that formal and prescribed elements have no place in their services. Yet it is not true that they do not have liturgy; every time people gather to worship, they do the work of honoring God, which, at heart, is what liturgy is. What they do may be in no particular order from week to week or season to season, it may take form differently each time. What is lacking in this stratagem is a sense of continuity, of order, and of permanence. It does little to connect the congregation with the tradition of the whole church, it is the antithesis of God's work in creating order out of chaos, and it does not provide much of a foundation for a balanced and cultivated spiritual outlook.

Because narrowing the liturgy to what is convenient stunts growth, it can be detrimental to cut and paste parts of the liturgy together according to the whims and passing fancy of either preacher or congregation, however deeply felt or momentarily useful that resulting collage may be. That we are people of a covenant is our distinctive stance among other denominations. We put deserved emphasis on our belonging with the cloud of witnesses gone before us as well as with those who believe in Christ around the world, regardless of their worship practices. Inasmuch as we share their practices, we witness to the unity of the wider church. Where we differ, we witness to the unique manifestation of the Holy Spirit among us. We do well to retain the fundamental tradition, including those parts which bind us to the rest of the Christian church, while making an effort to communicate deliberately with souls who are alive today and hoping for a relevant word from God. Reformed custom attempts to straddle the gap between the new and the old, just as our Lord described: "Therefore every scribe who has been trained for the kingdom of heaven is like the master of a household who brings out of his treasure what is new and what is old."[1]

Setting the Stage

While it would be nice to be able to offer a formula that would work from week to week, congregation to congregation, I don't have it to give. Instead let me place before you some general guidelines for the practice of liturgy, guidelines I hope will be helpful as you work out worship in your own context.

First, there is homework to be done. Before even starting to do the legwork necessary, get some competent and perceptive help from members of your congregation and maybe an outside friend or two. Your board of elders is a good place to begin to look for people who are willing to make the requisite inquiries and draw conclusions from their findings. If you have a worship committee, its members might also be a valuable asset in the assessment that you need to undertake. The qualities these folks need are an openness to hear what others have to say, some precision in reporting and thinking, and enough time and patience to see the process through.

[1]   Matthew 13:52.

Once you have a group of dedicated people, it's time to get down to brass tacks. First, ask questions of the people in the pews. Who is in your congregation? In what years were they born? How old are they? Notice that these are not necessarily the same question. What kinds of work do they do? Where and how do they spend their time off? What do they watch on television or listen to on the radio, I-Pod, or stereo? How do they naturally express themselves? What are their aspirations? What are they proud of, ashamed of, worried about? If you do not know the answers to these questions, find out, first hand. Draw up a brief list of questions. Have conversations with your congregation and also with people outside the church, in the neighborhood. Their answers can help you decide whether to embrace an element in the service that is less well known by the congregation in order to make outsiders more comfortable. Collate and discuss the answers you receive. This basic groundwork is essential to diagnosing the spiritual and worship needs of those who come to worship and those who may yet attend.

Next, appraise resources for worship. All we really need for Reformed worship is a place to gather, a Bible, and someone among the "we" who knows what she is talking about. Anything else is technically extraneous; nevertheless, everything that encircles us in worship says something about who we are when we are together and what we think and feel about the One we worship. Start with what you have on hand or what is easily available to use in the service. Take a good hard look at the room itself and listen for its acoustics. Consider the furniture, paraments, Bibles, hymnals, musical instruments to accompany congregational singing, the worship space, and seating. What messages are they sending to those who sit in the seats? What is in good condition, worthy to be put to use in service of the Omnipotent One? What needs fixing or polishing or cleaning? What should you toss altogether?

Now search for what is not there. What would take a little effort to have on hand but it is possible to get? A seasonal banner, for example, a token trinket as a reminder of the sermon, or a leaflet to guide people through the service. Further, what do you need that you do not have, things that would take some planning and expense to acquire but would be worth the effort? A viable sound system for ease of hearing and recording the service, a computer and projector with Power Point capabilities, a pipe organ with trumpets en chamade? What about people to use these things? Musicians, both instrumentalists and vocalists, technicians, donors, artisans, and craftspeople; all of these are necessary if these additions to worship are going to work. Does your church have the resources it needs? What is missing? What must be done to make up for that lack? Do you as a congregation have the will and ability to do it?

You have interviewed people, you have taken a hard look at your worship space, and now it's time to compare the answers you have found. How do the two categories match up? Does the character of your congregation mesh well with the character of the space of worship? Are there folks in the pews listening to classical music at home who feel bombarded with rock and roll in worship? Is it the other way around? Do you have aesthetically aware souls who sit in drab surroundings while adoring the God of the cosmos? Do you have technicians, donors, artisans, and craftspeople who would gladly share their gifts with their sisters and brothers in Christ but have not been invited to do so? If your surroundings are worn, shabby, and derelict, what does that communicate to those who come into God's presence in your sanctuary? If the architecture and furnishings are brash, shiny, and ostentatious, what does that say? Once you have heard the message you are sending, compare it to the message you want to send, the one that is consonant with the character of your understanding of the Reformed tradition, the members of your congregation, and their hopes of what God is calling them to be. Does the message imbricate with that character? If not, what needs to change and in what order of urgency? The recommendations you decide upon should then be presented to the board of elders or the whole consistory for their imprimatur.

Once approval has been granted, if there are changes to be made, it is a well worn rule of thumb that the congregation should be alerted to the change and why it is happening. Prepare answers to the questions, "What makes this new addition a good idea?" "What makes the change better than what it is replacing?" "Why should the congregation allow it—aside from the elders' and pastor's recommendation—and how does it benefit the community?" If you cannot come up with satisfying answers to these questions, perhaps the change you propose is not the "magic bullet" you were hoping for.

When you have answers to anticipated questions, make the recommendation to the congregation. This process takes time and patience. Remember that your team has already spent time—a whole lot of time—talking among themselves and with the congregation and examining the worship space, but others have not. Give them time to assimilate the information, to ask their questions, and to express their apprehensions. They may have valid points that the committee did not see that would be good to consider. This dissemination of information is not license for members of the congregation at large to stonewall the change; our polity dictates that decisions made by representatives are binding on the whole body, popular congregationalism notwithstanding. Keep a united front, respond with consistent answers, and most congregants will trust you enough to go along. Enlist the squeakiest wheels in the next round of deliberations.

In good time, that is, not too little that most people are confused by the change or too much that they've forgotten what you taught, make the changes. Note if there are strong objections and what the reasons are for those objections, but do not allow a few squeaky wheels to stop the truck. "The dogs bark at the caravan but the caravan moves on" is an old Arabic saying that applies here. Remember, too, that everything we hold dear was once foreign and new. A bit of time with the novelty usually cures most ills. Allow time for the newness to take root before considering reverting to what was.

It is important to say here that none of the decisions made up to this point have been matters of mere personal taste; they are sincere attempts to serve the members of the body and those outside of it. This principle is not quite the democratic "majority rules" mandate. Taking into account the lowest and the least is as essential as polling the high and mighty. If we are true to scripture, we must not give preference to one person or clique or another in formulating our plans.

Strike up the Band

The same concern for the whole body must be taken into consideration even with regard to the small details of the Sunday service. Music, both hymnody and performance pieces, is perhaps the most treacherous of all of those details. As such, it is best to know something about it and its place in the worship of God.

Let us first make clear the distinction between music, properly the tune and harmonies, and the texts which are sometimes attached to melodies. There is nothing intrinsically sacred about music, any more than there is anything intrinsically holy about any of the arts. The style of music used, whether Renaissance or Rap, is relatively immaterial. There are great and poor examples of both genres. Our challenge as those who plan worship is not to pander to the lowest common taste but to choose the best from among many things and offer only our best to God. To do this we do well to gain an understanding of what touches our congregation, what the people are apt to reject or accept, what will cause them to be open to the work of the Spirit in their own hearts. We also do well to have a sense of what makes a piece of music suitable for the purpose to which we put it.

To that end, a number of questions may be posed. First, is the piece true to its genre? Does it show characteristics of beauty that are essential to the kind of piece it is? This estimation requires knowledge about many species of music, perhaps best left to trained musicians. Second, is it suited to the use we want to make of it? Many solo pieces are so popular that they are used as congregational songs when in fact they are too complicated for untrained and unrehearsed singers to get right. The result is less than music, and I daresay less than worthy of offering to God. Third, does the music convey by its quiddity, its being what it is, what needs to be expressed at that particular time in the course of worship? Is its character indicative or is it coercive? Does it force people to feel something, manipulating them into a certain emotional state, or does it bring out what the devoted and attentive soul, of its own volition, would say if only it could find the right means? The latter is the better function.

Music is peculiar among the arts for worship because it is the easiest and most universal to press into service. If none of us carries a sketch book or carving tools to church every week, all of us do carry the instruments God gave us at our birth: our voices. To use these instruments normally requires that we put words with the music the voice makes. This necessity brings up the question: Which words? Our *Book of Church Order* requires that the hymn texts used in worship be in sympathy with our standards.[2] While this is not difficult to do if we confine our choices to pieces contained in hymnals that have the Reformed Church's imprimatur, the most recent one was printed in 1985.[3] Although many hymns in older collections are fresh and relevant to this day, the present plethora of materials and the ease of reproducing those works make the field far broader than ever before. We do well to exercise caution in our choices of texts.

To choose texts for public worship, there are a few guidelines. Look at the text itself as a piece of art. Does it reach the standard of poetry, is it merely verse, or is it a quotation of scripture without embellishment? If it is meant as poetry, does it use more than mere rhymes to clothe its ideas? Is there alliteration, assonance, metaphor,

---

[2]   Chapter 1, part I, section 2, paragraph 11.d. (New York: Reformed Church in America, 2005), 15.

[3]   *Rejoice in the Lord*, (Grand Rapids: Eerdman's, 1985). The more recent *Sing! A New Creation* is a joint effort among the Reformed Church in America, the Christian Reformed Church through its publishing arm Faith Alive!, and the Calvin Institute for Christian Worship. Both volumes are referenced in chapter 4.

onomatopoeia, simile, synechdoche, to name some literary devices that add interest? When was the text created? Is it still worthwhile? Are there arcane or passé expressions that sound dated or have lost their meaning? Are there unfamiliar words? If so, why are they there and what do they mean? Can their meaning be divined from the context, can you define it for the singers, or should this text be skipped in favor of a better crafted example?

If the text is merely verse, is it worth the time and energy to worry with it? Is there beauty and symmetry about it, or did the author try to do both music and text together, fitting one to the other with the result that both lose? Is there enough similarity and contrast within the text to help it wear well from use to use? Is it in accord with the natural rhythms of everyday speech? Does the work itself reflect creativity and effort worthy to offer to God? If not, why use it? If the text quotes scripture directly, is the paraphrase or translation suited to the character of worship? Is it redundant, repeating what was or will be spoken? How does it mesh with the other scriptures of the day?

As for content of what any text conveys, it is best to let the scripture lesson(s) of the day be the primary arbiter of what may be appropriate. Some hymnals or collections will have a scriptural allusion index that can help sort things out, along with an index of themes and theme words. I also commend to you William S. Smith's *Hymnsearch*,[4] keyed to the *Presbyterian Hymnal*, which contains scriptural allusions and references galore to the texts in that hymnal. The hymn texts are mentioned by name as well as number, so you can see whether the hymn you have chosen is in your hymnbook.

It may seem strange to point out, but each hymn has an author, whether the text bears that person's name or not. Every writer has a particular point of view, a particular theological slant, a particular way of seeing. If authors are allowed their own perspectives, then so are we, the people who sing their hymns. It is important to remember this because you may not agree with what the author has to say, even though the editor of the book or collection put it in the book. One of this author's teachers, Helen Kemp, has been known to caution: "If you don't believe it, don't sing it," and this is good advice. Hymns are insidious; they get inside your memory and are harder to oust than dandelions once they are established. There is less danger of singing an incredible hymn from books that have been well edited or endorsed by

---

[4]   William S. Smith, *Hymnsearch: Indexes for* The Presbyterian Hymnal (Jackson, Miss.: William S. Smith, 1995).).

a denomination; the selections have been thoroughly vetted by a panel of experts in theology, music, and poetry. Nonetheless, there are plenty of hymnals published just for the sake of selling a book. We do well to look critically at what the hymn says and whether we want it in our mental storehouse.

Recalling that we are a corporate covenant body at worship, a word about personal preference in relation to a hymn's appropriateness to a service is in order. Many people have written many hymns that are wonderfully expressive of the soul's yearnings and the relationship between the believer and the Lord. At face value, there is nothing at all wrong with these hymns, used in their best context. However, hymns that use exclusively the first person singular pronoun that refers to the singer often are too personal and too singular to be used when the whole church gathers. In addition to the many praise choruses that proclaim, "I will praise you...," the easiest picking in this category is the old chestnut "In the Garden."

> I come to the garden alone,
> while the dew is still on the roses,
> and the voice I hear,
> falling on my ear,
> the Son of God discloses.
> And he walks with me, and he talks with me,
> and he tells me I am his own;
> and the joy we share as we tarry there,
> none other has ever known.[5]

Besides the fact that, taken out of context, it could be any "he" at all who walks and talks with me and shares my joy (and what does that say about the males who sing this piece?), where are the rest of the folks with whom I am worshiping? Do they get a share in the conversation or the joy? Do they, too, belong to "him"? If so, doesn't that break up the party and defeat the idea of the hymn? If not, why are we singing this together? If it is useful for private devotions, by all means, use it, but as a hymn for the gathered people of God, it is substandard.

---

[5]   C. Austin Miles, 1912. Cited as Hymn #130 in *Tabernacle Hymns Number Three* (Chicago: Hope, 1929).

Un-Sung Words

The other, nonpoetic, words chosen for worship are also important. While we have listed the elements of worship before, it may be helpful to re-sort them according to their ilk rather than their function. Among the ingredients in worship are what may be called "speeches"; that is, words that have kept the same character and order every time they have been recited. In the Roman church these have been called "commons," since they are common to all services. We have, by and large, abandoned the five ancient liturgical commons in favor of our own; our examples of these speeches are the Lord's Prayer, the Apostles' Creed, and perhaps familiar psalms. Many members of the congregation are able to repeat the words to these speeches without thinking: they have learned them by heart. In contrast, some members, children among them, are too new to these forms to have committed them to memory, and the language in which they are cast seems foreign, even though it is the English an older generation is accustomed to using in worship.

Herein lies a volatile question: what form of these speeches do we use in public worship? Is it better to saddle the more liberal folks with outmoded language, sparing the more conservative ones the shock and loss of learning something new, or do we present ourselves both to God and to one another as the people we are now and speak the current language even though it may upset the apple cart? On what basis do we make this decision? Is there a happy middle ground?

Another batch of elements are those which, by nature of the changing seasons of the year, the lectionary cycle, or the ongoing life of the congregation are never quite the same in content week after week. Responsorial psalms, the scripture of the day, the sermon, the prayers of the people, and the hymns and anthems fall into this category. Moving beyond the question of inclusive language (which I fully advocate), what words best convey what needs to be said? Do you use the King James Version, the New Revised Standard Version translation, or *The Message* paraphrase[6] for public proclamation of the Word? If there is a hymn text that was written in the 1700s that is directly on point but whose diction is foreign, do you use it "as is" anyway, attempt to "fix" it, or try to find or compose something else?

While their content may change, the congregation's expectation is that their form will be stable most if not all of the time. It will be clear who says what sections of the responsive reading. The scripture

6   Eugene Peterson (Colorado Springs: Navpress, 2002).

of the day may be read from the lectern or from the pulpit Bible. There may always be a prayer before it. The sermon may be delivered from the pulpit. Hymns may always be introduced by playing the whole tune through. Every hymn may end with an "Amen" sung in a plagal cadence. You can name your own species of these things that change in content (and from congregation to congregation) but usually do not change in form or placement in the order of service. Will changing or discarding them have meaning? Is it the meaning you intend?

Finally, we have those things in worship that happen. They are not planned, not scripted, in fact they do not really belong in church, but they take place as everyday life takes place, except they happen in the gathering of God's people. John gets a bloody nose. Mary is having trouble making Emily stop crying. Barry needs more time in silence to pray this particular week. In these cases, it is important to remember that worship is practice for the reign of God. It is good to *respond* in the first place, and not to turn an embarrassed eye to what is happening. In responding, it is also good to do it with kindness rather than irritation. These are unexpected things but they can be seen in the light of worship rather than acted upon with the everyday reactions we might have.

Blocking and Choreography

Now that preparations have been made—the stage has been set for worship and all divisions of actors have done their work in making their parts ready—we may consider what happens during the time we spend in worship itself. Remembering that we have a script already, what is the best way to perform it? This is a matter of style more than substance, the addition of heart, soul, and strength to loving God with our minds. What follows are merely suggestions that might enlighten and enliven worship. You know your context of worship (you did your homework), so change and adapt and make up other ways as you see fit.

Approach:
- Involve the whole congregation in a procession into the sanctuary.
  - o Wave palm branches on Palm Sunday, alternately reciting Psalm 118 and singing an appropriate antiphon.
  - o Distribute red, orange, and yellow pennants on Pentecost for a parade.
- Speak the text of a hymn responsorially rather than singing it.
- Use an anthem rather than a congregational hymn for the hymn of praise.
- Recite the opening sentences from the entrance of the church,

the votum from the middle, and the salutation from the steps of the chancel.

- Lead the rite of confession from the communion table.
- Instead of a unison prayer of confession:
  o Have slips of paper and golf pencils ready in the pews for people to write their sins down. Collect and burn them in a thurible or charcoal grill with or without incense. Be sure you have enough draft to burn them completely.
  o Use jelly roll pans half full of sand in which penitents sketch or write their sins, and then have the elders smooth the sand over while giving the words of assurance.
  o Dance or pantomime one of the stories where Jesus forgave and healed someone, with or without narration.
- Sing the Decalogue or the summary of the law.
- Use musical settings of the responsorial psalm:
  o Taizé
  o Gelineau
  o Genevan psalter
  o Gregorian/Anglican chant
- Recite the psalm antiphonally (in two or more groups) instead of responsorially.
- Use the four corners of the room from which alternating leaders speak their verses of the psalm.

Word:
- Enlist lectors to read the Old Testament and epistles.
- Use actors to pantomime with narration, or dramatically read the scripture.
- Use recordings of someone else reading the passages of the day, whether or not the recordings were professionally produced. Shut-in members can be heard if not seen if they read the passage.
- Read a pericope with instrumental accompaniment; e.g. Bach's *Sheep May Safely Graze* with the parable of the Good Shepherd, or *O Voll Mit Blut und Wunden* during the reading of the crucifixion portion of the passion.
- Project on a screen images and pictures that embellish the reading.
- Preach peripatetically.
- Instead of a usual sermon:
  o Write a poem expressing your interpretation. Use a classical form such as a sonnet, epic, or ballad.

    o Compose an interactive piece with a cue line for which the congregation has to listen and to which they have a given response. The response need not be solely verbal.

    o Write in the style of another author: Dr. Seuss, Lemony Snicket, Charles Dickens.

    o Ask for another speaker and have a dialogue sermon with prepared questions and answers.

    o Allow a children's choir or acting troupe to perform a short musical or play on a biblical theme.

Response:

- Use portions of the Heidelberg Catechism, Our Song of Hope, or the Athanasian Creed instead of the Apostles' and Nicene Creeds.
- Sing the creed.
- At the offering, have people bring their gifts to the table rather than having ushers collect them.
- Use slips of paper for people to offer their time and talents as well as their funds.
- Sing a doxology that is not attached to "Old Hundredth." The final stanzas of many hymns are perfectly good doxologies.
- Display photographs or project slides of the faces of people for whom you are praying.
- Use responsory prayers in which a leader mentions a subject and individuals name that for which they pray within that topic.
- For smaller gatherings, have "seeing-eye" prayers, where instead of bowing heads, we keep looking at each other.
- Share prayer leadership by inviting individuals, sitting wherever they are, to introduce a section of the prayer time with a prearranged preface or one they make up themselves.
- Use a section of scripture as a responsive blessing, allowing the congregation to bless each other as well as the minister.
- Sing the benediction all the way out the door.

Reformed and Contemporary

When all is said and done, Reformed worship can be meaningful and relevant without disposing of its historic integrity or its attachments to the rest of the church universal. With preparation, thought, and care, it can help us practice virtue and glorify God, giving us on earth a pledge and foretaste of the feast of love of which we shall partake when God's reign has fully come.

A RESPONSE TO CHAPTERS 5 AND 6

Norman J. Kansfield

As we come closer to the conclusion of this volume, it is an honor to respond to two such outstanding chapters as Paul Janssen and Kathleen Hart Brumm have provided. The perceptiveness and careful scholarship they have demonstrated indicates that the future of worship within the Reformed Church in America is in secure and thoughtful hands.

Forty years ago my honored predecessor, Howard G. Hageman, quoted an assessment of the state of worship within the Reformed Protestant Dutch Church that had been presented to the General Synod of 1848. Hageman did that in order to make the point that liturgical laxness is not a new phenomenon. When Janssen, citing that same report to the synod, observed that the church in 1848 was barely two generations beyond the *Explanatory Articles*,[1] he helped us put in proper perspective the evaluation offered to the General Synod of 1848. Everything within the church's North American adventure was still so new, so unsettled, so exploratory. In exactly that same way,

---

[1] John H. Livingston, trans. and ed., *The Constitution of the Reformed Dutch Church in the United States of America* (New York: William Durell, 1793).

you and I need to remind ourselves that we are currently less than two generations—a mere thirty-eight years—beyond the monumental liturgy of 1968.

As Janssen suggested on other grounds, this asks us to take note of huge shifts in the liturgical behavior of the Reformed Church in America. For example, before the publication of *Liturgy and Psalms* in 1968, our communion liturgy said lots and lots and lots about remembrance. It said very little about communion. It said almost nothing at all about hope. The clear direction of the celebration of Communion was backward. Every theological "i" had been dotted and every "t" crossed within the enormous verbiage of the liturgy, but there was very little life in it. The communion liturgy before 1968 lacked any powerful statement of what Communion actually was intended to *be* for those who partook of it.

The liturgy of 1968 changed all of that. Howard Hageman's brief "Meaning of the Sacrament," as Christopher Dorn demonstrated in chapter one, changed all of that. Howard used only 263 words—200 of them words of only one syllable—to teach us to think more grandly and powerfully about what is going on when we celebrate the sacraments as genuine means of grace, in the mystical presence of Christ. But, since 1968, a whole host of other things have changed as well. Prior to 1968, the Reformed Church had very little awareness of the liturgical year. We made no use of the *Common Lectionary*. Such a thing did not exist. So, the *Liturgy and Psalms* created its own very wonderful four-year lectionary, including lessons from the Heidelberg Catechism during thirteen weeks of each year. And, before 1968, we had no treasury of prayers. We had only one prayer for each purpose. So the *Liturgy and Psalms* provided us with a rich resource of prayers.

The statistics about the current state of worship within the Reformed Church, analyzed for us by Janssen, demonstrate just how much has been gained in the years since 1968. That ought to encourage us truly to celebrate the publication of our new liturgy, the 2005 *Worship the Lord*, an accomplishment that suggests unmistakably that worship within the Reformed Church in America still has a strong and beautiful heart.

Western Seminary's professor, Tim Brown, whom I am honored to claim as my student, has urged the church to think of worship and preaching as acts of hospitality—"grace offerings of hymn and prayer, chalice and loaf, scroll and blessing" by which we may "remind the people of God who they are, and what great things have happened in their wilderness past, so that they might have confidence and hope for a promised land future."[2] The late Erik Routley, who gave so profoundly to the worship life of the Reformed Church, in his posthumously published book, *The Divine Formula: A Book for Worshipers, Preachers, and Musicians, and All Who Celebrate the Mysteries*,[3] spoke of worship and preaching as "team sports."

In the tradition of Brown and Routley, Kathleen Hart Brumm has urged us to understand worship as an egalitarian and inclusive effort. And yet, at the same time, she has asked us to seek to understand liturgy as a thoughtful, planned process by which we can honestly hope all present will be able to worship God. As she pointed out, we gather as a "we" to hear God's voice. No one, including (or, perhaps, especially) the pastor, therefore gets to do "solo" things in worship. My sense is that, in the words of poet Robert Frost, we still have "promises to keep and miles to go before we sleep" on that one.

Four brief additional suggestions regarding the future of creative and contemporary Reformed worship may be helpful. First, I ask each of you to reflect upon why it is that within the Reformed Church we have no genuine, uniform, denomination-wide commitment to the liturgies for baptism and the Lord's Supper. For myself, I think I have identified the source of the problem in four areas of functional doubt within the denomination:

1. We don't really believe that Jesus is specially present in the sacraments. We believe that the scriptures rise above other writings because Jesus is in them, but we can't really confess the same for the sacraments.

2. We don't really see the sacraments as anything more than a remembrance of Jesus' past acts.

3. We aren't ready entirely to hand the sacraments over to God, as God's acts, and to see them therefore as seals of God's faithfulness and of our being placed in union with Christ.

4. We aren't ready for them to be for us mystery, intended to move us, rather than to be theologically reasoned acts that we do. But how do you read the issue?

Second, it is my hope that in our worship we will make more use of *Our Song of Hope*.[4] While it was written in the 1970s and approved

---

[2]   "A Blueprint for Pulpit and Table," *Perspectives* (May, 2002), 9.

[3]   (Princeton: Prestige, 1986).

[4]   Eugene P. Heideman, *Our Song of Hope* (Grand Rapids: Eerdmans, 1978).

in 1978, it sings as if written specifically for our current context. This is an age that very much needs to know that

> Christ places the Lord's table in this world:
> Jesus takes up our bread and wine
> to represent his sacrifice,
> to bind his ministry to our daily work,
> to unite us in his righteousness.

as well as that

> The boundaries of God's love are not known,
> the Spirit works at the ends of the world
> before the church has there spoken a word.

Third, let's remember, please, that our beloved denomination and we who seek to be its faithful children don't have to invent every wheel anew and by ourselves. There is a wonderful variety of resources of which we can take advantage. For example, I invite you to consider joining two wonderful organizations that have been enormously helpful to me. The first is the Mercersburg Society. This ecumenical fellowship seeks to keep alive the theology of education, of liturgy, and of Christ's real presence inherited from John Williamson Nevin (1803-1886), Philip Schaff (1819-1893), and their colleagues within the seminary of the German Reformed Church in Mercersburg, Pennsylvania, in the middle of the nineteenth century. The society publishes the *New Mercersburg Review* and the *Mercersburg Practitioner* and holds an annual convocation for the sharing of research and renewal. The second is the Association for Reformed and Liturgical Worship. This association is now three years old and seeks "to cultivate, practice, and promote its *ordo*-centered vision of worship....worship that offers a foretaste of the fullness of God's reign." The association meets annually, typically concurrently with the Summer Institute for Liturgy and Worship, on the campus of Seattle University. In addition, there are powerful theological journals such as *Reformed Worship, Call to Worship,* and the *Hymn,* to which one can subscribe. These two organizations and these fine journals (plus a small but growing number of very helpful websites) provide points of access to an expanding wealth of research and reflection for the daily celebration of Reformed worship.

Finally, let's be clear that "among the thorns" is an always appropriate place both for the lily and our liturgy to be. We are called—always—to celebrate God's presence in all of the difficult and prickly places of our shared human existence; to take the good news of Jesus to precisely those persons for whom no one else cares; to offer cleansing, Eucharist, and healing in all of the pain-filled, unpeaceful places on our globe; remembering—always—that "Jesus places the Lord's Table in this world."

FOR FURTHER READING

James Hart Brumm

Just as this book is hoped to be but the start of a conversation about worship in the Reformed Church, it is also a mere beginning in terms of the resources available. Below is a list of titles that have been suggested by the contributors to this book, to guide those who are interested in exploring particular topics more deeply. While some of the older volumes are, unfortunately, out of print, they should be available through academic libraries and used book services.

General Worship

J.D. Benoit, *Liturgical Renewal: Studies in Catholic and Protestant Developments on the Continent* (London: SCM Press Ltd., 1958). These papers are significant for the view they afford of the impact of the liturgical movement on the French Reformed church, whose liturgical productions exercised a decisive influence on the committee members entrusted by the RCA with the revision of its liturgy during the era in which this book appeared.

Frank C. Senn, *Christian Liturgy: Catholic and Evangelical* (Minneapolis Minnesota: Fortress Press, 1997). Senn presents a comprehensive history of Christian liturgy in the West, from the Jewish antecedents to early Christian worship to the liturgical movement in the twentieth century. He concludes with a criticism of "contemporary" approaches to worship and with a reflection on the place of liturgy in a "postmodern" culture.

J.J. von Allmen, *Worship: Its Theology and Practice* (New York: Oxford Univ. Press, 1965). This is the great Reformed classic of a generation ago. Von Allmen offers a systematic theology of worship informed by the Reformed tradition and the insights of the ecumenical movement, in which he played a leading role. He combines a Calvinistic sense of discipline with a liturgical vision that is so high and miraculous that it actually includes the place of angels in our worship.

John D. Witvliet, *Worship Seeking Understanding: Windows into Christian Practice* (Grand Rapids: Baker Academic, 2003). A collection of essays reflecting theologically about various aspects of worship.

Reformed Worship

Howard Hageman, *Pulpit and Table: Some Chapters in the History of Worship in the Reformed Churches* (Richmond: John Knox Press, 1962). Hageman's Princeton lectures constitute one of the earliest attempts in English to provide an overview of the history of worship in the Reformed churches. From Zwingli's prone in Zurich and Calvin's liturgy in Strasbourg to the twentieth century liturgical renewals in the continental Reformed churches under the leadership of the *Liturgische Kring* in the Netherlands and *L'Eglise et Liturgie* in France, Hageman sketches the course of liturgical development in the Reformed tradition.

Alasdair I.C. Heron, *Table and Tradition: Toward an Ecumenical Understanding of the Eucharist* (Philadelphia: Westminster, 1983). Heron provides an overview of the eucharistic theology of the Reformers and suggests new directions in which to develop this theology in light of contemporary ecumenical progress toward the resolution of Reformation era controversies over the Eucharist or Lord's Supper.

Gregg A. Mast, In *Remembrance and Hope: The Ministry and Vision of Howard G. Hageman* (Grand Rapids: Eerdman's, 1998). Mast gives an account of Hageman's contributions to the identity and mission of the RCA. Germane to the subject of worship are the chapters in which Mast relates Hageman's understanding of the role of preaching and the significance of the Lord's Supper in a Reformed liturgy of "pulpit and table." The final chapter of the book, "Three Lectures," consists of Hageman's on the RCA *Liturgy* presented at Western Theological

Seminary in 1966. Part of The Historical Series of the Reformed Church in America.

Jack M. Maxwell, Worship *and Reformed Theology: The Liturgical Lessons of Mercersburg* (Pittsburgh: Pickwick, 1976). Maxwell presents an analysis of the controversial liturgical movement in the German Reformed church during the Mercersburg era, a movement that culminated in the publication of *An Order of Worship* in 1866. The author describes the theological and liturgical convictions of Schaff, Nevin, and their supporters, as well as those of their opponents.

Daniel James Meeter, *'Bless the Lord, O My Soul:' The New-York Liturgy of the Dutch Reformed Church, 1767* (Lanham, Md.: Scarecrow, 1998). Meeter's book contains a critical edition of the English liturgical forms of the Dutch Reformed Church in North America, published in New York in 1767. These are preceded by a historical introduction and followed by a commentary on the theological content of the forms.

James Hastings Nichols, *Romanticism in American Theology: Nevin and Schaff at Mercersburg.* (Chicago: Univ. of Chicago Press, 1961). Nichols's work remains the standard introduction to the productive theological and liturgical partnership of Nevin and Schaff at Mercersburg.

Hughes Oliphant Old, *Worship: Reformed According to Scripture*, rev. (Louisville: Westminster/John Knox, 2002). The best short introduction to worship, written for ordinary pastors and college students. Covers all the bases expertly. Treats Reformed worship as something not borrowed or second-rate, but with its own strengths and virtues.

Howard L. Rice and James C. Huffstutler, *Reformed Worship* (Louisville: Geneva, 2001). The authors aim to explain the history of the Reformed liturgical tradition and apply it to actual settings in the worship life of Reformed congregations today.

Lukas Vischer, ed., *Christian Worship in Reformed Churches Past and Present* (Grand Rapids: Eerdman's, 2003). This book consists in a series of essays by theologians and liturgical scholars who together present a wide-ranging survey of Reformed worship across time and place. The concluding section contains essays on aspects of worship that are of contemporary relevance for Reformed churches.

Baptism

Hughes Oliphant Old, *The Shaping of the Reformed Baptismal Rite in the Sixteenth Century*, (Grand Rapids: Eerdman's, 1992). Comprehensive and scholarly, but so thorough in its detail that just by reading it you get educated into how to read it.

Congregational Song

John L. Bell, *The Singing Thing: the Case for Congregational Song* (Chicago: GIA Publications, 2000). An anecdotal theological reflection on why we sing, and the place of singing in the life of the congregation.

Emily R. Brink, editor, *Sing! A New Creation Leaders' Edition* (Grand Rapids: CRC Publications, 2001). Includes articles and suggestions for incorporating contemporary hymnody, praise music, and world music in worship.

Emily R. Brink and Bert Polman, eds., *Psalter Hymnal Handbook* (Grand Rapids: CRC Publications, 1998). While this book is a companion to the official hymnal of the Christian Reformed Church, several of the articles address the heritage of psalmody and hymnody which is common to the RCA as well.

James Hart Brumm, *Psalms and Hymns of the Reformed Protestant Dutch Church: a Historical Companion* (unpub. diss., 2005). A complete examination of the first denominational hymnal produced in North America, the influences behind it, and the ways in which its development paralleled the development of what would become the RCA, over eight decades.

James Hart Brumm, *Singing the Lord's Song: a History of the English-Language Hymnals of the Reformed Church in America* (New Brunswick, N.J.: Historical Society of the Reformed Church in America, 1992). The most complete survey to date of RCA hymnals, from the "Collegiate" Psalter of 1767 to *Rejoice in the Lord*. A more thorough examination than is found in this book, although some of the research found here is more recent.

Erik Routley, revised by Paul Richardson, *A Panorama of Christian Hymnody* (Chicago: GIA Publications, 2005). An updated edition of a classic and invaluable hymnological resource, surveying the range of Christian hymn texts, with numerous examples.

Erik Routley, *Christian Hymns Observed: When, In Our Music, God Is Glorified* (Princeton: Prestige, 1983). Short history of the history of congregational song and the theology behind many of its major currents, by a leading scholar of his day.

Paul Westermeyer, *Let the People Sing: Hymn Tunes in Perspective* (Chicago: GIA Publications, 2005). An examination of musical, theological, and practical considerations of tunes for congregational song, including their historical development.

Brian Wren, *Praying Twice: the Music and Words of Congregational Song* (Louisville: Westminster/John Knox, 2000). A collection of essays reflecting on the theology and practice of hymnody and congregational singing.

Architecture

Donald J. Bruggink & Carl H. Droppers, *Christ and Architecture: Building Presbyterian/Reformed Churches* (Grand Rapids: Eerdman's, 1965). A lavishly illustrated volume. Includes a theological program as well as illustrations of an effective architectural presentation of those liturgical principles.

Donald J. Bruggink & Carl H. Droppers, *When Faith Takes Form* (Grand Rapids: Eerdman's, 1971). A follow-up to *Christ and Architecture*, illustrated exclusively with churches in the United States.

Corby Finney, *Seeing Beyond the Word: Visual Arts and the Calvinist Tradition* (Grand Rapids: Eerdman's, 1999). A historical overview of architecture and visual arts and understandings of them in denominations of the Calvinist tradition around the world.

Creative Contemporary Worship

Emily R. Brink, John D. Witvliet, et al., *The Worship Sourcebook* (Grand Rapids: CRC Publications, 2004). A large and thorough collection of prayers, sentences, litanies, and other portions of worship, along with explanations of their purpose and place in the liturgy and patterns for readers to construct their own materials. Includes a CD-ROM with all of the worship portions, so they can be easily copied into worship bulletins.

C. Michael Hawn, *One Bread, One Body: Exploring Cultural Diversity in Worship* (Bethesda: Alban Institute, 2003). A renowned student and proponent of world music for Christians examines the value and challenges of culturally diverse worshiping congregations and offers practical suggestions for congregations that wish to be more diverse.

Robert Webber, *Planning Blended Worship: the Creative Mixture of Old and New* (Nashville: Abingdon, 1998). A study in how to transform congregational worship without sacrificing tradition or dividing the congregation into niche market groups by adding new elements while respecting the old.

Wild Goose Resource Group, *Cloth for the Cradle: Worship Resources and Readings for Advent, Christmas, & Epiphany* (Chicago: GIA

Publications, 2000). A collection of creative worship materials for the Christmas cycle from the Iona Community.

Wild Goose Resource Group, *Present on Earth: Worship Resources on the Life of Jesus* (Chicago: GIA Publications, 2005). A third Iona volume, following the pattern of the two above.

Wild Goose Resource Group, *Stages on the Way: Worship Resources for Lent, Holy Week & Easter* (Chicago: GIA Publications, 2000). Another Iona volume, this one for the Easter cycle.

RCA History

Donald J. Bruggink and Kim Nathan Baker, *By Grace Alone: Stories of the Reformed Church in America*, no. 44 in the Historical Series of the Reformed Church in America (Grand Rapids: Eerdman's, 2004). A one-volume complete survey of RCA history, with copious illustrations and charts, useful for even beginning students of church history.

Periodicals

The Hymn: a Journal of Congregational Song (Boston: published quarterly by the Hymn Society in the United States and Canada). A regular publication of scholarly, practical, and devotional discussions of congregational song, along with regular notices of a wide variety of publications in the field. Subscription comes with membership in the society and invitations to its annual conferences, four-day festivals of singing, study, and fellowship. The Hymn Society in the United States & Canada, Boston University School of Theology, 745 Commonwealth Avenue, Boston, Massachusetts 02215-1401; 1-800-THE-HYMN; www.thehymnsociety.org.

New Mercersburg Review (York, Penn.: published semi-annually by the Mercersburg Society). A journal to promote theology in the Mercersburg tradition in scholarly, liturgical, and educational work. Subscription comes with membership in the society and invitations to its annual two-day convocations. Contact the Rev. Phyllis Baum, Membership Chair, 100 Haybrook Drive, York, Pennsylvania 17402.

Reformed Worship (Grand Rapids: published quarterly by Faith Alive Christian Resources). A journal to provide practical assistance in planning, structuring, and conducting congregational worship in the Reformed tradition. 1-800-777-7270, www.reformedworship.org, or subscriptions@reformedworship.org.

AFTERWORD

James Hart Brumm

As you have already been reading, the Reformed Church in America is a denomination of two minds about more than a few things. While being intensely proud of its own tradition, almost to the point of being insular, it is also evangelically open, almost to the point of denying its identity. While being cerebral and scholastic, it can also be pietist and almost anti-intellectual. While it holds its *Liturgy*—especially that for the Lord's Supper and baptism—to be constitutional and puts a great deal of thought and energy into producing and approving such liturgies, it also lets every congregation go its own way to a great extent. It even takes the position (which at least two of the foregoing authors consider ontologically impossible) that it is semiliturgical. While its song grows out of a Calvinian understanding that music is powerful and must be carefully controlled, it refuses to exercise any serious control whatsoever.

At its best, this state of divided inclination can result in marvelous creativity. From this ongoing paradox has come *Psalms and Hymns* and *Sing! A New Creation*, as well as the poetic beauty that filled *Liturgy and Psalms* in 1968 and the 2005 edition of *Worship the Lord*. When the varied voices abandon the hard work of dialogue, however, the RCA can devolve into camps of mutual suspicion. The failure to adopt some liturgical revisions and the tendency in the denomination to abandon some of its own hymn writers and even hymnals are symptoms of this distrust. Hard work is required to maintain creative tension and covenantal dialogue and, all too often, the denomination has seemed liturgically lazy.

Or maybe worship just isn't a priority for the Reformed Church. Jesus said, "Where your treasure is, there your heart will be also."[1] When I. John Hesselink recommended to the synod of 1996 that new worship resources were needed, the synod voted "to instruct the Commission on Christian Worship to produce worship resources which include supplemental forms of worship and hymns, songs, and choruses which reflect our faith and speak to our time."[2] What the synod did not do was appropriate any money to this enterprise. In some sense that may have inspired even greater creativity on the part of those who have done good work in the succeeding decade. Yet, if we are to assume that Jesus was right—a logical Reformed position—then this new worship initiative was less important to the church than many other activities of the church, for which there was a budget of $4,102,340.[3] Just over a decade before that, as was noted in chapter 4, a new hymnal was approved for the denomination without any investment in educational materials.

A decade later, participation in the "Liturgy among the Thorns" conference could be seen as another indication of denominational commitment or lack thereof. It drew, as such things go, a respectable turnout, but it was a very Caucasian group, mostly from eastern synods, mostly attached to congregations that use a rather traditional liturgy. Some of this has to do with the fact that the event was held in New Jersey, and, as Paul Janssen has already pointed out in chapter 5, most eastern congregations celebrate fairly traditional liturgies. However, people of color and those who use more praise-and-worship or "seeker" oriented orders of worship were invited to participate in this volume, and they declined. Janssen also points out that a higher percentage of congregations in the midwestern and eastern United States participated in the 2004 worship survey than did those in Canada and the U.S. Far West. Whether it be a sense of anti-liturgicalism or anti-intellectualism

---

[1]   Matthew 6:21.
[2]   *Acts and Proceedings,* 1996, 232.
[3]   *Acts and Proceedings,* 1996, 66.

or something else, such study and discussion does not seem to be valued in the Reformed Church.

Why does this matter? It is the same old discussion of denominational unity and the centrality of worship to who we are. If, indeed, as Hesselink posited, worship is central to our unity and identity, we need to have a common worship life, not a lock-step uniformity (which has, arguably, never been an element of RCA worship), but a common set of liturgical understandings and principles out of which each local expression arises. If, indeed, worship needs to continue to adapt to the needs of a changing world, and if, indeed, we are a covenant people and the *Liturgy* is a tangible expression of that covenant, then we need to be in conversation together about our continuing liturgical evolution. Covenant people have responsibilities to one another; as Hesselink reminded us, Reformed people cannot just "do their own thing."

It could be that this dichotomy is an essential by-product of a Reformed liturgical process. The creation of liturgy is an artistic process, and art is hardly ever created by committee.[4] The maintenance of covenant, however, is a communal process. We therefore run the risk of either spinning off in multiple directions following every creative impulse or having a worship of gray banalities born of a board process that reduces liturgy to the lowest common denominator.

Perhaps the best way to avoid both of these errors is found in the *Directory for Worship*,[5] which points out that "worship is both a dialogue between minister and congregation and between God and people."[6] In worship, we are called to be in constant dialogue. Does it not make sense, therefore, that, in preparing worship and formulating liturgy, we should also be in constant dialogue? Successful dialogue requires participation by all parties, active engagement in listening and sharing, not so that they might necessarily achieve uniformity, but so they might be able to walk together, as a synod should. It is hoped that this

---

[4] For an attempt at art by committee, one only need turn to the Invitation to the Communion in the 1987 *Liturgy*: "All those who have confessed their faith in Christ and are members of a Christian church are welcome at the Lord's Table." James R. Esther and Donald J. Bruggink, eds., *Worship the Lord* (Grand Rapids: Eerdman's, 1987), 9.

[5] The *Directory* was adopted by the General Synod of 1986. *Acts and Proceedings*, 1986, 170-82. The synod of 1988 referred an amendment that was approved by the classes which gave the *Directory* constitutional status alongside the *Liturgy*. *Acts and Proceedings*, 1988, 228.

[6] *Acts and Proceedings*, 1986, 170.

volume, by reminding us where we have been, might provide a common starting point for the journey forward—a "tie that binds," to quote the hymn of which the Reformed Church has been so fond. Let us worship God together!

INDEX

The Historical Series of the
Reformed Church in America
Recent Books

Donald J. Bruggink & Kim N. Baker
By Grace Alone, Stories of the Reformed Church in America
Intended for the whole church. After a consideration of its European background in an introductory chapter "Reformed from What?," the story of the Dutch and their church in the New World from the early seventeenth century to the present is told with attention paid to relationships to Native and African Americans at home and missions abroad. The movement of the church across the continent and immigration to Canada, as well as its ecumenical involvement, leads to a challenge for the future. Additional personal interest stories in sidebars, as well as time lines and resources, accompany each chapter. Pp. ix, 222, illustrations, index, 8 1/2 x 11". 2004. $29.

June Potter Durkee
Travels of an American Girl
Prior to WWII, June accompanied her parents on a trip through Europe to the Middle East and India. Her father, F. M. "Duke" Potter, was for thirty years a major force in mission policy and administration. The world and the missionaries, as seen through the eyes of a precocious ten year old who polished her account at age twelve, makes delightful and insightful reading. Pp. xv, 95, sketches, illustrations. 2004. $14.

Mary L. Kansfield
Letters to Hazel, Ministry within the Woman's Board of Foreign Missions of the Reformed Church in America
A collection of letters, written by overseas missionaries in appreciation of Hazel Gnade, who shepherded them through New York on their departures and returns, inspired this history of the Woman's Board. Kansfield chronicles how a concern for women abroad precipitated a nineteenth century "feminism" that, in the cause of missions, took women out of their homes, gave them experience in organizational skills, fundraising and administration. Pp. xiii, 257, illustrations, appendices, bibliography, name index, subject index, 8 1/2 x 11". 2004. $29.

Johan Stellingwerff and Robert P. Swierenga, editors
Iowa Letters, Dutch Immigrants on the American Frontier
A collection of two hundred fifteen letters between settlers in Iowa and their family and friends in the Netherlands. Remarkable is the fact that the collection contains reciprocal letters covering a period of years. While few have heard of the Buddes and Wormsers, there are also letters between Hendrik Hospers, mayor of Pella and founder of Hospers, Iowa, and his father. Also unusual is that in contrast to the optimism of Hospers, there are the pessimistic letters of

Andries N. Wormser, who complained that to succeed in America you had to "work like a German." Pp. xxvii, 701, illustrations, list of letters, bibliography, index, 6 x 9", hardcover, dust jacket. 2005. $49.

James C. Kennedy & Caroline J. Simon
Can Hope Endure? A Historical Case Study in Christian Higher Education
Hope was founded as a Christian college. How it has endured to the present without slipping either into secularism or a radical fundamentalism is the account of this book. The course has not always been steady, with factions within the school at times leaning either to the left or right. The account can perhaps be instructive in maintaining Hope's traditional centrist position. Pp. xvi, 249, bibliography, index, 6 x 9". 2005. $28.

LeRoy Koopman
Taking the Jesus Road, The Ministry of the Reformed Church in America among Native Americans
The ministry began in the seventeenth century, carried on by pastors who ministered to their Dutch congregants and native Americans. After the Revolutionary War, ministry moved from pastors to missionaries, increasing in activity following the Civil War. Koopman does not shy away from multiple failed government policies in which the church was often complicit, but he also records the steadfast devotion of both missionaries and lay workers who sought to bring assistance, love, and the gospel to native Americans. Pp. xiv, 512, illustrations, appendices including pastors, administrators, other personnel, and native American pastors, index, 6 x 9", hardcover, dust jacket. 2005. $49.

Karel Blei
The Netherlands Reformed Church, 1571-2005
translated by Allan J. Janssen
Beginning with the church's formation in 1571 during the upheavals of the Reformation, Karel Blei's *Netherlands Reformed Church* follows a dynamic path through over 400 years of history, culminating in the landmark ecumenical union of 2004. Blei explores the many dimensions of the Netherlands Reformed Church's story including the famous splits of 1834 and 1886, the colorful and divisive theological camps, and the hopeful renewal of the church in the mid-twentieth century. Also included are incisive explorations of new confessions, church order, and liturgical renewal. Pp. xvi, 176, index, 6x9, 2006. $25.

Janet Sjaarda Sheeres
Son of Secession: Douwe J. Vander Werp
Janet Sjaarda Sheers has written a moving, sympathetic, and exciting biography of Douwe Vander Werp, one of the key figures in the Netherlands *Afscheiding* of 1834 and a principal minister in the early development of the Christian Reformed Church. Credited with having founded ten congregations, Vander Werp was a man zealously committed to his understanding of God's Word and its implications for his life, even when it required the painful sacrifice of three secessions. Sheeres's sociological observations add interesting insights into

Vander Werp's fascinating and fractious times. *Son of Secession* is a challenge to our understanding of the historical origins of the Christian Reformed Church as well as that church today. Pp. xxii, 210, appendices, bibliography, index, 6 x9 ", 2006. $25.

Allan J. Janssen
Kingdom, Office, and Church. A Study of A. A. van Ruler's Doctrine of Ecclesiastical Office.
A. A. van Ruler is one of the most influential twentieth-century theologians from the Netherlands. One of the many challenging aspects of his work is his theology of the kingdom of God and its relationship to the church and its ecclesiastical offices. Allan J. Janssen draws on extensive pastoral and ecclesial experience as well as closely reasoned analysis to set forth the implications of van Ruler's theology for the church today. Christo Lombard of the University of the Western Cape writes: "when theologians grappling with the realities of the new millennium are re-discovering the exciting and challenging work of one of the most original theologians of our time. . . .anyone interested in the way forward for the church in an age of post-modernity and globalization, should read Dr. Janssen's book, based on meticulous scholarship and a passion for God's work in and through us as God's partners." Pp. xvi, 319, bibliography, index, 6x9", 2006. $35.

Corwin Smidt, Donald Luidens, James Penning, and Roger Nemeth
Divided by a Common Heritage: The Christian Reformed Church and the Reformed Church in America at the Beginning of a New Millennium
A quartet of social and political scientists from Hope College and Calvin College have drawn a picture of their two denominations, based upon comparative surveys of laity and clergy and their theological perspectives, creedal awareness, religious practices, ethical emphases, congregational loyalties, ideological issues, and current political and social issues. The book helps readers understand the broad areas of agreement between the two groups and the issues that still divide them. Pp. xiv, 226, tables, bibliography, appendix, and index, 6 x 9". 2006. $24.

James A. DeJong
Henry J. Kuiper: Shaping the Christian Reformed Church, 1907-1962
Written by the president emeritus of Calvin Theological Seminary, the biography of H.J. Kuiper reveals his influence on the CRC, influence that resulted in many of the positions still manifest in *Divided by a Common Heritage*. DeJong presents an objective biography of Kuiper as pastor, ecclesiastical politician, and editor of the *Banner*, positions from which he promoted Christian schools, reform of liturgy and hymnody, city missions, and above all, Reformed orthodoxy. Pp. xviii, 270, illustrations, appendix, bibliography, index, 6 x 9". 2007. $28.

Jacob E. Nyenhuis, ed.
A Goodly Heritage, Essays in Honor of the Reverend Dr. Elton J. Bruins at Eighty
The festschrift honors Bruins for his career as pastor, college professor and administrator, and founder of the Van Raalte Institute. There is a biography of Bruins as well as a bibliography of his writings by Jacob Nyenhuis. The

fifteen contributors are colleagues and former students, now professors and presidents. Essays, under three sections representing the primary areas of interests in Bruins career, include

Church History & Theology:
"Singing God's Songs in a New Land: Congregational Song in the RCA and CRC" by Harry Boonstra;

"Ancient Wisdom for Post-Modern Preaching: The Preacher as Pastor, Theologian, and Evangelist" by Timothy L. Brown;

"Extra-Canonical Tests for Church Membership and Ministry" by Donald J. Bruggink;

"Dr. Albertus Pieters, V.D.M.: Biblical Theologian" by Eugene Heideman;

"Scripture and Tradition—A Reformed Perspective: Unity in Diversity—Continuity, Conflict, and Development" by I. John Hesselink;

"'No One Has Ever Asked Me This Before': The Use of Oral History in Denominational History" by Lynn Winkels Japinga;

"Richard Baxter: An English Fox in a Dutch Chicken Coop?" by Earl Wm. Kennedy;

"A Decade of Hope and Despair: Mercersburg Theology's Impact on Two Reformed Denominations" by Gregg Mast;

"A Century of Change and Adaptation in the First English-Speaking Congregation of the Christian Reformed Church in Holland, Michigan" by Jacob E. Nyenhuis;

"What Happened to the Reformation? The Contentious Relationship between History and Religion" by J. Jeffery Tyler;

The Life and Heritage of the Reverend Albertus C. Van Raalte, D.D.:
"Civil War Correspondence of Benjamin Van Raalte during the Atlanta Campaign. 'My opinion is that much will have to happen before this campaign is concluded. Whoever lives through it will have much to tell.'" by Jeanne M. Jacobson;

"Albertus C. Van Raalte as a Businessman" by Robert P. Swierenga;

Hope College and Holland, Michigan
"Will the Circle Be Unbroken?: Essay on Hope College's Four Presidential Eras" by James C. Kennedy;

"The Vexed Question: Hope College and Theological Education in the West" by Dennis N. Voskuil;

"The Joint Archives of Holland: An Experiment in Cooperative Archival Preservation and Access" by Larry J. Wagenaar.

Pp. lii, 412, illustrations, index, 6" x 9" hardcover, dust jacket. 2007. $49.